MW01156735

www.wadsworth.com

Choral Concepts

Donald Neuen

University of California, Los Angeles

Illustrative Material by Piero Bonamico

SCHIRMER

THOMSON LEARNING

Australia • Canada • Mexico • Singapore • Spain • United Kingdom • United States

SCHIRMER
THOMSON LEARNING

Publisher for the Humanities: Clark Baxter
Assistant Editor: Julie Iannacchino
Editorial Assistant: Jonathan Katz
Marketing Manager: Mark Orr
Project Manager, Editorial Production: Jerilyn Emori
Print/Media Buyer: Judy Inouye
Permissions Editor: Robert Kauser
Production Service: Forbes Mill Press

Text Designer: Robin Gold
Illustrators/Autographers: Piero Bonamico, Marc Riley
Cover Designer: Carolyn Deacy
Cover Image: Paul Cherfils/Stone/Getty Images
Cover Printer: Phoenix Color Corp.
Compositor: Forbes Mill Press
Printer: Quebecor World Book Services, Iowa

Printed in the United States of America

2 3 4 5 6 7 06 05 04 03

For more information about our products, contact us:
Thomson Learning Academic Resource Center
1-800-423-0563

For permission to use material from this text, contact us by:
Phone: 1-800-730-2214   **Fax:** 1-800-730-2215
Web: http://www.thomsonrights.com

Library of Congress Cataloging-in-Publication Data

Neuen, Donald.
    Choral Concepts / Donald Neuen ; assisted by Piero Bonamico.
        p. m.
    ISBN 0-02-864749-1
    1. Choral conducting. 2. Choirs (Music) 3. Choral singing--Instruction and study. I. Bonamico, Piero. II. Title.

MT85 .N48 2002
782.5'145--dc21   2001057656

Wadsworth/Thomson Learning
10 Davis Drive
Belmont, CA 94002-3098
USA

Asia
Thomson Learning
60 Albert Complex, #15-01
Singapore 189969

Australia
Nelson Thomson Learning
102 Dodds Street
South Melbourne, Victoria 3205

Canada
Nelson Thomson Learning
1120 Birchmount Road
Toronto, Ontario M1K 5G4
Canada

Europe/Middle East/Africa
Thomson Learning
Berkshire House
168-173 High Holborn
London WC1V 7AA
United Kingdom

Latin America
Thomson Learning
Seneca, 53
Colonia Polanco
11560 Mexico D.F.
Mexico

Spain
Paraninfo Thomson Learning
Calle/Magallanes, 25
28105 Madrid, Spain

This book is dedicated to all those who read it
and venture confidently into paths of artistic excellence,
inspiring both musicians and listeners to heights greater
than they ever had imagined possible.

Contents

Preface

This book is the result of nearly fifty years of choral conducting. The ideas and concepts presented here draw on personal experience and have consistently worked well in various choral situations: teaching and conducting elementary, secondary, university, symphony, and church choruses; festival and workshop choruses; chamber singers; jazz and show choirs; men's and women's glee clubs; opera; Broadway musicals; bands; and symphony orchestras. The perspective is broad, the approach is realistic, and I try to combine practicality with the highest ideals of creative imagination and standards of excellence.

I admit to being an energetic, passionate, even occasionally evangelistic teacher, conductor, and therefore, writer. I try to write very enthusiastically about those concepts that I firmly believe. Although we all need to keep growing, we must do what we are doing now with solid faith in ourselves, great confidence, zeal, and contagious enthusiasm. That is the only way that really wonderful things happen!

I will frequently and intentionally repeat basic conceptual thinking that I believe is important. My intent is to reaffirm these points and remind you of their immense value. The key words that you will see frequently are impact, conviction, crucial, intensity, always, should, communication, must, commitment, importance, significance, and making a statement. I will also make frequent use of italics and boxes to emphasize my thinking and help you hear me speak directly to you.

To sing, and to conduct singers, is to work with the instrument of nature. There should be nothing unnatural or gimmicky—no "tricks of the trade." Vocal techniques and methods, therefore, should be based on reason, common sense, and practicality. I hope to present worthy ideas that work, solid concepts of fine singing that will apply to any and all choruses, young or old, amateur or professional.

Nevertheless, remember the following advice when it comes to implementing the concepts that follow: *Any good idea taken to extreme immediately becomes a bad idea.* In other words, don't overdo anything. A technique that we implement so much that it draws attention to itself and away from the music has become a negative technique. Techniques and interpretation should enhance music, not distract from it. Listeners should simply enjoy the composition, without a glaring awareness of the techniques.

As you study, consider setting aside your current ideas and concepts. They are fine and valuable, but, for now, just put them on hold. Make room in your mind for the possibility of something new or different. Approach each idea with the expectation that it might help you to serve better the composers, singers, and audiences in your future. Eventually, you will bring back those ideas that have been on hold and integrate them with new insights. Gradually you will form your own special perspective of, and approach to, choral conducting. Conductors at all levels of experience should cultivate a continual process of growth and evolution as they develop their artistic contributions to the choral field.

> To absorb anything new or different, one must be completely open-minded, positive in nature, and generous of spirit.

When reacting to, or trying to implement the ideas presented here, remember that if they are to be effective, you must be comfortable with them. They must be natural for you, and you will have to find your own way of doing them—which may not necessarily be the manner prescribed in the book. You may simply have to work with them for some time before they can become yours.

Remember that most new concepts usually feel a bit unnatural at first. As with new and different methods of playing golf, tennis, or anything else, it usually takes a while to get comfortable with the new method before it can become effective and productive. So, be patient. Furthermore, although the basic concept should work, you may have to learn to do it your own special way. That, of course, is as it should be. Whatever you do, you must do it convincingly, and with complete confidence in yourself. Your methods must be yours, coming from within you.

Conductors sometimes forget the responsibility that results from the immense privilege of spending a lifetime in the choral art. We must find a way to serve that art, and the singers (and players) who entrust it and themselves to us. We must serve with indescribable effort, knowledge, wisdom, creativity, energy, passion, and downright hard work!

It can seem very lonely opening a new score for the first time, trying to plan rehearsals, and uncovering the myriad pitfalls awaiting your chorus in the preparation of a major work. I hope that this compilation of my experiences will ease this process and help you to more easily understand, teach, and perform great music.

Artistic Musical Conducting

I deliberated at great length before adding Chapter 11 because many full-length books have been written on the subject. I decided to do so because a book on choral concepts would be incomplete without specific reference to the art of conducting. Still, to condense this subject into one chapter necessitates a highly selective conceptualization of those tools that a conductor will need to develop as he or she moves toward the highest levels of conducting excellence. But if clearly formulated—as I have tried to do—and well established in the reader's mind, these basic ideas are crucial to our development and consistently abound in the work of many great conductors.

Developing truly artistic conducting techniques.   The development of skilled, refined, and artistic conducting technique should be as high a priority for the conductor as a fine violinist's right hand and bowing technique. Most conductors have studied the actual art of physical conducting and choral techniques less than any other discipline in their musical training. Most have spent much more time with their major instruments and in the study of theory, counterpoint, form and analysis, and music history. For many, the serious study of conducting amounts to at most three semesters—seldom on a private-lesson basis—or possibly no study at all.

There are two obvious reasons: (1) some college curriculums offer only two or three semesters of conducting and one of choral techniques and methods, and (2) most musicians who are physically coordinated and possess a good basic sense of rhythm feel confident conducting with minimal training. It is often felt that although it takes years of rigorous training for a gifted person to become a fine singer, instrumentalist, theorist, or musicologist, "anyone can conduct." We see the results of this thinking in many ways: Professional singers and instrumentalists who, in their later years, attempt to begin a conducting career; organists who, without sufficient conducting or vocal and choral techniques training, conduct church choirs; singers and pianists who do the same thing with school and community choirs; the professional symphony orchestra conductor who began as a pianist, became an opera coach, then an opera conductor, and finally a symphony orchestra conductor, and who, in some cases, never studied conducting at all.

These examples, together with the fact that choruses, orchestras, and bands strive for fine performances despite poor conducting, account for the acceptance of this pathetic situation. Many ensemble members have never performed under a truly fine conductor—and don't even know the difference. Thus, the conductor (if there is any awareness at all) has no incentive to improve or change his or her technique.

The reader will need to separate the study of this chapter from the typical conducting class with its full-length textbook and instructor who explains, demonstrates, and teaches each principle, technique, and fundamental. I will present *concepts*. At times, they will be quite general and broad; others will be very specific and direct. I hope, however, that all will have substance and lasting value, and form the basis for a lifetime of further study and development.

> The video of my conducting and teaching, which is produced by the Choral Excellence series, goes into more detail on conducting technique. On those tapes you will be able to see these and many additional concepts in action. This video is available through ChoralExcellence.com Web site or the Wadsworth Web site at www.wadsworth.com.

A Special Note to Instructors

A final comment regarding the use of Chapter 11, "Artistic Musical Conducting." The approach to teaching both ourselves and our students should come from two separate perspectives:

- Developing artistic conducting

- Gaining the knowledge to teach choral/vocal techniques and methods

We can more effectively teach each perspective when we focus on only one, and not both. That is, teach conducting as an individual art, not associated with the teaching of choral and vocal techniques and methods, then teach the latter. Finally, put the two together in live rehearsal conditions. It is often counterproductive to ask the student to rehearse a chorus while he or she is still concentrating on learning the basic art of conducting, or vice versa. In the developing stages, the student can seldom do both effectively.

Choral concepts: teaching them.   I frequently use the term *concepts* throughout this book. That is certainly by design. If we teach concepts successfully, and with greater consistency, we will need to teach specifics much less. If a chorus thoroughly absorbs and understands the concept of syllable inflection and is motivated to make it a true priority, we would seldom need to mention it in specific instances. So, too, with any number of other aspects of successful performing.

How do we successfully teach a concept? We teach it in such a manner that the chorus will understand, absorb, retain, and recall when needed:

- **Understand.** If the chorus does not completely understand a subject or technique, nothing productive can follow. It is not just that a subject or technique must be intellectually understood, it also must be *functionally* understood. The singer must actually know how to physically do it—and how to consistently succeed at doing it. That is complete understanding and necessitates masterful teaching.

- **Absorb.** Absorbing a new concept takes a conscious desire and effort to do so. The person has to really want to. The singer must put forth great effort to mentally absorb the process. This is true in learning anything new: tennis, golf, business procedures, anything at all. We must motivate our choruses to be positively consumed with the new ideas. That is total absorption.

- **Retain.** One of the most difficult things to accomplish with any chorus is retention. I am speaking of the retention of both basic concepts, and of music rehearsed from one rehearsal to the next (especially with ensembles that rehearse only once each week). I constantly find it necessary to admonish my choruses to make a greater conscious effort to retain that which we have rehearsed. Retention must be an important factor in their attitude toward singing. It will not happen accidentally. They must want to remember and they must feel that it is imperative to remember. *They must know that forgetting is not an option.*

- **Recall.** To recall when needed is something that we must train the brain to do. This is very similar to self-hypnosis. The conductor cannot legislate singers' recollection in performances of what they learned in rehearsals. However, one can continually challenge them to think in performances, to think, and consciously do what they need to do with each syllable, word, and note. Every pencil mark they have made on their scores must come to life in the performance. In the end, it is totally up to each individual singer to activate the brain, think, and do it right. With proper practice and preparation, students can convince themselves that their brains will recall—and it will happen.

Putting it together.   Before every performance, I remind the chorus that "a chorus that does not work hard in rehearsals has to work extremely hard in performances.

But the chorus that has worked extremely hard in rehearsals has 'paid its dues' and can now relax, be 'loose,' and really enjoy performing with inspired communication and conviction." I don't believe that singers, or I, can ever work too hard. Within reason, there is no such thing as working too hard. Hard work is the true path to success in any and every endeavor. But, when it comes time for the concert, that hard work has made it possible to now be free to perform!

Despite this, singers and conductors must still think. Performance is not completely right-brained but, rather, a continual process of the marriage of both the left- and right-brain activity. Obviously, in the earlier rehearsals it is more left than right—intellectual rather than emotional. But as the chorus masters the music and the concert approaches, the process becomes much more right-brained and the emotional intensity (passion) of the performer takes over—on a solid foundation of intelligence and conscious thinking.

Acknowledgments

I extend special, unending gratitude to my loving wife Lisa, whose indescribable support, encouragement, knowledge, and love were the underlying foundation of my five-year effort in writing this book.

Then, I would like to acknowledge those who have so generously taught me the important choral, musical, and spiritual concepts that form the basis and foundation of my life in music. Some go back as far as high school, some during my collegiate training, others during my life as a teacher and conductor—either by example, tutorial, or both. Degrees of success, as varied as they may be, are achieved only through the help and encouragement of others. No one does it alone. To these great people, who were there when I needed them, I say, "Thank You."

Freeman Burkhalter	Robert Shaw
Christine Purves	Julius Herford
F. Lemuel Anderson	Alfred Mann
Robert Hargreaves	Roger Wagner
Seth McCoy	Robert Fountain
Raymond Mac Afee	Frank Pooler
Lara Hoggard	Paul Salamunovich
Timothy Noble	Jester Hairston
Robert Milford	Westin Noble

It was Robert Shaw who, after observing a 1964 rehearsal of Bach and Schubert that I was conducting, called his teacher, Julius Herford (then the head of graduate choral studies at Indiana University) and asked him to "take care of this boy." I was thirty-one. He did take care of me. I studied with him until his death in 1981. I was devastated by the news of the death of this great teacher. I was beginning the first of my twelve years on the faculty of the Eastman School of Music. Yet, at that very moment, also on the Eastman faculty, was the highly respected musicologist and choral conductor Alfred Mann, whom Herford had often quoted with great admiration. He graciously and generously opened his arms to "carry this boy" on from the point at which Julius had departed. I cannot adequately describe my appreciation to each of these wonderful men for their sincere friendship, generosity, and invaluable teaching. Without them, this book would never exist.

There have been so many more, who, during my education and career, shared their knowledge, and served as examples of excellence—colleagues, singers, players, students, and spiritual leaders. My unending gratitude goes out to them all.

Robin Gold, the text designer and copyeditor, is the one to whom boundless gratitude is extended for patience, encouragement, and extreme professionalism. The final presentation of the book rests with her creative attention to detail and effective communication of the English language.

Of course, I owe an important acknowledgment to Piero Bonamico whose critical reading, good advice, and splendid photographs, diagrams, and layouts illustrate so many of the concepts discussed here. In addition, I am delighted to be included in his Choral Excellence Series of videos.

Lastly, I thank my parents, Erma and Leland Neuen, who, through their example and encouragement, instilled in me the all-important foundation of freedom of expression, commitment to music, the potential for *excellence* in every rehearsal and performance, and the incredible *joy* that we find in the that processes.

Good luck, and best wishes for inspiring rehearsals, great performances, and continued growth. Bless you for caring about your growth in the choral art.

Artistic Excellence

When we accept the role of conductor, we commit ourselves to artistic excellence in everything we do. Without this commitment, we can create nothing worthwhile. Art has been beautifully described as "the soul's yearning to find meaning in existence." Notice that the yearning comes not from the mind but reaches deeper—to the soul—and that the soul does not search but, rather, *yearns* to find meaning in this often-chaotic earthly existence. The sole purpose of art is either to express or receive *feelings,* in sound, movement, form, writing, pictures, and design.

> ## The Characteristics of Great Artists Are within Our Reach
>
> Intelligence • We've got it
> Talent • We've got it
> Knowledge • We can get it
> Creative Imagination • We can develop it
> Skill • We can develop it
> Hard work • We can do it

The artist actively combines intelligence, knowledge, talent, creative imagination, skill, and hard work to express feelings sensitively and effectively. True artistic accomplishment is not an accident. It results from a commitment to artistic integrity and artistic excellence.

Conductors and the members of the ensembles they lead are *potential artists.* To turn this potential into reality, each performer must make a commitment to artistic excellence. Pause for a moment and consider the words *intelligence, knowledge, talent, creative imagination, skill,* and *hard work.* Take a moment to apply them to yourself and evaluate your own special potential as an artist. Remember that you *have* or can *acquire* everything you need to become a great and artistic conductor. If you are committed to excellence and hard work, everything will eventually fall into place. It is simply a matter of awareness and commitment—awareness of what it takes, and a commitment to develop and do it. Remember: We are limitless.

In this chapter, we will describe choral excellence, the attributes of choral success, the commitment necessary for excellence, and qualities conductors must have to inspire choirs.

✍ Every Aspect of a Choral Program Must Be Excellent

Vocal methods and techniques

Musicianship

Musicality, phrasing, and expression

Dramatic communication/diction/passion

Score study and preparation

Rehearsal pacing and planning

Artistic conducting

Organization and discipline

Recruiting and promotion

Comprehensive program development

Programming and concertizing

Appearance, attire, and stage decorum

Facilities and equipment

✍ Establish Your Priorities

Truth: Believe in truth, integrity, and God—or whatever you envision as universal strength and direction.

Self: Nurture and give yourself true quality care—so you will be able to serve others fully.

Family and friends: Treasure those who will be there through the ups and downs of your life and career (mission).

Music: Think of it not as your career but, rather, as a *mission* to enhance people's lives through music.

Choral Excellence

Every aspect of a great choral program must be based on the pursuit of excellence. If the chorus lacks vocal or musical security, fails to make an impact on an audience, or looks unprofessional, it will block the full realization of expressive feelings—the *art*. So let's not fool ourselves. If the rehearsals and performances are not based on a foundation of consistent excellence in *all things,* neither our singers nor we are performing as *artists*. Let's not forget that all conductors and choruses have the ability to perform artistically. It is simply a matter of knowledge, desire, setting priorities, discipline, and hard work. *The only limitation on a chorus is its conductor, and there is absolutely no limit to the growth and progress of a conductor.*

Any chorus will reflect the quality of its conductor. Bring in a better conductor tomorrow, and the chorus will be better tomorrow. Bring in a worse conductor, the chorus will immediately be worse. The chorus is *always* a reflection of its conductor and will always be capable of attaining new heights of greatness and quality if the conductor is capable of leading them there. Because the conductor's growth and progress are unlimited, every conductor—with sufficient dedication, commitment, and hard work—can deliver great, artistic performances.

The Attributes of Success

Success is the consistent execution of excellence. A successful program will have properly executed rehearsals, exciting and well-attended performances, an expanding roster of singers, and expanding budgets for program development, equipment, facilities, and music.

We can never underestimate the power of positive thinking. To succeed, we have to really want to. We must have the inner drive and desire for it. It has to be one of our very top priorities; then it will happen. We are what we think. We are the results of our thoughts and priorities.

Priorities do become realities, so we must select them carefully. Furthermore, we must put them in the right order. Many people have succeeded at the expense of their integrity, well-being, family, and friends. Our music is often a reflection of our lives, so we must carefully consider our values. With a clear set of priorities in place, we can begin to outline the specific attributes and qualities that will enable us to succeed as conductors.

Make Things Happen

Thrive on being a doer. Make things happen; don't wait for someone else to do things for you. Especially in the younger, formative years of your work, do it *all* and say an enthusiastic "Yes!" to almost everything that comes your way. You're not too busy, and if you don't know how to do something, learn.

Dedicate yourself to the work you're presently doing. Dedicate yourself 100 percent to your current job. Never have one eye on a better, more prestigious job, or consciously use the present one as a stepping-stone. If you do, you'll only produce half a job where you are and no one will want to offer you a better one. If you give 100 percent to your current position, you won't have to seek a better position. It will seek you.

Grow, learn, and expand your musical knowledge. Grow continuously in all aspects of life but—for our purposes here—especially in *musical substance.* There will always be more to learn about the voice, conducting, scores, and musicology. The musicologist should be the conductor's best friend. When conducting Bach, seek out a Bach scholar; when conducting Brahms, seek a Brahms scholar. No matter what substantial composition you may be performing, you can find a musicologist who, having specialized in the work of that composer, knows more about it than you or I and would love to share that knowledge.

Contact the scholar, ask for private study, and extend an invitation to attend your rehearsals (for a fee). Let everyone benefit and learn. Invite the scholar to make appropriate suggestions about style and interpretation, even in front of the chorus. If the scholar communicates, and you listen, in a positive, generous manner, it can be an incredible education for all concerned.

We should always have teachers to help us mature and develop musically. Remember, the day we stop getting better is the day we start getting worse. If we are truly committed to excellence, our own personal musical growth will be a major part of the process.

The Commitment to Excellence

When we are committed to excellence—and there is no reason not to be—we are ready to pursue the actual knowledge and skills that will make us great choral conductors. A world of information is available to us, and we will pursue that knowledge for the rest of our lives. The question becomes, "Where do I begin?" We will start by creating a framework of knowledge. This framework is based on three simple questions. What is excellence? How do I teach it? How do I inspire others to want it?

Knowledge is the cornerstone of success. We must *know* before we can *do.* We must be able to identify great tone quality, intonation, phrasing, understandable diction,

> ### ℘ Three Fundamental Questions
>
> What is excellence/greatness?
> How do I teach it?
> How do I inspire singers to want it?

✑ *Areas of Excellence*

1. Knowledge
2. Conducting
3. Inspiration
4. Hard work
5. Order
6. Singing
7. Accuracy
8. Phrasing
9. Diction
10. Communication

and the many other critical attributes of fine singing. If we are going to attempt to conduct great choral music, we must be familiar with the performances of great singers and conductors.

It is our responsibility to listen to and learn from both live performances and professional recordings of singers and choruses who consistently sing beautifully, lyrically, and in tune, with accurate stylistic interpretations, clear diction, and effective personal communication. *We must be intimately familiar with what they do.*

We must know what great singing is in general, but also very specifically for each of the four sections—sopranos, altos, tenors, and basses; for young singers and older ones; and for many different styles and genres. If we don't know what greatness is, we have no frame of reference from which to begin. There can be no progress toward excellence if we don't know what truly great singing really is. We must have examples of great singing in our minds as we hear and see the ensemble with which we are working. We need to know the differences between the world's greatest choirs and our own.

Excellence for the Conductor

The following six categories of excellence relate specifically to the conductor who must master them to produce excellence with a chorus.

1. Knowledge of vocal techniques and artistry
2. Knowledge of the score and stylistic interpretation
3. Conducting artistry—expression and passion with clarity and precision
4. Inspiring personal communication
5. The ability to create a positive, hardworking attitude in the performers
6. Order, organization, and consistency

Excellence for the Choir

Organize choral excellence in your mind—for example, the "umbrella of excellence" (Figure 1.1). Notice that the umbrella has five main categories. These categories appear in their order of importance so that you will be able to envision the critical areas of choral excellence in a concise and logical way.

If you focus on accomplishing these five categories you will succeed. Let's describe each in more detail.

1. *Singing.* Teach people to sing, really SING! *This is the most important and significant thing we do.* The chorus must sing with a sound that has the potential to thrill and make an impact on the listener. Whether *forte* or *piano, allegro* or *grave, fuocoso* or *tranquillo,* the chorus must sing with passion and enthusiastic energy.

Figure 1.1

Umbrella of Excellence

2. *Accuracy.* Every singer must consistently sing the right pitch at the right time. Musicianship, the mechanics of music-making, must be solid for every singer, every note, every word, and every syllable.

3. *Phrasing.* The chorus must sing every note, syllable, and word *musically* and *expressively*. We will consistently strive for musical, and expressive performances. These qualities transform mechanics into true musical art.

4. *Diction.* The chorus must sing the text in a manner that is understandable. Solid diction takes full advantage of the *entire color spectrum* of the language. Without effective delivery of text, the audience would rather hear an instrumental ensemble. Many conductors (and voice teachers) take English diction for granted. The result: it doesn't exist.

5. *Personal Communication.* Songs project and communicate a direct message. Singers must deliver the emotion and drama of a song in a manner that realizes the song's full potential to affect the listeners. This communication moves directly from the hearts and minds of the singers to the hearts and minds of the listeners. Although it is the responsibility of every singer in the ensemble, this communication will happen only if the conductor leads by example, consistently teaches it, inspires the singers to do it, and accepts nothing less.

We will discuss in later chapters how to execute all the concepts discussed so far. For now, review the *areas of excellence* (in Figure 1.1) and begin to absorb them as part of your musical life's blood. Embed them in your mind and you will have a clear roadmap toward success.

Teaching Excellence

We have all heard of fine singers who were not fine teachers, or fine athletes who were unable to become successful coaches. Teaching is an art and, probably, a calling. Certainly, fine teaching is a rare gift. At the very least we can say teaching is a highly developed skill that relies on an enthusiastic and communicative personality.

To teach effectively, we must know our subject thoroughly. We must also be able to put ourselves in the student's place to determine how to present our knowledge

✒ *A Conductor Is a Teacher*

We must positively embrace the concept that every conductor is essentially a teacher. The choral conductor is a full-time voice teacher and a full-time music teacher. In Italian, *Maestro* means teacher.

in a manner that will be *easily understood*. We must decide what to teach first, enabling the student to understand what follows. Being an effective teacher is not automatic. It takes a great deal of thought, concentration, skill, knowledge, experience, talent, and desire.

In this text, you will see many lists that are usually quite short. We need to learn to *organize* and *condense* our ideas into elements that are compact, meaningful, and *easy to understand and remember*.

How do I inspire others to want excellence? In many ways, the answer to the question "How do I teach effectively?" is simply "Inspire the students." If you can inspire the student to want to learn the material, and the material is of *real substance*, solid learning *will* happen. How, then, do we inspire them?

Students and singers *want* to be inspired and motivated. Fortunately for us, few areas of life are as potentially inspiring and motivating as the arts in general and singing in particular. Conductors, by responsibility and obligation, should provide inspiration and motivation in their presentations. Their success rests on two qualities: personality and knowledge. We have pointed out previously and will continue to mention the significance of a solid and broad base of knowledge. Without an inspiring personality, however, all the knowledge in the world will be quite useless. If a conductor's personality is less than inspirational, it is essential to improve it.

With focus and honest desire, we can succeed at being friendly, cheerful, and positive in ways that communicate with and directly affect others. This will produce stimulating results. We must really love the music, enjoy feeling that love, and develop a desire to share it with our singers. This text is not intended as a self-help book, but we must realize that all the technical knowledge we can acquire will be of little use without an infectious love for the music, the singers, and the opportunity to teach and "make great music together."

This infectious love comes from deep within us. Some say it cannot be taught. But I believe this is a limiting philosophy. In fact, human beings have a limitless potential for growth and development in all things. Study your own personality. Study those who seem to be incredibly inspiring, and begin to follow their examples consciously.

The Elements of an Inspirational Personality

After years of conducting and teaching conducting, I have concluded that an aspiring conductor must have or develop a few very critical attributes to teach and communicate effectively.

A conductor must have a genuinely positive personality. People do not *have* to be in a chorus. They choose to sing because they want to have an exhilarating, positive, and fulfilling experience. The degree to which that happens depends not only on the conductor's knowledge and teaching qualifications but also on the motivational, supportive, and encouraging aspects of the conductor's personal communication with the chorus. Singers cannot sing and perform well with either a passively boring or an angry conductor on the podium. The voice comes from within, and if the conductor's manner makes the singer either bored or tense and nervous (rather than relaxed and free), all efforts to sing will reflect this inner tension.

There is a fine line between a conductor whose rehearsal manner is positive yet very intense, fast-paced, totally business-like, and completely productive and one who crosses over that line into the realm of debilitating, demoralizing anger. Record your rehearsals and listen to them. Would the conductor on the tape inspire you? Or would you be, at one extreme, nervous and tense, or, at the other, bored and empty? Remember, it's all up to the conductor. The buck stops at the podium every time for every thing. Yes, there have been highly successful conductors who have been overly stern, negative, and angry with their choruses, even to the point of being abusive. But that's a style of past decades when singers were willing to put up with it. We can be thankful those days are gone. Singers will no longer abide it, and we have found that it is unnecessary. Relentless intensity? Yes. Anger? No!

> ### ✑ *Robert Shaw*
>
> During my tenure as Robert Shaw's assistant conductor with the Atlanta Symphony Orchestra and Choruses, I asked him how he felt about guest-conducting choruses who weren't well prepared. He said, "I simply teach them the notes. That's my job. . . . The pitches and rhythms *must* be accurate. If there is only one place in the Western Hemisphere where singers sing the right pitch at the right time, let it be Atlanta!"
>
> Robert Shaw worked harder than any person I've ever known. He would not give up until it was right. He worked meticulously with the Atlanta chorus for 100 percent accuracy. It didn't matter how long it took, or how often it had to be repeated, he would never settle for less, and said, "90 percent will never be good enough!" He was relentless in the pursuit of excellence—whether working with the Collegiate Chorale in New York City, the professionals in the Robert Shaw Chorale, the Cleveland Orchestra Chorus, the Atlanta Symphony Orchestra Choruses, guest conducting throughout the world, or even on the infrequent occasions when he worked with high school singers. He demanded *absolute excellence* on every note in every phrase of every song.

Conductors need to have a genuine love for people and music. Conductors must find working with people not only comfortable but also really enjoyable. The depth of their love for music must be at a profound level of intensity. When teaching, rehearsing, and performing, the conductor must be completely consumed by the music, as if there were nothing else in the entire universe at that moment—except the opportunity to share it with others.

Conductors should find hard work a stimulating pleasure. Achieving great heights of musical excellence does not result from natural phenomena and God-given talent. It results from hours and hours of HARD WORK. It has been said that when Robert Shaw's mother was asked if she thought her son was a genius, she replied, "No, he just works harder than anyone else." When Mr. Shaw was asked how much time he spends studying scores, he answered, "Every waking hour." Everyone is talented; some work hard enough to develop that talent fully.

All the categories listed under our umbrella of excellence involve an incredible amount of hard work. The main point, however, is that this hard work must be a real *joy* for a conductor. There is no happier way to earn a living than to spend one's life making great music. To make mediocre music is a horrible existence. To make and to help others make great music is sheer ecstasy.

Conductors must continue the quest for knowledge. Knowledge enables conductors to present their ideas to the ensemble with confidence. This knowledge and sense of security allows the conductor to accept responsibility for making all the decisions about the musical environment over which he or she presides. The conductor is trained, experienced, and qualified to make these decisions, and he or she must accept the responsibility to do so. A musical setting is not a democracy. The conductor makes the decisions, whether they have to do with tone, musicality, music selection, concert appearances, seating arrangements, performance attire, rehearsal decorum, or anything else. Good decisions reflect knowledge and wisdom. They also show respect and sensitivity to the singers. But no matter what the decisions, the *conductor makes them.* So we better know enough to make the right ones. (Occasionally the conductor might ask for input from the singers. This is healthy, but it should be very rare and carefully selective.)

Conductors must see themselves as professionals. See yourself as a *professional*. Traditionally, leaders of orchestras have been called "conductors," and the leaders of choruses, "directors." Why? And why have we named our professional choral organization the American Choral *Directors* Association? For decades, the instrumental world considered singers and choral conductors second-class musical citizens. In most cases, choral musicians were not as extensively trained as were instrumentalists, who began private lessons in the second or third grade. Thus, often, singers and choral conductors were not as experienced in areas of musicianship, musicality, technique, and stylistic interpretation.

Fortunately, and deservedly, perceptions have changed and are continuing to change. The forces behind these changes were basically the teachings of Julius Herford and the conducting and performances of Robert Shaw. The result is that choral conductors, whether they are in elementary, middle, or high school, or church, university, and symphony choruses, can now truly think of themselves as professional choral *conductors.* It is simply a matter of studying and working hard enough to deserve the title.

If you dedicate yourself to the principles of excellence and success that we have been talking about in this chapter, you are a professional. Don't think of yourself as a "choir director" or "chorus teacher." At this point, you have made a commitment to excellence. You are trained and qualified. You are paid. You are a *professional* and you are a *conductor!*

Summary

We have or can acquire everything it takes to succeed. In this chapter, we discussed the affect of pursuing excellence in all that we do:

- Without excellence, there is no art because *feelings* will not be sucessfully communicated.

- Excellence is necessary and *attainable* for every aspect of our work.

- We, the conductors, are the only limitation of our ensemble's progress toward excellence.

- We have no limitations except those we place on ourselves.

- We must know what greatness is, how to teach it, and how to inspire others to want it.

- The umbrella of choral excellence specifically includes (1) great singing, (2) accuracy and solid musicianship, (3) musical phrasing, (4) effective diction, and (5) dramatic, personal communication.

- Conducting excellence includes (1) knowledge of the score, style, and techniques of the forces, (2) conducting artistry, (3) inspiring and passionate communication, (4) creation of a positive work attitude in the singers, and (5) order, organization, and consistency.

- Personal attributes for success are the following: (1) Be a *doer*—make things happen, (2) always continue to grow and learn, (3) develop a positive attitude and personality, (4) love people and love music, (5) find hard work stimulating, and (6) see yourself as a true, professional choral conductor.

A Soloistic Approach to Ensemble Singing

2

We are now ready to begin thinking about singing and address the question: "How will we teach the chorus to *sing*?" It is critical that choral conductors have a clear concept of fine singing. This chapter will begin the process of just that. We will discuss an effective approach to the development of a great choral sound in general, then specifically each of the four sections (soprano, alto, tenor, and bass). We will then talk about breath support and control, which is the foundation of all fine singing.

Great Soloists Can Make Great Choral Singers

Think of the finest vocal soloists that you have seen and heard. How do they sing, how do they look, what do they do? They are the finest examples that we have of great singing. If our choral singers sang with that same quality, focus, and concentration, we would have a phenomenal chorus. We should base the concepts we teach on these examples of the finest professional singers because they represent the epitome of great singing.

Our singers, young and old, experienced and inexperienced, can safely strive for a high professional standard of singing excellence. Although many of our singers, especially the younger ones, cannot and should not attempt to sing with the same strength and upper range as accomplished soloists, they can successfully emulate the *standards of excellence* set for us by these great singers. The finest examples of energy, posture, vowel formation, diction, vocal placement, expressivity, sensitivity, and effective communication are all within reach of any singer who is inspired to strive for them.

> ☙ Teach musicianship, musicality, sensitivity, and naturally free and beautiful singing, and blending will quite naturally result. Fine vocal soloists singing with *sensitivity to the score, each other, and the conductor* are capable of producing the finest choral ensembles.

Fine professional singers do not sing anemically, sit or stand lazily, look bored, allow their minds to wander aimlessly, or lack energy, vital animation, zeal, and interest in what they're doing. Their approach to everything is completely professional. Their dedication to the highest standards of excellence is obvious in every aspect of their behavior. Our singers can do the same thing. It is simply up to us as conductors to see that it happens. Remember, as professional choral conductors we have already accepted the responsibility of *knowing what greatness is, knowing how to teach it, and knowing how to inspire our singers to want it.* Now, we must add one final element: We must train ourselves to be *unable to accept anything less.*

In the United States, Fred Waring's Pennsylvanians, the Robert Shaw and Roger Wagner Chorales, the Metropolitan Opera Chorus, and other professional ensembles composed entirely of fine soloists established the concept that great soloists can make great choral singers. In Europe, choruses made entirely of professional soloists have produced wonderful results for many years. Despite this overwhelming evidence to the contrary, however, many conductors remain needlessly wary of soloistic singing in their choirs.

Our singers are individuals. They deserve to be respected and treated as individuals. They should not be manipulated into some kind of mass unit that has no individual identity. They are all human beings. They will sound similarly beautiful, and surprisingly uniform, if they sing naturally, freely, energetically, and with sensitivity. They need not be forced to sound like someone else, or manipulated into a "special sound" for which the conductor wishes to be known.

Characteristics of Fine Soloists

Fine soloists share many characteristics. Reading these characteristics off the page is absolutely no substitute for actually hearing and seeing them, but it should help serve as a guide to what to *listen for* and what to *teach.* You will see that everything a fine soloist does has a parallel in the pursuit of excellence in the choral setting.

Positive attitude.   Professionals exhibit an attitude that is 100 percent positive. Our singers can do this too. They must commit themselves to the expression of positive energy regarding the music, the other singers, and the total environment in which the singing is taking place. When you ask professional singers what their favorite song, opera, or major work is, they almost always respond by saying, "The one I'm doing right now." With that attitude, they are sure to give it their very best. Inspire and teach this kind of attitude in your ensembles.

A focus on the beauty of sound.   A soloist works to create beautiful sound and constantly improve the quality of that sound. This is a conscious responsibility that is accepted along with the solo. Our singers must be aware of *their* sound and continually strive for a *naturally beautiful sound.* They must have a clear awareness, achieved through our teaching and their intense sensitivity, of the process of creating beautiful sound.

If singers with naturally larger voices sing with a consistently beautiful tone, they need not "walk on eggs" worrying about singing softly enough to blend. If they don't sing louder than the composer's dynamics indicate, and sing beautifully, the ensemble will simply sound as though it has more fine singers, not one who is offensively sticking out.

Assertive leadership. Soloists have to depend on *themselves* for everything that is to be done, not on those around them. Ensemble singers must be able to sing with that same musical security and leadership. All singers should feel as though they are *leaders*—being assertive in every aspect of singing. They will make mistakes. That is to be expected. But let them be magnificent mistakes! Instill this kind of confident and free singing in every singer. This is a *major* responsibility of a choral conductor.

Responsibility. Soloists accept the responsibility of learning everything they possibly can about the score. As conductors, we can train our singers to do the same. The accuracy of pitches, rhythms, and intonation, printed and conductor-requested directives, musicality, diction and dramatic personal projection of the text are all part of a singer's job, none of them are optional. We can train and inspire our singers to accept this responsibility.

> ## ℘ The Singer: ⅓ Technician, ⅓ Musician, ⅓ Dramatic Actor
>
> The instrumentalist is half technician and half musician. That is, half trumpet technician, half violin technician, or half keyboard technician—and half musician. The singer, on the other hand, is one-third vocal technician, one-third musician, and *one-third dramatic actor or actress*.
>
> The singer has to do everything an instrumentalist does plus create impacting drama to communicate the text. This is an incredibly important aspect of soloistic singing in any situation, including in the chorus where it is often ignored. This manner of singing and performing has to be consistently taught right along with pitches, rhythms, intonation, phrasing, diction, and everything else.

You might hear people say "But this is only a volunteer chorus, we aren't professionals." We might respond by politely informing them that a chorus under our direction will strive for musical and vocal excellence, whether or not anyone in the ensemble is paid. Remind them that the only real purpose of art and music is to express feelings effectively, and that feelings can only be meaningfully expressed when every member of the ensemble is dedicated to excellence. Therefore, members of our chorus must be dedicated to both excellence and the highest standards of musical professionalism. Why would anyone do otherwise?

Effective communication. Great soloists communicate musical and textual ideas. When performing, their entire bodies should resonate with passion and conviction. Singers need to communicate both the music and the text with this personal conviction and passion, which includes *appropriate facial animation*. The face must dramatically reflect the meaning of the text. Fine soloists do this, but ensemble singers seldom do. It is not enough to simply sing well; the singers must *perform*! As the great American tenor Seth McCoy said, "When you perform, make a statement—with conviction!"

Pencil markings. Every singer should always have a pencil and mark every applicable directive given by the conductor—absolutely every one. Our singers can't remember everything. Pencil marks help to establish directives and concepts firmly in the mind and are a visible reminder the next time the song is rehearsed. If the conductor gives directives of substance regarding phrasing, inflection, breathing, accents, stresses, and other nuances, these pencil marks will help make it possible for the singer to transcend the mechanics of the piece into beautiful music. Soloists' scores are always well marked. My directive to choruses: "If I talk about it, you write about it!"

Singing posture.   Posture is the first important element of fine singing. Without proper posture, our singers simply cannot sing up to their full potential. As with all our standards of excellence, we must react swiftly and relentlessly to signs of poor posture.

Study the posture of the finest oratorio and recital soloists: You will never see them slouching. Our singers, too, should sit or stand with the highest standards of soloistic posture. *The singer sings with the entire body.* The body is the instrument, and anything done to constrict the voice/instrument will limit its potential.

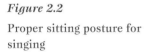

Figure 2.1

Proper standing posture for singing

When singing while standing, stand as though you were against a wall with the outside of your shoulders and the back of your hips touching the wall (see Figure 2.1). The middle and lower back do not touch the wall. The chest is up and out. The stomach is as flat as is natural for you. The head is erect, looking straight ahead. One foot is slightly ahead of the other. Music is held out chest-high, with the arms not touching the sides (rib cage). When looking at the music, only the eyes look down to see it. The head doesn't bend. Then the eyes look back at the conductor (or audience if there is no conductor). Anything less will result in rounding the shoulders and compromising fine posture. This concept of posture might be thought of as regal, or with a great presence of dignity. (It is not related to the *tension* of militaristic posture. It should be done with a very relaxed and comfortable body.)

When *sitting,* the only way to maintain the same standards of posture that we

Figure 2.2

Proper sitting posture for singing

have suggested for *standing* is to sit on the front half or third of the chair, with the upper half of your body feeling exactly like it did when you were standing (see Figure 2.2). Place one foot slightly in front of the other *as we should do while standing,* so balance can be maintained while you lean *slightly* into and out of phrases. The singer is not a mannequin. The full body, appropriately and within reason, may subtly move with the music and singing. We should never do this to the point of distraction, just enough to allow the body to function freely, as one, with the voice.

Facilitating Soloistic Singing—The Soloistic Environment

The *Choral Concepts* video provides more information on posture.

We need to establish some specific concepts that revolve around the environments in which our singers will be asked to rehearse and perform.

Like any living thing, singers need to have an environment that supports their endeavors. If we are to expect special (soloistic) results from our singers, then we must provide a *special atmosphere* in which they sing. They must legitimately *feel* special, if only subconsciously.

Keep the rehearsal room neat and organized.   We cannot expect singers to behave and produce as professionals when the work environment does not support a professional atmosphere. Our rehearsal space must be neat, clean, and orderly. There should be comfortable and well-maintained chairs, and preferably risers for them to sit on. The floors should be clean, and any trash should be removed. If no one else can do it, we must. *Our rehearsal room is a reflection of our standards of professionalism and excellence and respect for our singers.*

Allow sufficient space within the ensemble.   The singer deserves to have a "solo area" in which to function effectively while rehearsing. Good posture and vocal production will be impossible if the singer doesn't have enough room. Allow at least four inches between chairs, ideally, six. Even more space can be given in smaller chamber ensembles. It may be difficult for large choruses to have this kind of spacing (four inches), but every effort must be made to do so, or the productivity level will definitely be diminished by the crowded seating arrangement.

In addition, remember that it makes no sense to space the singers properly during rehearsals and then have them in a crowded situation for the performance. We must think and plan ahead for suitable seating arrangements in both circumstances. (More about seating arrangements later.)

Singers should have their own copies of music. Within this concept of the individual soloistic significance of each singer, we should mention the importance of all chorus members having their own music. Sharing music not only negates the overall concept, but also destroys efforts toward correct posture. Each singer deserves to have personal music, with personal markings. (If the only way this can happen is by the conductor finding, raising, or contributing the extra monies to do it, so be it.)

The Relationship between Conductor and Singer

Although we have spent a great deal of time explaining that we want our singers to rehearse and perform like soloists, it is important to define the role of the singer,

> *Singers owe the conductor nothing. The conductor owes singers everything. Everything singers do, they do for themselves, the composer, and the audience.*

the role of the conductor, and the relationship between the two. Conductors, while asserting confident leadership and directives, must make a regular practice of reminding the chorus of their confidence in them as responsible leaders, in this team-effort of respected individuals. Chorus members are to sing like fine soloists, but within the context of teamwork and ensemble. There is an assemblage of *individuals,* all contributing to the fullest extent of their abilities toward a common goal of making beautiful music.

Remind chorus members, also, of their responsibility to the score and the ensemble. If they study privately, you want them to sing in this ensemble exactly as they would sing in a solo appearance. (See Chapter 4 for remarks about soprano volume.) Conductors and private teachers continually give corrective advice. Just because chorus members sing the way they do in the studio or recital does not mean that it is *acceptable for your choral ensemble.* No singer is perfect, and all singers need teaching or coaching in most every situation. Furthermore, as conductor you are ultimately responsible for the overall performance of the ensemble. Your training and unique perspective enable you to lead. If there is a discrepancy between what you are asking them to do and what their voice teacher has taught them, the latter takes precedence (yes, the latter). Mention, however, that in such cases you would appreciate an opportunity to discuss these differences, giving you the option of accepting them or asking that the singer simply not sing during those special and exceptional instances. Thus you don't ask a singer to perform in a way that is contrary to the voice teacher's instructions, but you don't have to accept singing that does not complement your ensemble.

This *entire soloistic concept* will endear you to voice teachers. It will also remove barriers that might arise between those advanced singers studying voice, and the conductor. I have never found this concept to fail, nor to cause a problem in the rehearsal. We will discuss developing a great singing sound further in Chapter 3.

Singers show respect to conductors who earn it. A conductor earns respect by possessing knowledge, effective teaching, and showing respect to the singers. Successful conductors will demonstrate respect not only in the manner in which they treat their ensemble but also in the way they dedicate themselves to their craft. An ensemble will respect the directives and criticisms of an individual who takes responsibility for what he or she does and continually demonstrates knowledge based on study, experience, and hard work.

We need to instill in the minds of our singers that their efforts toward excellence are not done for the conductor. These efforts are done for

1. Themselves—they *deserve* excellence and greatness.

2. Composer/score—without whom we would have nothing to sing. We *all* strive to serve the *score.*

3. Audience—the audience deserves the very best we can give. They deserve nothing less than the highest standard we can deliver.

With this concept honestly and firmly established, the conductor can be incredibly demanding and relentlessly exacting in all areas of choral discipline, rehearsing, and performing. This is not done for the sake of a dictatorial conductor, but for the singers, composers/scores, and the audience. This is crucially important. It must be solidly (and frequently) embedded in the minds of the singers. All work between singers and conductor rests on this perspective. Explain it thoroughly and often.

Breath Support

Most voice teachers seem to feel that teaching proper breathing is the foundation on which all further vocal progress securely rests. We will discuss breath support first and follow that with breath control. There are many methods of teaching this, but we will focus on one that seems to work especially well with ensembles because a large group of singers can comfortably grasp each concept and master it without being confused or needing individual instruction. The method we use should appear to be easy, logical, and based on common sense.

Methods of Breath Support

There are two widely used methods of breath support: the German and Italian. They both agree on the first part, expanding to inhale. They differ on the second, in that the German method teaches the singer to further push out the abdominal muscles to achieve support, and the Italian method instructs the singer to contract the abdominal muscles to support the tone.

The German method originated with brass players who sat somewhat slouched-down in their chairs, and for the support of their tone, pushed the abdominal muscles out and slightly downward, while tucking in the muscles of the buttocks. The German opera singers adopted this.

> ✒ **The Italian method of breathing: Expand to inhale and contract to exhale.**

It works very well for those who choose to use it; however, this method needs very careful attention by a private teacher, in a one-on-one situation, to achieve it properly without causing tension in other parts of the body.

The Italian method of *contracting* to support, which we will discuss and recommend here, is far more easily understood, especially by large groups of singers. This concept also appears to be more logical. The overall concept is that we *expand to inhale and contract to exhale.*

In expanding, we fill up with the air needed to sing. We do not suck the air in by focusing entirely on inhaling. We expand the abdominal muscles and the rib cage. We do not simply push the stomach out. There is a full expansion around the midsection, including the rib cage, toward the middle of the singer's back. This expansion "inhales for us."

This expansion does not include the chest and shoulders, which should be consistently up in the position of the *recommended posture*. It should, therefore, be unnecessary and practically impossible to raise or expand them any further. All movement in breathing should take place below the chest and shoulder area. There is no movement, related to breathing, in the upper chest and shoulder area at all.

During this expansion, you can think of the torso as the shape of a pear or light bulb and as though the lungs were two balloons filling up entirely down through the waist. Once this expansion has taken place, and the lungs are filled with air, a natural process of contraction takes place as the singer sings.

Conscious contraction, however, can take place to physically *support* the tone, especially during an ascending leap. In this case, an active contraction of the abdominal muscles will result in the air stream supporting the upper tone, enhancing both quality and pitch. It is not necessary, for the purposes of this book, to describe the technical physiological aspects of the diaphragm muscle, situated between the thoracic and abdominal cavities, used in respiration. Here, it is simply important to know that *contraction can support tone.*

This correct function of the abdominal muscles (expanding and contracting) is natural in the breathing process of babies. It also happens naturally with older children and adults lying on their backs asleep. When awake, however, most people tend to do just the opposite. They raise their chest and shoulders and pull in the abdomen to inhale, then let the chest and abdomen drop as they exhale. So the challenge is to re-teach singers how to breathe properly after years of breathing improperly.

The Teaching Process

When teaching breathing to ensembles, do so in a manner that will be completely understood and easily applied by each individual singer. The directives must be easy and obvious, nothing complicated or hard to envision. To tell the chorus members that they must now begin to expand-to-inhale and contract-to-exhale, and then expect them to do it, is unreasonable and practically impossible. My experience has shown this is a very difficult concept for singers to understand and immediately perform.

I will now outline a process that has proved very workable with choruses of any age and level of experience—beginning at the age of fourteen. Younger singers could be given things far more productive and practical to learn than how to properly breathe (such as animation, diction, vowel formation, and beginning to learn to read music). I think learning breathing techniques is better left to somewhat more advanced singers.

We conductors and teachers should also realize that most singers do not come to rehearsals to learn how to breathe. They come to *sing.* We can, however, teach breathing techniques without their even knowing we're doing it. We might not specifically tell them what we are about to undertake but, rather, will simply work it in as a part of physical warm-ups. If, however, more advanced singers *are* eager to learn proper breathing techniques, discuss the significance of breathing properly and explain that the learning process is about to begin.

Your common sense will dictate whether teaching breathing techniques to a *very* advanced, experienced chorus is unnecessary. To varying degrees, the members will know and understand the process, and you need not waste their time and yours. Spend valuable rehearsal time teaching breathing techniques when the choruses actually need it. You be the judge.

Long-Range Plan for Teaching Breath Support

In many situations, we would not plan to teach breathing on a given day or during a given week but, rather, over many weeks (with or without the singers' awareness), very slowly, one step at a time. We may teach breathing in the fall, winter, or spring. Following is a five-week plan for developing breath support. If your chorus is not meeting several times a week, you might want to extend this over a longer period of time.

Week 1.   We will begin in a typical rehearsal with the usual warm-ups and vocalizing. After the physical stretching and loosening up that precedes vocalizing, we will insert the first step toward proper breathing without making any reference to breathing at all, let alone *proper* breathing. We simply ask the singers to stand with their best singing posture and, using their hands, slowly push all the air out of their stomachs. For now, let the air come flowing out of their mouths in an *audible manner*. Ask them to push their stomachs in until every ounce of air is gone. Do this very physically two or three times. Then move on to regular vocalizing and rehearsal of songs. They will think of this as a mere extension of the physical warm-ups. We teach them contraction first because pushing the air out is something they can readily do. To try to teach them expansion first is often futile.

During the remainder of this first week, follow the pushing-out-of-the-air with the added directive to let the belly flop out *quickly and fully* while they completely fill up with air. Then on again with vocalizing and rehearsing.

Week 2.   During the second week, ask the singers to let the *full abdominal area* (no longer referred to as the "belly") and including the rib cage, expand and *slowly* fill up with air—as slowly as they previously had pushed the air out. Use a moderately slow count of four for each direction. Begin with "one-two-three-four" to push the air out, and then "one-two-three-four" to fill up.

Explain that, when expanded full of air, they should *imagine* themselves in the shape of an upright pear or upside down light bulb. Remember to consciously breathe through the mouth—because that is the way to breathe most productively—and (for now) rather loudly, so that everyone can really feel it together.

Although they are not aware of it, they are now actually *controlling* the action of the abdominal muscles for both *contraction* and *expansion*. Remember that we are not "teaching breathing"; rather, say that we are just doing physical exercises.

Week 3.   Now that they have actually *controlled* what they are doing in both areas of contraction and expansion (by doing it slowly over four counts), we are at a point when they can be asked to switch these two, *beginning with expansion* over four counts. They now will be able to do that quite well. They are able to *expand to inhale and contract to exhale*, although they might think it is just a physical exercise.

Week 4.   Beginning this week, we will ask them to do the full exercise but in half the time. That is, they should fill up completely with full expansion, but over only *two counts,* and contract completely, also over only two counts. The entire procedure is just twice as fast. They should "fill up as big as a barrel," and then contract "until the air is completely gone"—on just two counts each.

In addition, suggest that they no longer push the air out with the hands. They now place the hands on their rib cages, with the thumbs pointing toward the back, and the index finger pointing toward the front, with the other fingers not touching their sides (so the posture will remain up). The hands in this position will allow them to experience the rib cage expanding in addition to the abdominal area. Both must take place during the expansion. From now on, this will be the position of the hands for these breathing exercises.

Week 5. This week, we will ask the singers to cut the time element again. Do the full expansion followed by the complete contraction, but on only *one count*. Just as much energy is expended, as much abdominal movement occurs, and as much air goes in and out, but it happens on only one count each way. As before, we do this each day for the entire fifth week (or, for several rehearsals if the chorus does not rehearse daily).

The Breathing Exercise

We may now begin the sixth week by telling the chorus, if you haven't already done so, that they have completed learning the process of correct breathing. We can outline the breathing exercise that they have developed over the past five weeks.

The Complete Breathing Exercise

- Expand fully over four counts. The result: a full inhale.
- Contract fully over four counts. The result: a full exhale.
  (Do this four times)

- Expand fully over two counts, resulting in a full inhale.
- Contract fully over two counts, resulting in a full exhale.
  (Do this four times)

- Expand fully over one count, resulting in a full inhale.
- Contract fully over one count, resulting in a full exhale.
  (Do this four times)

This three-step breathing exercise can now be done regularly, if deemed necessary or appropriate, as the final step of the *physical* warm-ups, and just before the *vocal* warm-ups. When teaching this procedure to a private student, the assignment should be to practice it eight to ten times daily for several weeks. Ideally, this manner of breathing, in a natural and less exaggerated manner, becomes the way we breathe habitually, whether singing or not.

Proper Breathing as a Support for the Singing Tone

Now we can explain and show how the preceding breathing technique can be employed to actually support the tone, especially in the upper range and for ascending leaps.

Step 1. Use the third part of the breathing exercise, in which we expand and contract on only *one count each*, but this time, ask the singer to produce a rather loud and somewhat boisterous "ha!" on the contraction of counts two and four: (1)

expand, (2) "ha!," (3) expand, (4) "ha!" This tonal "ha!" must be produced solely by the abdominal contraction and *not vocally from the throat*. Furthermore, its tonal placement should be in the head, *not in the throat*.

Step 2. The next step is to employ this support during the singing of a legato melodic line that uses the scale tones of 1-3-5-3-1. Sing this melody on *la*, but in a very lackadaisical and anemic manner. Repeat in the same manner, but on the top note (the fifth scale tone), employ the abdominal contraction used on the previous "ha!" This buoyantly supports the top tone with a lifting spirit. The result will resemble an accent or sforzando.

Step 3. Do the exercise again, but this time, contract on *both* the *third* and the *fifth* scale tones while ascending. Then contract on the third, fifth, and third. The singer does not continually contract at these three points; think of it more as a panting action.

Step 4. The last step is to use this panting contraction on five scale tones—1 2 3 4 5 4 3 2 1—ascending and descending. By now the contraction movement will be very slight and will lessen with the degree of rapidity at which the exercise progresses.

I would *not* suggest singing a rapid succession of notes *in a song*, using this method of support for each *note*. Melismatic passages are to be sung *melodically* with the brain simply changing pitches, *not* with diaphragmatic activity on each note. This action is solely for the purpose of building and strengthening the abdominal muscles, while developing the ability to support a tone when it is appropriate and needed.

Once the support system has been fully developed, the singer need not consciously employ it. For the *advanced singer,* it is simply a matter of *thinking* support. The body will quite naturally take care of the *physical production* on its own. There will be a slight flick in the area of the diaphragm. It will happen, almost involuntarily, as a result of consciously *thinking* support. Notice that we have not mentioned the word *diaphragm* until the very end of the process, for a very good reason: it is *involuntary*. You cannot *make* it work, and it can be very confusing to members of an ensemble, especially an ensemble of young singers.

Breath Control

Breath control is the ability to control the amount of air being used in a breath. It takes a certain amount of breath flowing past the vocal chords to activate them into producing a singing sound. I'm sure no one knows how much. The problem is that some singers use too much breath, far more than is needed to produce a desirable sound. The result is breathy tone quality and the inability to complete a phrase of normal duration. Others use too little breath, which results in weak anemic sounds that are seldom in tune or pleasing. We will use the following exercise to demonstrate the potential for optimum breath control.

Step 1. Inhale, then—over as long a time as possible—allow the breath to exhale in a soft hissing sound. Time yourself or the chorus and see how long you or they can keep the hissing sound going. Have the singers stand to begin this process, then sit as they run out of air. You may call out the number of seconds they have been hissing, in five-second intervals, so they will know where they were at the time they sat down.

Step 2. After resting a moment, do it again, but this time,

- Inhale fully, as in the two-count portion of the breathing exercise.

- Make the hissing sound only loud enough to be heard; don't over-hiss.

- Consciously keep the abdominal area *expanded*. Remember the pear/light bulb shape we mentioned earlier? *Remain expanded* until the point (number of seconds) at which you ceased hissing the first time. Don't let the abdominal area contract as it normally would during singing (hissing).

- Now, *slowly contract the abdominal are*a (as if there were a reserve tank of air for you to use), thereby extending your original time by as much as ten to fifteen seconds or more.

The chorus will have made significant progress in just one attempt. Consistent practice of this exercise will greatly extend breath control. Granted, it takes more air to produce a sustained *singing tone* than this hissing sound. However, it is relatively easy to develop the hissing time to 45 to 60 seconds. If singing takes twice the air, one could learn to sustain the singing tone for at least 20 seconds. Surely that is sufficient for the duration of any reasonable phrase. It is quite easy to expand the singers' potential breath control to the point of quite comfortably singing most phrases intended to be sung in one breath. There are many more exercises to improve breath control, but the one recommended here seems to be practical for ensemble situations.

Organized Staggered Breathing

When the phrase length cannot possibly be sung in one breath, employ staggered breathing. Regular staggered breathing, during which the singers breathe any time they wish, can be inconsistent and unreliable. *Organized* staggered breathing better serves the situation. This is a method in which the individual singers are *assigned* a beat on which to breathe.

1. If the passage is in four beats to the measure, have the ensemble number-off in fours, that is 1234,1234,1234, and so on; if the passage is in three, they number-off in threes. The time signature determines how they number-off.

2. They may breathe in any measure, but *only on the beat that corresponds to their number*: the ones breathe on any beat one, the twos on any beat two, the threes on any beat three, and the fours on any beat four. (The exception to this is an instance in which you, the conductor, do not want anybody to breathe on a given beat for the purpose of strength, crescendo, rubato, tenuto, or some other nuance on that particular beat.)

3. After assigning the numbers, have the chorus sing through the phrase, breathing on any appropriate beat and *marking with pencil* where the breath was taken. Instruct them to breathe at that point, with consistency, throughout all following rehearsals on this phrase. The result will be reliable, consistent, and effective staggered breathing.

Summary

Be aware of exactly what great professional singing really is, then teach it, and relentlessly expect singers to perform at a consistently high standard.

Singers should (1) have a positive attitude, (2) focus on beautiful vocal sound, (3) assert aggressive leadership, (4) accept musical and vocal responsibility, (5) communicate effectively, and (6) sit or stand with correct singing posture.

Conductors should

- Treat each singer as an *individual,* an individual *soloist,* allowing and expecting the singers to perform as great solo artists who are *sensitive to each other, the music, and the conductor.* Teach (and demand) that they contribute with the same confident and *aggressive* vocal and musical output that they would present as professional soloists. All this can result in the finest possible choral ensemble.

- Provide all singers with their own music—no sharing; be sure each has sufficient space.

- Tell singers to pencil-in every directive you give them.

- Understand the relationship between conductor and singers: "The singers owe the conductor nothing; the conductor owes the singers everything." The singers do what they do for themselves, the composer (score), and the audience.

- Emphasize that the major breath support concept is "Expand to inhale and contract to exhale. " Let the abdominal muscles and rib cage do the breathing for you.

- Teach the recommended process slowly over a period of time, not in a single session.

- Use only enough air to sufficiently produce beautiful tone, but no more.

- Control the use of air and its flow.

- Organize staggered breathing by numbering-off the singers according to the time signature (1, 2, 3, or 4 in 4/4 time), then instruct them to breathe on their assigned beat number in any measure.

Developing a Great Singing Sound

3

The most exciting aspect of any great chorus is the wonderful quality of their singing sound. The first priority in our "umbrella of excellence" is singing, and singing will always be the most important thing we teach. We will start this chapter by briefly examining the development of choral singing in America and establishing the principles of fine singing and tone quality. Then we will present a clear and effective means of creating that tone quality within our choruses.

The Development of Choral Singing in America

America is home to a wide variety of singing styles that reflect the great diversity in American culture, religion, and ethnic backgrounds. Within the field of choral music, there is, and has always been, an enormous range of opinion about how a choir should sound. Within the relatively narrow range of classical choral music, two dominant schools of thought established themselves in the early twentieth century; these two schools resided on opposite ends of the spectrum of choral sound. One came from the choruses of the Lutheran church and university tradition largely established by Olaf Christiansen, and the other came from Westminster Choir College under the direction of John Finley Williamson. The Lutheran tradition was designed for the performance of sacred a cappella music and advocated a pure and perfect approach to singing where a full range of dynamics, emotional expression, and individualism was avoided in favor of controlled beauty, unified tone production, and absolute perfection. The Westminster tradition was developed for the purpose of singing larger, often romantic works with professional symphony

> The American choral pioneers did a phenomenal job of establishing and developing the foundation of what we now enjoy as the American tradition of great choral music. We owe all of them, especially the two American professional giants, Robert Shaw and Roger Wagner, an enormous debt.

orchestras. The style was considered by some to be overly dramatic and artificially dark. Regardless of personal taste, the Westminster sound was easily defined as full-bodied, mature, and powerful. In both instances, the identifiable style of singing carried over into the bulk of the repertoire performed by these two choruses. Choral directors who had the opportunity to hear performances of these groups (or groups directly inspired by one of them) would often emulate one or the other depending on their preferences. Other choir directors were left in the unenviable position of having to reinvent the wheel on their own.

During the 1930s, 1940s, and 1950s, most graduate programs in choral conducting had yet to be established, and organizations like the American Choral Directors Association and the Music Educators National Conference were either in their infancy or not started. There were few choral workshops at which people could gain and share new ideas. Lack of information forced individual conductors to develop their own concepts and methods in a vacuum.

Bringing American Choral Music to the Center

So we were left with a chasm between the Lutheran tradition of Olaf Christiansen and the Westminster tradition of John Finley Williamson. As with most extremes, each was well suited to certain repertoire and certain ensembles but not to a comprehensive style of vocal singing or teaching.

In this vacuum of centrist thinking three of our nation's most significant choral figures arose. They, with the help of others, established a balanced and versatile style of choral singing. Robert Shaw and Roger Wagner in the professional world and Robert Fountain at Oberlin College sensed the need to bring the choral sound from the extremes of Christiansen and Williamson toward a more centered approach. The new sound was based on complete vocal freedom; it was healthy, natural, unaffected, and unmanipulated. Singers were not directed to sound exactly alike. They were asked to be *sensitive to each other, the score, and the conductor.* Priority was given to naturally beautiful vocal production that, when combined with an energetic spirit, solid musicianship, expressive musicality, and textual communication, produced excellent well-balanced sounds. This sound gave each singer the freedom to sing with full expressive assertiveness. They could perform without compromising their voices.

Developing Singing Styles

I recommend that there be one basic manner of physically singing and that this manner not be *drastically* altered to sing in different styles. I do believe in allowing the music itself to subtly encourage the singer to minimally modify the vocal sound when changing styles. But to *completely* change the way of *physically singing,* when changing from Palestrina to Brahms to Stravinsky, is neither musically necessary nor vocally healthy. Singers should not consistently avoid vibrato, nor should they use an overweighted Wagnerian style. Certain things equate to simple musical *common sense:*

1. To varying degrees, minimize vibrato and dynamics for earlier music (composers of the Renaissance period and earlier) and occasionally use a straight tone (without vibrato) for certain cadences and their gradual approach.

2. Sing in a fuller, freer style for the music of later composers (beginning with Baroque, more with Classic, and then with special depth for the music of Romantic composers).

3. Occasionally eliminate vibrato for tone clusters and other appropriate moments in contemporary music.

Allow the voices to blend naturally. Singers who use a healthy, naturally beautiful, sensitive approach to vocal production will produce voices that blend. In fact, if they are singing like this, the word *blending* seldom needs to be mentioned. Think back for a moment to the wonderful sound of the Robert Shaw and Roger Wagner Chorales. They both consisted totally of professional soloists, yet blended perfectly. There wasn't a conductor's stylized *vocal manipulation.* To manipulate the voice of a singer is to partially paralyze a singer's ability to think, feel, and fully express themselves. We can use the examples of Shaw, Wagner, and Fountain as a basis for the way we develop the sound of our chorus. Remember, when conductors create an artificial manipulated choral sound, they are doing a disservice to the singers.

Do not manipulate the tone quality of singers. The human voice is capable of a tremendous range of vocal styles and colors. It would be a mistake not to use this wonderful variety of sound. However, consistent manipulation of the voice, or the deliberate training of singers to sound a "certain way," is both wrong and potentially harmful. The sound of every good choir should be quite similar: free, healthy, natural, vibrant, beautiful, expressively musical, and personally communicative. The only differences should be in areas of vocal development and maturity, *not in one conductor's style over that of another.* Singers should sing like natural human beings, not like a conductor's conception of how they might be transformed, manipulated, or manufactured into something else!

Encourage natural vibrato. The vibrato is one of the most obvious elements of tone quality that conductors seem tempted to manipulate. It can also be the most dangerous. If young singers from approximately fourteen to sixteen years of

A Famous Partnership

Julius Herford was a great musician and teacher. He escaped from Hitler's Nazi Germany with his wife Hanna and came to New York in the late 1930s. He had been the conductor of the Berlin Philharmonic Chorus, a concert pianist, and musicologist. Composer Lukas Foss introduced Julius to the young American choral conductor, Robert Shaw.

Shaw suggested to Herford that in return for teaching Herford English, Herford would teach Shaw music. Thus began a teacher-student relationship that lasted until 1967. Herford would play masterworks at the keyboard into the early hours of the morning ("until my fingers would bleed") and Shaw, in return, would read English poetry to teach Herford the language of his newly adopted country. In addition, Julius served as musical advisor for every serious piece of music that Shaw conducted and eventually for the Robert Shaw Chorale. Herford literally taught Shaw, phrase by phrase, piece by piece, most of the great choral masterworks.

Herford and Shaw became an inseparable team, appearing throughout the country, with Herford lecturing on the major work Shaw was conducting. More than anything else, this unique partnership influenced quality choral music in America. Shaw was phenomenal—extremely intelligent, gifted, curious, and open to Herford's teaching. Herford's teaching became widely known and respected because of Shaw's remarkable execution of Herford's musical ideas. Those of us in American choral music will always be grateful for their groundbreaking achievements.

age are taught and encouraged to sing freely, without strain or forcing, they will usually develop an involuntary, *natural* vibrato. It is *unnatural* to prevent this from occurring. Granted, as singers progress and mature, they sometimes push a naturally pleasing vibrato into an offensive wobble. This most frequently arises as a result of oversinging or an attempt to sing in a false manner, older than is appropriate for the age of the singer (for example, sopranos who as young girls tried to sound like older women). This is offensive to their fellow singers, the conductor, and the audience. Relaxation and conscious listening by such a singer can usually help correct this problem.

Singers should be encouraged to allow the natural vibrato to function normally. The only exceptions are tone clusters of contemporary music, some phrase endings and cadences in renaissance music, and, very rarely, for *momentary* special effects in other music. I strongly oppose the total elimination of vibrato, in a consistent manner, for *any* style of music. Through simple sensitivity, the vibrato may be encouraged to somewhat lessen or strengthen, as desired, for different stylistic periods of composition, but it should never be totally omitted as a consistent way of singing. A final reminder: Just as vibrato should not be totally eliminated, it should never be forced to happen either. Vibrato is a natural evolution of relaxed singing.

Defining and Teaching a Natural Choral Sound

We must make the concept of a natural choral sound as simple as possible. When we simplify concepts, they become more effectively taught and learned.

Think of adjectives that appropriately describe fine singing and tone quality. As you do, you will discover that they all fall into three basic categories: energy, beauty, and placement. (Remember that *placement* is crucial to *resonance* and should be thought of as one unit: "placement/resonance.") Table 3.1 will help you to get started.

Table 3.1   Words Describing Energy, Beauty, and Placement

Energy	Beauty	Placement
alive	clear	brilliant
animated	floating	focused
buoyant	beautiful	forward
energetic	free	full
exciting	lovely	rich
lifting	lyrical	ringing
spirited	natural	resonant
vibrant	pure	round
vital	relaxed	warm

You may be able to come up with more. If the words are specifically descriptive (rather than general terms, such as colorful, artistic, and mature, which could be applied to any of these words, in Table 3.1) they will also fall into one of these three categories of *energy, beauty, and placement.*

Energy

The voice is the only living instrument. Life is energy. The voice is energy. Energy, therefore, must be the very foundation of vocal production. We might go so far as to say that energy is 80 percent of great singing, and everything else is contained within the remaining 20 percent. This energy holds within itself everything from attitude and posture to breathing techniques to the animated, vital human being we will discuss now.

Most important, singers shouldn't have negative thoughts while singing: no negative thoughts about the song, the voice, fellow singers, the conductor, or any other situational surroundings. Everything must be positive. We are what we think. If we think negatively, our bodies respond negatively, affecting our voices. The first priority is being a totally positive person. *The conductor must create a positive environment in which the voice can truly live.*

The conductor is the example of positive energy. Energy is reflected in inspiration and motivation, facial expression, love and enthusiasm for the music and singers, and the overall work output. The singers will always be a reflection of the conductor, positive or negative. The conductor can never expect anything for free. Results will only come through knowledge, example, teaching, and inspiration. The very sound of the conductor's speaking and singing voice will enhance the productivity of energy from the singers or detract from it. Videotape yourself and check the level of energy from which your singers might draw.

Let your energetic tone create energetic sound.   Let's begin with you, the conductor. Practice speaking. What does it sound like to speak in a manner that is alive, animated, buoyant, energetic, exciting, lifting, spirited, vibrant, and vital? Speak as though you are abundantly happy, as though you have the best possible news to share with someone and can hardly wait to express it. Be completely positive and spirited! Practice, over and over, speaking that way. Make up some positive thoughts and really deliver them! (If this concept is overdone, the conductor would sound ridiculous. Do not exaggerate it.)

Now sing a vocalise in this same manner, without compromising the energy, on 1-3-5-3-1 (*yah*). Raise your eyebrows and let your eyes sparkle! Through this simple vocalise on *yah*, communicate the happiest, most positive message possible. Continue in ascending half steps.

Then repeat the exercise, singing *mp,* but doubling the energy. Repeat it, again doubling the energy level, but now singing *piano*, and then, *pianissimo*. Remember that your enthusiasm cannot diminish. It must increase. This is *energetic singing*! The feeling should be incredibly stimulating.

Teach energy.   If it is difficult for you to do this exercise without being inhibited, how will you inspire your singers to do it? First, you will absolutely have to master it. We must be the prime example, always, of everything. *We are the source.* That means we must lose all of our inhibitions and become totally consumed by this energetic process. Then, and only then, will we have the potential to become a useful example and teacher for the singers.

Now, how to get *them* to do it? We will have to be creative and imaginative. Invent exercises that will allow them to be completely uninhibited and aggressively physical.

The following exercise has worked quite well for me with every chorus with which I have worked. It is very important that it be done at a lightning-fast pace, hardly giving the singers time to think— spontaneously, they'll do it very well. If we linger during the process, giving them time to think about it, their inhibitions will take over and the entire process will fail. Here it is, word for word.

Step 1: "Chorus, I want you to imagine that there is an empty seat next to you and that your best friend (with whom you really enjoy singing) comes into the room. Now, before your friend has the chance to sit anywhere else, you enthusiastically invite him or her to sit beside you. You really extend yourself, and make sure that your friend knows you want him or her to sit beside you, and nowhere else!"

Step 2: "Now, pretend that I am that best friend. On my cue, I want you to enthusiastically invite me to come and sit in that imaginary empty chair beside you. Sit up with good posture, but with a stone-sober face, and on my cue, light up with incredible energy and invite me to come and sit beside you, by saying a most enthusiastic 'Hey, come here and sit down!' Say it with your entire being!"

You will notice that the physical energy and personal communication extended in this invitation is very similar to the assertive delivery and projection used in the successful singing of a joyful phrase ("Gloria in excelsis Deo," for example). The feeling within the singer is basically the same. The *outward* physical energy may be somewhat lessened, based on the demands of the phrase. Remember, however, that energy does not depend on dynamics. This energy we're speaking of should be the foundation of all singing, from *ppp* to *fff*.

Returning to the exercise, the chorus will respond with varying degrees of energy. Some will really do it. Others will do it half-heartedly. So, you give them another chance.

Step 3: "Chorus, this time I'll be looking around the room to spot those who just can't seem to bring themselves out of their inhibited shells, those who can't animate sufficiently to the point of really inviting me to come and sit next to them. And, those who can't get it will stand and do it alone, until they *do* get it! So now, let's try it again."

This time they all will give you 100 percent with a most energetic *"Hey, come over here and sit down!"* (We would never follow-up on the threat to single out some to do it alone. That would be embarrassing and counterproductive. But, it did serve its purpose. They all really got with it!)

The next step in this process is to change this *imaginary situation* to one in which the rehearsal has already begun; everyone is focused and concentrating on the music, and there is absolutely no talking permitted. (Keep it moving fast!)

Step 4: "We'll do the same thing again. There is an empty chair next to you. Your best friend enters, and you want him or her to sit next to you. This time, however, you cannot be disruptive with abundant bodily movement and sound. You must manage to get your friend's attention with only a whisper and minimal bodily movement. You must double the original energy and intensity, but invite in a much quieter manner. On my cue, *do it*!" They will.

Immediately put this energetic action into singing. Before they can even think another thought, have them sing a vocalise (1-3-5-3-1 on yah or nee-ay-ah–) in this same *extremely animated manner.* And, sing it softly, demonstrating how energetic soft singing can really be. More than just *forte* singing can be filled with energy; energy is even *more* important in soft singing. Many choruses perform soft passages, especially in slow tempi, in a lifeless manner. The result is disastrous. If properly energized, soft singing can often communicate more effectively than louder dynamic levels do.

> ## ✎ *"Sing the hell out of the louds and sing the hell out of the softs!"*
>
> Here's a lesson I experienced as a young conductor. I was beginning my career in choral conducting when I asked a mature and experienced university conductor to tell me the reason all his ensembles always sounded so exciting. He answered, "Because we sing the hell out of the louds and we sing the hell out of the softs!" This was one of the best descriptions of energy I have ever heard. Obviously, we should never push energy to the point of destroying healthy tone quality. But every single note of every single phrase of every single song should be filled with this primary human and spiritual energy. The degree to which it is intensified depends on the song, its style, and potential emotional impact.

Can you imagine a chorus that consistently sings with this kind of energetic wide-eyed enthusiasm singing flat, with lifeless tone, or lacking effective projection and communication? The potential of all other qualities rests on *energy first!* After decades of observing lifeless choruses in which singers had no concept of the energy needed to sing well, it is clear to me that without specific training a chorus will not sing with energy. In fact, I have seldom worked with a chorus of any age and experience level that didn't need this exercise. I have never found the exercise to fail. Try it, or come up with one you like better.

Teach buoyant singing. Another very important aspect of energetic singing is the presence of a *lifting, buoyant, singing tone.* The tone should not be forced straight ahead. It should lift, almost as though coming out of a trampoline in slow motion. Living things tend to go upward: trees, flowers—growth of any kind, including people. The voice is the only living instrument. Let it also ascend with an upward feeling, a buoyant feeling. This concept is absolutely paramount to great singing, yet buoyancy seldom exists.

Although appropriate in all styles and dynamic levels, when singing *forte* or *fortissimo,* caret-accents (ᵛ) placed above the notes (indicating a *lifting buoyancy*) will do much to bring life to these notes that can so easily sound forced and straight. I cannot overemphasize the significance of this concept. It can make a truly amazing difference in achieving a vital, energetic sound.

We might close this portion on energy by saying that the danger will almost always be in the direction of not enough energy rather than too much. Sufficient energy within the total being of each singer, throughout every minute of every rehearsal and concert, is singularly the most difficult quality to achieve and maintain.

Never take it for granted. And remember, without it, the singing might be beautiful but it will most certainly be boring, flat, and lifeless, quite similar to a beautiful person who has no personality. The key is always energy first; then all other things at least have the potential to be added to it. Use wisdom and judgment, and always remember one of our most important concepts— *Any good idea taken to extreme immediately becomes a bad idea.*

Beauty

Beauty is not as relative as some may think. If several singers came into a room, and each one sang the same solo, those listening would probably tend to agree about which singers sang beautifully, and which ones, if any, sang with an offensive tone.

It may be easier to identify a tone that would be considered offensive or ugly— tones characterized as harsh, edgy, shrill, breathy, strained, forced, dull, or strident. A conductor must become conditioned to respond immediately to such sounds. Our response should be similar to the sight and sound of fingernails being scraped down a chalkboard; ugly tones must be literally *impossible* to accept.

Therefore, when we hear an unacceptable vocal sound, we stop *immediately* and correct it. Two things will take place: the singers are taught (or re-taught) the proper way to sing, and they soon learn that we will not accept anything but a beautiful tone. Singers who sing too loudly create the majority of offensive sounds. Therefore, establish a simple rule: *Singers should never sing louder than they can sing beautifully.* Teach it and enforce it.

The conductor must use this concept of beautiful tone to channel the enthusiasm of the choir. If we are incredibly inspirational, our singers, if left unchecked, may oversing. Singers under dynamic and inspirational conductors want to give as much as the conductor seems to require. In such cases, the well-intentioned conductor is usually not aware that he or she is demanding an inordinate amount of vocal output, a result of the intense passion of the musical moment in which everyone seems to be entrapped. The result is oversinging.

Singers must be told to take the same energy and enthusiasm and direct it toward diction, facial animation, breath support, and sensitive listening, rather than toward sheer volume. Unbridled energy should never be allowed to distort the tone, causing it to become close to an uncontrolled shout. The singing tone must be beautifully exciting or spirited, beautifully passionate, beautifully tranquil or serene, beautifully *fortissimo* or *pianissimo*. Always beautiful.

How to teach beautiful singing. Beautiful singing is clear, floating, flowing, free, lovely, lyrical, natural, pure, and relaxed. The most important words are *lyrical, free,* and *natural.* A lyrical cantabile approach to all singing, with an open and free throat, is the foundation of beauty. Even more dramatic and powerful singing should be done on this foundation of lyricism if the voice is to last and remain beautiful throughout a long singing career.

As with energy, examples of lyrical, free, and natural singing should be presented for the singers to emulate. A conductor should develop his or her voice to the extent that vocal examples demonstrated for the singers (which are worth more than the proverbial thousand words) are done in this recommended lyrical manner. A conductor does not need to be an accomplished vocal soloist to do this, but must develop the basic ability to demonstrate properly. Further examples may be given to the singers by having them hear fine soloists perform, either live or on recordings. Encourage this. The singers chosen to serve as role models, however, must sing with a beautiful lyrical quality (such as Kathleen Battle singing Mozart).

Our singers need to have the appropriate sound, the ideal sound, firmly established in their mind's ear before they can reproduce it in their own singing. They should be striving for this ideal sound throughout every note of every rehearsal and concert. If they do, they will be moving consistently toward the goal of beautiful tone. If they don't, they will simply be learning more songs with the same vocal quality with which they sang last week, last month, and last year.

With this recommended process, singers will consistently improve, and someday they may reach or even surpass their role models. This is not to say they should sound exactly like someone else. It simply makes good sense to have a sound goal in mind for which a singer continually strives. I will frequently remind the chorus, "Don't sing like you, sing like someone much, much better—always."

One more thought on lyrical singing: *all singing* should be based on a lyrical foundation. Avoid oversinging in an attempt to develop a more dramatic style. Lyrical singing is the best singing, whether the voice is powerfully large, very light, or anywhere within that range. True dramatic singing, by a mature singer qualified to do it, is also done in a manner that could be described as lyrical.

The ideal overall choral sound is based on the following qualities within the four sections (soprano, alto, tenor, and bass):

- A soprano sound based on the quality of a lyrical first soprano
- An alto sound based on the quality of a lyrical mezzo with *warm tone quality,* not an overly dark, manufactured, contralto
- A tenor sound based on a lyrical first tenor
- A bass sound based on the quality of a lyrical baritone

This approach will give a consistency to the over-all sound of the chorus, giving it the potential to be in tune, unified, natural, and beautiful. Don't worry about those singers who are, in fact, true low basses, mature altos, second tenors or second sopranos. The lyrical approach *will not compromise their true sound.* They will simply sing with their own sound, but do so in a more natural, unaffected manner.

Placement

The placement of sound within the head is the primary determining factor in the production of great resonant singing, second only to the basic ingredient of *energy.*

As with many aspects of singing, imagery will also be of great importance in this area. You can't *really* place the voice in the head, or anywhere else. But you can direct it, *through imagery,* to be anyplace you want it to be: the head, the chest, back or forward in the area of the mouth and throat, the cheekbones, or the nasal area.

Tonal production, whether speaking or singing, takes place through the process of air activating vocal chords in the throat. So even though we spend a lot of time and effort telling singers to "get the sound out of the throat," that, in reality, is exactly where it originates. The goal, however, is directing the sound, originally created in the throat, to other areas of the head for the purpose of enhancing its quality and to eliminate the potential of singing *only in the throat,* causing harmful muscular tension in the throat and undesirable tone quality.

Creating and maintaining the use of head tone. Through this method of imagery we will create a manner of singing in which all singers can sing with effective *head tone.* This means that the tone is thought of as being produced in the area from the hairline down to the jaw and chin. At first, emphasize that the tone should be mentally placed only from the *hairline down to the nose and cheekbone* area (for a substantial period of time and, in many situations, indefinitely). Lowering to the jaw and chin area should wait until the higher placement is very securely established.

Using imagery to explain placement. To help singers understand the concept of placement, use imagery to describe placement and its use. With the use of creative imagination, the tone can be placed exactly where we want it to be. I have done this with my own singing, and have seen it succeed 100 percent of the time with literally thousands of other singers with whom I have worked over past decades.

Figure 3.1

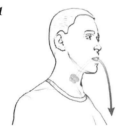

Image 1: The throat is a hollow tube, without vocal chords; it is simply a passageway for the airstream. When we talk, this airstream activates the vocal chords, and sound comes directly out of our mouths in the form of words. Their sound is neither sustained nor projected, as it is when we sing, but simply falls over our lower lip onto the floor (see Figure 3.1).

Figure 3.2

Image 2: When we sing, we picture our head as a hollow cavity with the vocal chords located in the area of our brains. Now we imagine that the airstream continues up the *back of the neck,* into the head, and connects with the vocal chords in their new location (see Figure 3.2). It is important to establish with our imagery that the placement of the vocal chords and the pathway of the airstream are radically different when we *sing* than when we *speak.*

Figure 3.3

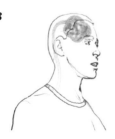

Image 3: The resonance that now can take place in the upper portion of the head is similar to the vibrating and resonating of the strings of a guitar, violin, or piano with the soundboard and body of the instrument. When the airstream connects with the vocal chords in their new singing position, they vibrate and so does the entire head. This creates a resonance similar to the guitar, piano, or violin. This resonance, beginning in the forehead and temples only, can later be developed to vibrate throughout the entire area of the head—forehead and temples first, nose and cheekbones next, and then jaw and chin (see Figure 3.3). Eventually, this area of the full head becomes the singer's soundboard.

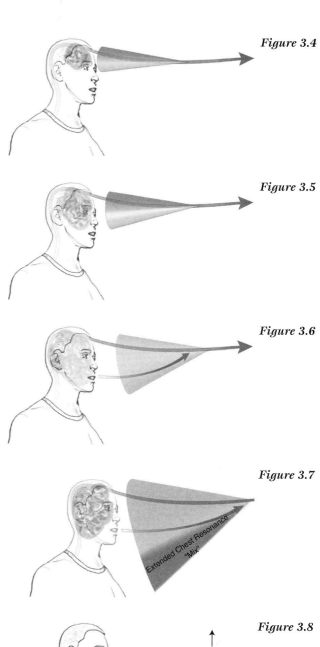

Figure 3.4

Figure 3.5

Figure 3.6

Figure 3.7

Extended Chest Resonance
"Mix"

> 〰 As the forehead area of resonance and placement lowers, it does not bring the top down with it. The lowering process is an *extension,* not a replacement, of the top-most areas.

Image 4: The tone does not come out of the mouth—it comes at first straight out of the forehead. This highly resonant tone is no longer falling over the lips and onto the floor but, rather, is emanating from the *forehead* and envisioned as a large, rounded cone (see Figure 3.4). This cone is similar in shape to that of a unicorn's horn. At the point of this "cone-of-tone," we will have a beautiful, resonant, ringing, and highly focused tone.

Images 5, 6, and 7: These involve expanding the cone eventually to encompass the full head and chest resonance.

Once this forehead area is well established, we can use our imagery to further lower the *bottom* of the cone to encompass the nose and cheekbone areas as well and, eventually, the full head. (Advanced singers, studying privately, will also develop this extension to include a mix of head tone with full or partial chest resonance.)

Figure 3.5 shows the resonating area as the forehead, temples, nasal region, and cheekbones. Imaging is the most productive and frequently used method of producing vocal tone placement and can be taught in any and all choral situations. Although we begin with the forehead only, that is a preliminary step to the more comprehensive area. Ideally, singers will consistently sing from the cheekbones upward through the head. In fact, we might say that *no singing takes place below the cheekbones.* It's all in the top half of the head until, with further study, lower area resonance may be mixed in—as can be seen in Figures 3.6 and 3.7.

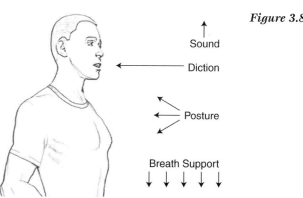

Figure 3.8

Sound
Diction
Posture
Breath Support

Allowing each region of the body its own function.
Because we want to encourage singers to use their entire bodies while singing, it is important to establish roles for the various parts of the body (see Figure 3.8).

This concept is appropriate and applies to *singers of all ages.* This method keeps the workload of singing out of the throat, which causes tension, strain, and a multitude of vocal problems. Over and over again in my experience, this technique has been proven to enable singers to

- Sing beautifully, well into older age
- Produce a brilliant, full, ringing tone without forcing and straining
- Rehearse and perform the demanding works of composers such as Beethoven without becoming vocally tired

In addition, vocal power can be achieved with great uniformity of sound. This will result in a tone that is brilliant, focused, forward, full, rich, ringing, resonant, round, and warm—all the adjectives mentioned in Table 3.1 under *placement*.

Exercises to Help Establish Head-Tone Placement

Exercises 3.1 and 3.2 need only be used minimally for female and young male singers to begin conceptualizing head tone. These exercises are, however, the foundation of great singing for more mature (over 17-year-old) male singers. Exercise 3.3 is basic and appropriate for all singers.

Exercise 3.1.   Instruct the singers to say the expression "uh-huh." Have them say the first syllable "uh" out of the head, coming straight from the throat and chin area. Have them say it with the head slightly tilted back to help them actually feel it coming from this area. The sound should be very shallow, immature, and rather bright. Then have them follow that with the second syllable "huh," tilting their heads slightly forward, encouraging the tone to come up the back of the head and out of the forehead. This second syllable can be led with breath through the nose, as though the breath is actually leading the tone, or the tone is following the column of breath.

Have them do this several times, until you feel they are really experiencing the *difference* of out-of-the-head and in-the-head. Follow this by asking them to produce the second syllable tone (huh) on an ascending pitch (the interval of a perfect fourth is effective). Do this first with a slow glissando to the upper pitch, as in the following Exercise 2, so they can really feel and hear the tone leaving the throat and entering the head.

Instead of "uh-huh," now use "ah-uh." The "ah" will more easily demonstrate the difference in beginning out of the head, placing the tone in the throat and chin area for a shallow and bright "ah," and then into the head for a "ringing tone" of more substance, on "uh. The "h" originally used in "huh" is no longer needed. Move from the first sound "ah," to the second sound "uh," in a legato manner as you slowly glissando upward (see Example 3.1). Finally, sing it using only "ah" for both notes: "ah------ah."

Example 3.1

ah — uh   ah — uh   ah — uh

Exercise 3.2.   Now, *gradually* increase the speed of the glissando until there is simply the articulate interval of a fourth. Ascend from the lower (out of the head) note to the upper (in the head) note in a moderate tempo. Again, *first* use "ah------uh," and *eventually only* "ah" ("ah------ah").

Example 3.2

ah — uh   ah — uh   ah — uh

Exercise 3.3.   Next, ask the singers to sing nee-ay-ah-ay-ee completely in the established head tone, on a sustained pitch (F natural, mid-range), ascending by half steps after a breath. They should place their fingers under their cheekbones, helping them relate to *singing above the hands in the head.* (Be sure the elbows are up and out, away from the sides, so that the posture remains as it should be.)

After a few of these, have the singers begin again, this time alternating each exercise, one in the head, above the hands, the next out of the head, below the hands. Encourage them to feel extremely *positive* when singing in the head and above the hands. They might be told to feel a bit *negative* when singing below the hands, in the throat and chest area. This will teach them to consciously *feel, know,* and *appreciate* the *difference.* Use both bright (Example 3.3[1]) and dark (Example 3.3[2]) vowels, alternating with each ascending half step if you wish.

In Example 3.3, the arrow pointing to the right is for the purpose of establishing forward motion at this moment in the exercise. More will be said about forward motion later; for now, simply feel the first three notes as *one* musical group, and the last two as *another,* all within the *one single phrase.*

Example 3.3

1) nee - ay - ah - ay - ee   1) nee - ay - ah - ay - ee   1) nee - ay - ah - ay - ee
2) noo - oh - aw - oh - oo   2) noo - oh - aw - oh - oo   2) noo - oh - aw - oh - oo

As we will see in more detail later, it is very important, in warm-up vocalizing sessions, to *begin* with an emphasis on *head-tone placement.* This needs to be reinforced on a regular basis. Develop your own additional exercises for this purpose. Completely solidify head-tone placement in the singers' minds. This is very simply *the way we sing.*

Summary

Three elements—energy, beauty, and placement—all necessary to produce a great singing sound. Energy without beauty and placement can easily become chaotic and sound like yelling. Beauty without energy and placement will be lifeless and dull. Placement without energy and beauty can become weighty and droning. As conductor, your role is to bring these three elements together:

• Understand each element thoroughly, demonstrate each effectively, and teach them with clarity and inspiration. We don't teach them once, twice, or a few times. We teach them every single day for the rest of our lives.

- Avoid extremes of any kind.

- Do not manipulate the singer's tone quality to become your own recognizable "choral sound."

- Do not force the elimination of vibrato—it is a healthy, natural manner of singing.

- Challenge singers to *think*—the voice has no brain, but it will do what the brain tells it to do. Consistently employ the process of imagery to emulate great singers and their manner of singing and to progress as effectively and quickly as possible toward this vocal excellence. Have the proper image in mind, then command the voice to produce it—the voice will follow the directive. Don't give the voice an option of doing otherwise.

Individual Section Characteristics, Problems, and Solutions

*W*e have already discussed vocal and choral tone in general. We will now become specific, addressing each of the four voice parts (soprano, alto, tenor, and bass). As the title of this chapter suggests, each of the four has very individual characteristics, problems and solutions. To be an effective teacher, the conductor must have thorough knowledge of each vocal category.

Knowing the needs of our performing forces is both fundamental and paramount. As we will discuss later in Chapter 12 on conducting, the conductor is a servant, serving the singers/players, the score, and the audience. *To serve the singers fully, we must know* **how to teach voice** *and the specific techniques necessary for the singers' success.*

This immediately brings to mind the potential problems facing the keyboard specialist who eventually becomes a choral conductor. I do not mean to imply that keyboard specialists cannot become great and effective choral conductors. I have known many that are. They simply must be aware that the choral conductor is a *voice teacher* in every rehearsal. The choral conductor must see effective voice teaching as the *first* priority.

In this chapter, we'll also discuss vibrato and problems associated with its use, and we will evaluate two concepts of choral section balance and review vowel formation.

Vibrato

As we noted in Chapter 3, vibrato is a natural phenomenon for singers who sing freely, naturally, and in a healthy manner. Instrumentalists must *learn* vibrato, but singers *acquire it naturally.* To force its elimination from the developed voice is unnatural. To do so in a consistent manner simply limits the potential beauty and freedom of the singer. Remember, it is appropriate to minimize it in certain instances and briefly eliminate it in others. Just don't eliminate it altogether.

Vibrato Problems

Problems usually arise in one of two categories: too wide and slow, or too fast and fluttery. The latter is more serious. Either situation is caused by tension or being vocally out of shape.

Too fast. If the vibrato is too fast and sounds nervous and fluttery, the problem is very serious. The singer should probably *not* sing in an ensemble, but should seek private study for a period of six months to a year and consider the following procedures:

1. Relax the throat and neck area, allowing all tendons and muscles surrounding the vocal chords to be at ease. Keeping the back of the throat open and relaxed is so important to naturally beautiful singing. Be aware of slightly raising the soft pallet (a feeling similar to the climactic moment of a yawn).

2. Sing softly, *mp* at first, then, as the singer improves, gradually progress to *mf*.

3. Consistently place the voice in the head. This is extremely important and will eliminate potential throat and neck stress, which negatively affects vocal chords and vibrato. (See the discussion of head voice in Chapter 3.)

4. Spend at least four to six months singing very easy vocal exercises and songs— in a slow, patient progress toward fixing this problem.

(Sadly, if progress with qualified professional guidance, patience, and controlled practicing seems impossible, it may be that the singer will simply need to seek another activity.)

Too slow. A vibrato that is too slow and wobbly can usually be remedied in the ensemble rehearsal (and with private study if possible) through the following procedures:

1. Completely relax the throat and neck area.

2. Sing somewhat more softly (*mp* to *mf*).

3. Consistently place the voice in the head area.

4. Use the voice and get it in good condition with regular ensemble participation and private practice that places special emphasis on flexibility exercises.

5. Consciously relax, listening for a beautiful, natural vibrato—and nothing more.

Generally speaking, the solution lies in relaxing and listening, placing the tone in the head, and not forcing or straining, especially in the upper range. If you ask a singer (usually a soprano) to "Sing that again, but this time relax, think of minimizing the vibrato to a normal beautiful sound, and listen to yourself," there will be an immediate, marked improvement. You are not actually teaching something specific, just asking the singer to listen, relax, and think. The problem of slow, wobbly vibrato usually arises from thoughtless oversinging (too loud in the upper range, especially with younger sopranos) or because the voice is simply out of shape as a result of aging, inactivity, or both. The singer's conscious mind is the first step in correcting the problem; physical conditioning is the next.

The conductor must listen carefully to the chorus, especially the soprano section, and simply not allow vocal sounds in which the vibrato becomes a distraction from fine singing. Be aware, and when you hear a negative sound of *any kind,* stop, teach, and correct it before you proceed.

> ℘ Remember, do not accept bad sounds. If you accept offensive sounds, you'll get them. A bad vocal sound should be something you simply cannot abide and will not tolerate.

Singers, eventually, will not do those things that are consistently unacceptable to the conductor/teacher. We're in charge. We make the rules. We enforce them. We determine the resulting output of our chorus. If it is great, we deserve the credit. If it is bad, we deserve the blame.

Think back on the general and specific areas of producing a fine vocal sound. Clearly organize the concepts in your mind. Formulate your own thinking about the *singing sound*—what it should be, how to present examples of it, how to consistently teach it, and how to inspire the singers to want to do what you teach.

Individual Section Characteristics

Sopranos

Sopranos are like the first violins of an orchestra and the first trumpets in a concert band or wind ensemble. They most frequently have the melody, and as the upper voice, they are most easily heard. As with a weak violin or trumpet section, if the sopranos do not sing well, the entire ensemble will sound weak and will struggle to do well. What are the keys to establishing a quality soprano section? In addition to everything we have already discussed, certain concepts pertain to the soprano section specifically.

Sing lyrically. Sopranos should possess a somewhat youthful freshness with great clarity, flexibility, and warmth. "Youthful freshness" means that the sopranos will sing with an animated youthful spirit without losing a healthy body of tone. All too often, sopranos attempt to sound like older professionals (perhaps in a conscious or unconscious approach to emulate an admired voice they have heard). High school singers often try to imitate thirty-year-olds, and college singers aim for the sound of forty-year-olds. The obvious result? They all sound old and manufactured, and by the time they actually are forty, they sound sixty. It is fine to emulate *professional excellence,* but not to imitate "older" sounds.

I often ask high school sopranos who are oversinging to try to sound like "the finest ninth-grader in the nation." Repeat, *finest* ninth-grader. They immediately sound naturally beautiful and lyrical. With older women who sound labored, weighed-down, and a bit wobbly, I ask them to do an impression of the "finest eighteen-year-old in the nation." Repeat, *finest.* They, too immediately begin to sound lyrical and naturally beautiful.

Although we want sopranos to sing with a full-bodied, natural sound, *less is often more* for the soprano section. Their naturally bright tone color and position at the top of the choral range make it likely that the soprano section will easily dominate the other voices. This is not a fault, just a fact. If the conductor encourages the soprano section to sing with sensitivity to the other sections of the choir, they will balance well. The conductor should not attempt to guard against poor balance by intimidating the soprano section into singing with an anemic, immature, or lifeless tone. Simply encourage beauty and sensitivity.

To a greater extent than with altos, tenors, and basses, all the characteristics listed in Chapter 3 under the category "beauty" apply to the soprano section. Never let sopranos' minds and ears dismiss the words *lyrical* and *beautiful*.

Do not sing forte above the staff.   Thoughtful composers who are knowledgeable about the voice will not write *forte* for sopranos above the staff. Neither will they make difficult textual demands for sopranos above the staff.

The soprano section should never sing louder than *mp* or *mf* above the staff. Even if the sopranos were all true professionals with splendid voices, *forte* singing above the staff would totally obliterate balance with the rest of the chorus and create an unpleasant sound for the audience. If the composer writes *f* or *ff* for the entire chorus, the sopranos must still sing only *mp/mf* above the staff. The resulting sound will be both balanced and pleasing. In addition, the sopranos will not destroy their voices by singing too loudly in their upper range.

Compromise soprano diction above the staff. Certain vowels and many consonants cannot be produced in the upper range of the soprano voice without causing vocal strain and unpleasant tone quality. In most instances above high F♯, sopranos should compromise all sounds toward an "ah" opening of the jaw.

In higher passages, above G♯, the sopranos should just simply sing "ah" instead of the printed text, returning to the text when the melody descends into the more comfortable range within the staff. We might point out that coloratura sopranos seldom sing words when singing in their top range. They sing a vowel sound that is comfortable for them in that range and melodic line. This same principle applies to our sopranos when singing above the staff. The diction will not suffer because the other sections of the chorus can pick up that responsibility, and it seldom lasts more than a few notes. If the sopranos were singing alone in such an instance, the problem, of course, would be magnified. A quality composer, however, would not write in that manner. (This is one of the few differences between ensemble and solo singing.)

Drop the jaw on ascending leaps.   All singers, but especially sopranos, need to drop their jaws slightly on ascending leaps into the upper range. In addition, slightly raising the soft pallet (a feeling similar to the climactic moment of a yawn) will enable higher notes to be sung with the same warmth and beauty as those in the lower range. To keep the jaw rigidly in the vowel formation of the lower note can cause the higher one to become tense, brassy, piercing, or tight. Here again, we slightly compromise the purity of the vowel toward an "ah" for the higher note.

Don't allow early oversinging to cause a wobbly vibrato. Because of often oversinging in their younger developmental years, the sopranos are the most likely to suffer from wobbly vibrato problems. The conductor needs to be very sensitive to this potential problem when listening to the sound of the soprano section. When it appears, the conductor needs to correct this problem with the procedure described earlier in this chapter.

Leading tones must be in tune. Because sopranos often sing the melody, the soprano line will more often include leading tones (for example, scale degree 7, F♯ in the key of G, or C♯ in the key of D). Leading tones are notoriously flat, so the conductor needs to alert the sopranos to this danger and remind them of it as often as necessary. A flat leading tone results partially from a lack of awareness and musicianship. A lack of sufficient energy to combat the natural gravity that pulls pitch down is also a major reason for singing under pitch. Conductors who explain the function of leading tones—that is, taking us "home" to the tonic—will help singers understand the significance of this problem.

Vocalize sopranos within a reasonable range. It is unnecessary and unwise for sopranos to vocalize any higher than high B♭ in an ensemble situation. Most choral repertoire does not include soprano passages above high B♭, so there is no real need to vocalize above that. Consistent vocalizing above B♭ can cause serious vocal stress and eventually harm the voice. This is especially true in situations in which the conductor is working with many singers who cannot be individually heard. *Preserve* the voice; don't overwork it or damage it.

Conclusions. Sopranos, without losing their spirit, vitality, and overall energy, must "take it easy." They must sing in a very relaxed and open manner and should not try to sound older than they are. Encourage them to sing lyrically with a naturally beautiful and spirited tone.

Altos

The altos are the most neglected section of the chorus. They are often the best musicians and readers, so the conductor seemingly has less to worry about with them. The result is that, for the most part, the conductor ignores the altos and permits them to proceed without teaching them fine singing, musicality, and expressivity. Altos need particular attention and help on the following issues.

Develop one continuous voice throughout the entire range. Many altos (and mezzo-sopranos) develop a break in the voice between the lower chest voice and the upper head voice. In the treble clef, this break lies in the area of G, A, and B♭. Below that area, altos often sing in what has become a manufactured chest voice, and above it, they sing in their natural top voices. Young alto singers develop this lower chest voice in an attempt to gain more volume in the lower range. They simply want to sing as full, or loudly, as everyone else. This results in a sound that is a combination of extra breath and forced singing. This sound is seldom beautiful, and

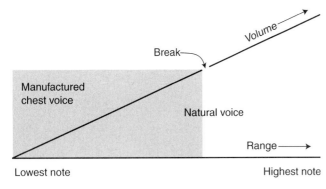

Figure 4.1

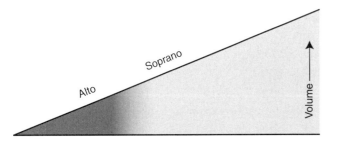

Figure 4.2

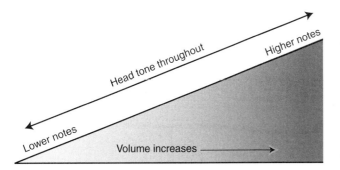

Figure 4.3

it becomes even less beautiful as the woman gets older, with the break becoming more and more pronounced.

Young men can easily smooth the breaks in their voices when using falsetto (discussed in the section on tenors). Women cannot. In Figure 4.1, a chest voice has been placed over the natural lower voice to produce more volume. Notice the break.

As with all singers, altos should use only the top voice, bringing it all the way down through the lower range and singing in one voice from top to bottom. There will be a noticeable decrease in volume as the singer descends into the lower range. That is as it should be—and the way the human voice is designed. Strength and volume increase as the singer ascends and diminishes as the singer descends.

Figure 4.2 shows the difference between the areas most generally used by both sopranos and altos. Notice that the area the sopranos use is considerably louder than that of the alto section. This is why the altos feel the need to increase the volume of their lower range.

Bring the upper voice down. The conductor can solve this problem by asking the altos to sing on "ah" and, beginning on a high note—perhaps, high G—descend the scale two octaves to low G. Remind them to be absolutely sure to stay in the high voice, the top head tone. Do not allow the voice to go into the manufactured chest voice at any point while descending.

In Figure 4.3, you will notice that, beginning at the left (the lowest part of the range) the natural voice is at its softest. Then, as the singer ascends, the volume naturally increases. The vocal range should be continuous from top to bottom. There is no break.

To accomplish this, the singer will have to decrescendo on the way down, or the voice will go into the heavier chest sound. The lower notes of the top head voice will be rather soft. They are supposed to be. But they may be even softer than normal if they have not been used in years. These natural lower notes will gain in strength through usage. They will never be as strong as the top of the range, but they will become stronger (louder) through proper use.

Women (not just altos) should sing entirely in their top head voice. Their voices will last for decades and be consistently beautiful in the process. The exception to this is when an advanced singer, in private study, is very carefully taught to *mix* the head voice with lower chest resonance. This is for increased sound in the lower range—usually for singing over an orchestra in operatic arias. This is inappropriate and unnecessary for most choral singing. In rare situations, however, it may be briefly and carefully employed. Basically, singers should almost *always* sing in their top head voice.

Encourage altos to sing musically.   Altos tend not to sing musically. Nor do they project a soloistic approach to their melodic line. They seldom sing with mature, beautiful tone quality. Basically they've been ignored and seldom, if ever, asked to sing beautifully. The conductor must become fully *aware* of the members of the alto section and their potential for musical and beautiful singing.

Consistently teach altos to *sing!* Teach them to sing with a beautiful, warm, rich, full tone. That is not an overly dark "older" tone but, rather, a beautiful, lyrical sound that is *consciously produced.* It is not breathy, anemic, shallow, or meaningless. The throat is open, and the tone is well placed. (Review the illustrations in Chapter 3.)

Altos, like all the other singers, are involved in communicating an important melody and a significant message. The alto's sound (like that of *all* singers) should make an impact on the listener. The alto part, although not always as melodically interesting as others, still must be sung with feeling, expression, and musicality. Altos' sounds need to come from their "hearts" as well as from their intellects.

I often ask altos to "sing like a woman, with a fully resonant, operatic sound." If they don't overdo it, and are sure to keep the tone placed in the head, this new sound is usually very beautiful, representing the manner in which they should always sing, whether *p* or *f.* The reason? By doing this, they are actually *producing tone.*

Do not sing the way you speak.   Far too many singers—especially altos—*sing* the way they *talk.* They are unaware that there is a critical difference in vocal production. When singing, they produce the same anemic sound appropriate for casual, conversational speaking. Although effective for certain types of pop and rock music performance with huge amplifiers and speakers, this style is *not* appropriate for singing choral music. In legitimate choral singing, altos must *produce* the sound as we have described it here.

Speak a phrase or sentence casually. Now speak it with great authority, sustained quality, resonance, projection, and dignity (as a great Shakespearean actor might speak it). Notice the elegant, regal difference that begins to approach the production of the *singing tone.* At first, inexperienced singers feel a bit awkward or self-conscious adopting this style. It is the conductor's responsibility to teach this until it becomes second nature to each member of the chorus, as the *only way to sing!* We talk in one manner, *we sing in an entirely different manner.*

Of all the hundreds of choruses I've heard, the major source of most problems comes from the conductor permitting singers to sing in the same informal manner they speak. Singing is hard work. Choruses need to *think* about singing, *focus* on it, and *produce* it. Just as oversinging is never good, neither is *undersinging.* Overdoing full, healthy singing until it becomes a shout, or preserving and caring for the voice until the sound is meaningless—either extreme is disastrous to great singing.

Never consistently sing tenor.   Altos should never, absolutely never, consistently sing tenor! The tenors are singing in the middle of their range while the altos will be singing at the lowest extreme of their range, which will force the altos to manufacture a chest voice to make any significant contribution at all. Singing tenor is the single most detrimental thing an alto can do to her voice.

It is, however, perfectly safe for altos to occasionally sing a few high tenor notes to strengthen the tenor line when it goes above the staff. These notes would fall in the middle of the alto range (G, A♭, A, and B♭). We will discuss this more later.

Insist that young girls switch regularly from alto to soprano.   Young girls in elementary and middle school should not be assigned to sing alto on a permanent basis. Real altos don't develop until much later. A procedure that will allow *all* girls to develop the full potential of their vocal range, and the ability to read music, is to divide the girls into two groups, then alternate their parts on every other song. Thus, each group sings soprano half the time and alto the other half.

Conclusions

- Altos must bring their head voices down throughout the entire range. Although there will be a decrease in volume both initially and ultimately, natural tone quality demands it.

- Under no circumstances should altos sing tenor consistently. This will ultimately harm the voice and, in the short term, may result in an offensive tenor sound.

- Conductors must not take altos for granted. Although they may seldom have an interesting melody, the conductor needs to encourage altos to sing with all the passion, energy, and enthusiasm of any other section. Even if they sing four bars of repeated pitches, they must sing them beautifully—musically.

- We must make sure that altos constantly use a *singing* tone. Too often altos sing with their chest voices and essentially *speak* on pitch and in rhythm. Remember, *we do not sing the way we speak!*

Tenors

The young tenor voice is the most fragile of all musical instruments. It is the most easily damaged. Many adult baritones with limited ranges would still be tenors if choral conductors had not demanded too much volume in their early years of development. These tenors' high notes were lost because of the constant forcing and straining to sing louder than they were naturally able. Young tenors (in middle school, high school, and the first year or two of college) must *substitute vitality for volume*.

That is the key phrase: *Substitute vitality for volume.* Young tenors do not need to sing loudly. Their naturally bright sound will, if properly projected with vital spirit and energy, carry to the back of any hall and balance with other (even larger) sections. This is the most important concept we can present concerning young tenors. If we do not preserve the young voice, a mature tenor will not follow.

Young tenors can sing a "relative forte" in the range-area from first-space F to fourth-space C. Above that, the dynamic range should lessen with each scale-step: D = *mf*, E = *mp*, and F-and-above = *p*. Remember that these lesser dynamic levels must be sung with *abundant energy*, or the tenors will sound anemic, like a plant looks when it needs to be watered.

Sing falsetto for high notes.   Tenors should sing with a highly spirited but very relaxed, lyrical approach. The sound should show no sign of tension or strain. The adult tenor can extend the top range, adding strength and power to it, by further developing the head-tone resonance we discussed earlier. Younger tenors need to use falsetto for high notes.

Not only is falsetto acceptable for younger tenors (and basses), but it is also *necessary*. Falsetto is the light sound, used by young male singers, to sing high passages in which the regular voice cannot properly function. It is similar to the sound of a boy-soprano, or the lighter sound of a female singer. To produce falsetto, only the edges of the vocal chords resonate. Generally speaking, falsetto cannot withstand a crescendo and does necessitate a break in the voice when going into it from the regular voice. This break can be smoothed out through vocalizing exercises, however, to the point that it is totally unnoticeable (compared with the *obvious break* in a woman's voice going from chest voice into head tone). Young tenors and basses should be encouraged to use the falsetto voice any time they wish to do so. In fact, they should be *directed* to do so by the conductor, in most high passages, depending on the singers and their range of maturity. When using falsetto, most boys can vocalize up to B♭ with sopranos, thus developing the falsetto and smoothing over the "break" until it is unnoticeable.

Develop the full male head tone.   We will now discuss the most important factor in male singing: the head-tone placement of the male voice. Without this technique, there will be *no real progress in the vocal development of men*. The potential of the top-range will simply never be realized. (Although not always the case, it may often take a male singer to successfully teach and demonstrate for other male singers concerning this technique.)

Maturing male singers, eighteen and older, will not progress properly without the full development of the male head tone. Falsetto must give-way to head tone. This is a technique peculiar to men. Women do not do this. Women can successfully sing from their lowest note to their highest, while remaining in basically the same voice: the top, head voice. If a male does this, the voice eventually turns into a shout. The male has only two effective choices, the falsetto and the *extended head tone*.

The extended head tone is based on the very same procedure that we described earlier in the discussion on placement and resonance (in Chapter 3). In Exercises 3.1 and 3.2, we began with the "uh-huh" exercise. When doing this with singers in general, we simply placed the tone in the head and let it go at that. We ask maturing males to add *considerable strength* to that head resonance. We will attempt to get the tone *fully ringing in the head*. Once this is achieved, the male's top tones will be produced with increased range, consistency, strength, and beauty.

In the following exercise, begin out of the head on the upbeat with an "ah," and then, slowly at first, go into the head during the ascending leap on "uh" to the tonic and back out of the head to "ah" as you descend to finish the exercise. Second, do it with ah–*oh*–ah.

Exercise 4.1.   In addition to the head tone exercise suggested earlier, also work with this exercise (see Example 4.1): 1-3-5-8-5-3-1. Begin with *yah*, out of the head, on a legato 1-3-5, then slowly glissando from 5 to 8, into the top tone, going into the head during the process. During the glissando, change (again slowly) to *oh*. This sound seems to help get the tone into the head. Hold the top tone in the head for a moment, then slowly glissando back down to the fifth scale-tone, bringing the tone

Example 4.1

ah - uh-ah_____   ah - uh - ah_____   ah - uh - ah_____

back out of head to *ah* (the shallow tone produced in the throat and chin area with which we began the exercise).

Tilt the head slightly back to begin, and slightly forward to ascend to the top tone, and back again for the lower tones. As with the "uh-huh" exercise, the male singer must literally *feel the tone*:

1. Begin out of the head (on "ah")

2. Move slowly into the head (to "uh" or "oh")

3. Set solidly in the head, then

4. Slowly move out of the head (to "ah")

5. Once again, be completely out of the head

The singer needs to *understand* and *feel* the difference. Apply this in Exercise 4.2, singing both ways: "ah-uh-ah," and "ah-oh-ah."

Exercise 4.2.   See Example 4.2.

Example 4.2

ah_____   uh - ah_____

ah_____   uh - ah_____

ah_____   uh - ah_____

Conclusions

- The singer must definitely feel and understand the experience of going in and out of the head tone. Male singers should sing all tones in the upper third (or more) of their range in this fully extended, ringing head tone (in all dynamic levels).

- Mature tenors, singing properly with head tone, can comfortably sing any dynamic called for throughout the top range. The sound will be brilliant and wonderful.

- A minor but important point is this: Tenors should not stick their chins up to help them sing high notes. Keep the head level, drop the jaw, use falsetto or head tone, and employ proper breath support.

Basses

Develop the head tone.   All that was said regarding falsetto and extended head-tone for tenors applies to basses and baritones. They may begin head-tone exercises with the higher pitch being B♭ (a step below middle C) and ascend to bring the high note up to E♭ or F, and eventually up to A♭ for mature advanced baritones. Tenors may begin with the high note being middle C, ascending to G, A, or B♭, and occasionally on to high C for advanced, mature tenors. (Basses may be encouraged to use a chest-mix regarding resonance on low notes.)

Don't allow overly dark singing.   Basses and baritones tend to desire a "woofy" tuba-like approach to singing everything. This causes problems with tone, pitch, rhythmic clarity, and diction. Here again, the important word is "lyrical." Lyrical basses and baritones need to use the recommended head tone and a very *forward* feeling to their singing. This forward feeling might be thought of as being in the "mask," that is, the area of the cheekbones, nose, and upper gums. Combining this with the forehead-area-concept will usually achieve the desired tone.

The ideal comparison is with the tone quality of French horns and tenor trombones, not with tubas. If all the basses sing with a lyrical *baritone* approach, the best overall sound will be achieved. This will not negate a good bass sound from true basses. It will simply enable them to sing with a refreshing sound that will be compatible with the beautiful lyricism of the rest of the chorus. In some cases, they might not want to do this and might even quietly rebel. Basses often want to sound older, more professional, and "mature." Stick with it. You'll eventually win them over, and the effort will be well worth it (for both basses and everyone else).

Don't allow growling or yelling.   Basses must avoid shouting on high notes and avoid growling on lower ones. Those notes in the lower extremes of the range are not intended to be sung loudly. The basses, therefore, should sing low Gs and below no louder than *mp/mf*, and often *p*. If the chorus is singing in tune, even one bass singing softly can be clearly heard because of overtones. Loud singing in the lower range is not only unpleasant to hear, it is totally unnecessary. But here again, the basses will want to do it because it feels and sounds masculine. Again, just stick with it. They'll eventually come your way, and the results will be beautiful.

With this in mind, *young basses* should follow this guideline regarding dynamics: within the octave of second-line B♭, to B♭ just below middle C, they may comfortably sing *f*, or even *ff*. Above and below that they must taper rather quickly to *mf*, *mp*, and *p*. Mature basses and baritones may, of course, sing fully in the top range, as long as the tone is beautifully produced in the head. No shouting!

Watch out for awkward head and neck positions.   The basses need to guard against tucking the chin in to help sing low notes, and sticking it up and out to sing higher ones (this is similar to the tenor problem). Teach them to keep their heads erect while singing and let the *jaw* do the moving.

Conclusions.   Keep the tone lyrical and naturally forward, emulating a French horn, not a tuba. Prioritize beautiful singing in both extremes (high and low) of the range. Keep the head erect, avoid stretching the chin up for high notes and tucking it in for low notes.

Lyrical Singing for All Singers

We have established that the sound of all voice categories (sopranos, altos, tenors, and basses) is to be refreshingly forward, clearly placed in the head, with a consistent focus on lyrical singing. This is a unification of healthy, natural, singing based on *energy*, *beauty*, and *placement*. The sound will be unified, brilliant and ringing with warmth and depth. This sound has the potential to be both powerful and dolce/tranquil (a cappella) and will be heard easily over the largest orchestra playing the music of such composers as Beethoven, Verdi, and Brahms—without straining or forcing the voices.

Concepts of Choral Section Balance

Two well-established concepts address the best relationship among vocal sections to produce choral balance. These concepts originated with the two foremost American professional choral conductors: Robert Shaw and Roger Wagner. Roger Wagner's approach was a "pyramid of sound" (see Figure 4.4), with the soprano dynamic level being the least, gradually increasing the sound of the altos and tenors, until, finally, the basses would be the strongest.

Although Roger Wagner's sound might have been a bit bass-heavy, it was absolutely beautiful. It just had a little extra emphasis on the lower sections of the chorus. He told me that, occasionally for recordings, he would add one string bass to a cappella singing, softly doubling the bass section of the chorus to help achieve this desired sound.

Robert Shaw, on the other hand, agreed with the idea of slightly diminished soprano sound but preferred a uniformity of dynamic sound from the altos, tenors, and basses (see Figure 4.5). This resulted in a somewhat more natural, unaffected sound (in which the conductor is not recognizable by the stylized sound of the chorus). The Shaw sound was also extremely beautiful, but in a completely natural manner that never drew attention to any aspect of itself.

These two sounds were (are) both very beautiful. The first manipulates the sound ever so slightly to overemphasize the bass quality. The second does not, holding that the natural instrument, the human voice, is sufficiently beautiful unto itself and does not need to be manipulated even slightly in any direction.

Let the sound be completely natural, based on the following:

1. A soloistic approach to ensemble singing

2. Solid breath support and control

3. Energy, beauty, and placement

4. Appropriate section characteristics

5. Logical unified vowel formation (see the following material)

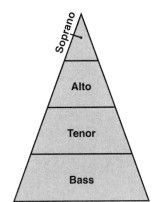

Figure 4.4

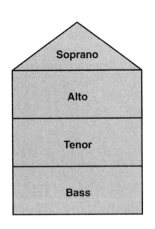

Figure 4.5

6. A solid foundation of musicianship, musicality, and personal communication

7. Common sense, reason, and good taste, taking no idea to extreme

A Unified Approach to Vowel Formation

Nothing will more quickly improve the overall quality of sound produced by a choir than the unification of vowel formations and sounds. We must first establish that all vowels are not formed similarly. They are not formed with the same position of the jaw and lips. Vowel sounds should be unique, each having its own individual color and sound. The orchestra has a wide color spectrum of sound from the many different instruments: French horns, triangles, English horns, cellos, tubas, piccolos, and so on. The chorus has only the human voice, and only four sections of those, similar to the string section of an orchestra. That limits the potential of color. Therefore, we must take full advantage of every aspect of the *language* in which we are singing. The language, in large part, is our color.

We will now address the fact that all vowels are not created with the same jaw and lips formation. Some vowels are formed with an open jaw, some relatively closed, and some fall in between. This is not a manipulation of vowels but, rather, a manner of shaping them, which results in a natural yet unique sound for each one.

Take a few moments to experiment briefly with the shape of your mouth, lips, and jaw while producing vowel sounds. You will find vowels sound right only in the right formation of the jaw and lips. For example, open up too much for *oo* and it becomes distorted; close for *ah* and it becomes distorted. We will try to determine which is exactly right for each vowel frequently used in the English language. It is impractical to go through the entire phonetic alphabet, so we will select those vowels most commonly used. If the chorus can remember to do them well on a consistent basis, we will have scored a major victory.

Six Basic Vowel Sounds

We will select six basic vowel sounds (*ee, ay, ah, oo, oh, aw*), and then add three additional sounds (*ih, a* [in cat], *uh*). We will discuss their color—bright or dark—the shape of the lips—round or vertical and their jaw opening—minimal (one finger between teeth), extended (slightly more than one finger between the teeth), and maximum (two fingers between the teeth).

Bright vowels. The bright vowel sounds are *ee, ay* (actually *eh,* because *ee,* the second sound of the diphthong *ay* [eh-ee], has already been categorized), and *ah.* The additional vowel *ih* falls in the category with *ee,* and *a*

> ✑ *All vowel sounds should be produced in either a round (dark vowels) formation, or vertical (brights vowels) formation.*
>
> This concept is paramount in achieving a great singing sound. Second only to energy, this is the most significant aspect in the development of tone quality with real depth, substance, and maturity. Teach it immediately and consistently in the rehearsal process of any chorus, young or older, inexperienced or very experienced.

(cat) falls in the category with *ah*. The singer produces the bright vowels with the lips *slightly flared vertically*, allowing the *lower edge* of the upper teeth, and the *upper edge* of the lower teeth to visibly be the opening of the mouth. This lip-position will help to give these vowels *ee, eh (ay)*, and *ah*, a *naturally* bright sound. (We do not need to add additional false brightness to them.) Think of these openings as vertical. Although horizontal mouth formations seem to be a consistent part of our casual speaking, *we never use the horizontal formation when singing*.

Dark vowels.   The dark vowel sounds are *oo, oh,* and *aw*. The additional vowel *uh* falls in the dark category with *oh*. Produce the dark vowels with the *lips in a circular formation*. The lips are very relaxed, but extended in a slightly pursed position, with the opening being *round*. Think of the *oo, oh,* and *aw* openings as those of a dime, nickel, and quarter. The potential problem is that singers tend to open barely wide enough for a soft-drink straw for *oo,* and progress accordingly. Let the jaw open freely, producing a comfortable *open* sound. In the case of these dark vowels, the *lips* will be the opening of the mouth. There will be no teeth visible. The sound will be naturally dark. *We do not need to consciously darken them.*

Pictures of Vowel Formation

It is important to understand that singers' jaws, mouths, and lips vary in size and shape. They might not all be able to form these recommended vowel formations in exactly the same way. Teach the basic concept and encourage the singers to do it as similarly as possible, allowing for slight variations among the individuals singing. I have found that great similarity is, indeed, possible and certainly worth striving for. The closer we get to it, the better the sound, pitch, and diction will be. See Table 4.1 and Figure 4.6.

Table 4.1   Unified Vowel Formation

Jaw Opening	Dark Vowels		Bright Vowels	
Minimal jaw opening (one finger between teeth)	○	oo	☐	ee (& ih)
Extended jaw opening (drop the jaw slightly)	◯	oh (& uh)	☐	eh (ay = *eh*-e)
Maximum jaw opening (drop the jaw to two fingers between teeth)	◯	aw	☐	ah (& a as in cat)

Exercises for Vowel Uniformity with Dark and Bright Vowels

Dark vowel exercises

- Practice singing *oo* using the backs of your hands gently to push the cheeks forward, helping your lips to purse out just a bit, relaxed and rounded, in the shape of a dime. Establish this concept first.

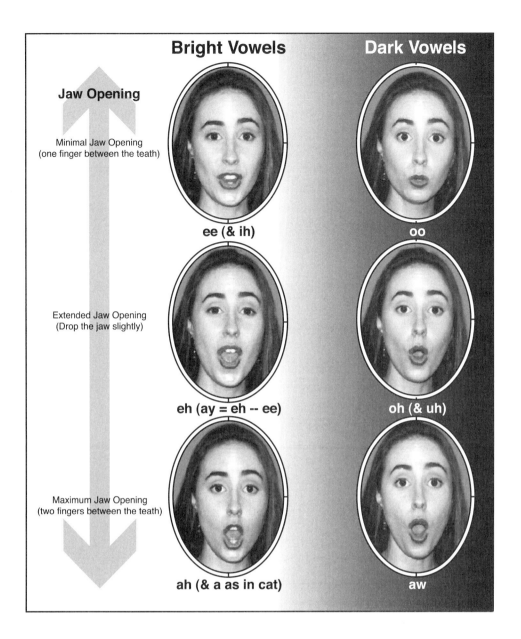

Figure 4.6

Bright Vowels   **Dark Vowels**

Jaw Opening

Minimal Jaw Opening
(one finger between the teeth)

ee (& ih)

oo

Extended Jaw Opening
(Drop the jaw slightly)

eh (ay = eh -- ee)

oh (& uh)

Maximum Jaw Opening
(two fingers between the teeth)

ah (& a as in cat)

aw

- Now go directly from this *oo* to a slightly vertically flared *ee* on a comfortable sustained pitch, retaining the same jaw formation (one finger-width between the upper and lower teeth). Go back and forth several times, experiencing the difference of the rounded *oo* and the vertically flared *ee*. Retain the warmth of the *oo* in the sound of *ee*. This is crucial to a beautiful *ee* sound with substance and depth.

- Actually, it is a good idea to feel that there is a slight *oo* warmth in *all* vowels, bright or dark, minimum, extended, or maximum, but especially in *ee*.

- Do the same back-and-forth exercise with both *oh* to *eh*, and later, *aw* to *ah*. This will continue to establish the physical difference and sound difference between the circular dark vowels and the vertically flared bright vowels.

- Sing straight down the dark vowel column—*oo, oh,* and *aw*—consciously thinking dime, nickel, and quarter-sized, rounded-lip formations. Now, on a sustained pitch, sing *noo-oh-aw-oh-oo*. Repeat this exercise, progressing with ascending half steps, for each new beginning. *Do not exaggerate the dark quality of these vowels. If produced naturally, they will be sufficiently dark on their own.*

Bright vowel exercises

- Begin with an *ee* that comes from an *oo.* Sing *oo* as described earlier, then immediately go into *ee* by slightly flaring the lips vertically. Sing, on a sustained pitch, *oo-ee, oo-ee, oo-ee,* establishing the unique sound of the *ee* coming from the warm sound of an *oo. Important: retain this warmth in the* ee. There will always need to be "*oo*-warmth" in *ee* vowels so they will sound beautiful. Another reminder: Beginning with *ee,* the bright vowels are formed in a manner that will show the slightest lower edge of the upper teeth and the slightest upper edge of the lower teeth.

- Now, beginning with this established *ee* sound, sing *nee-ay-ah* on a sustained pitch. Drop your jaw for *ay* and *ah.* Be sure to take the lower lip with you when you lower the jaw. It is possible to lower the jaw, and leave the lower lip in the previous position, resulting in a compromise between a dark and bright vowel: The jaw went appropriately down, but the lip remained up, covering the teeth, as is appropriate for the formation of a *dark* vowel.

- Repeatedly sing, on a sustained pitch, *nee-ay-ah-ay-ee,* and ascend by half steps each time. The feeling of the "*oo*-warmth" retained in *ee* can also enhance the beauty of *eh (ay),* and *ah.* We may actually think of this "*oo*-warmth" being present in *all* vowels for depth, substance, and beauty of sound (as long as the concept is not carried so far that it distorts the natural sounds, especially of the bright vowels).

- Last, alternate the bright vowels with the dark vowels, on sustained pitches, raising a half step with each alternation: *ne-ay-ah-ay-ee, noo-oh-aw-oh-oo,* and so on. Establish firmly in your mind the vivid difference between those vowels that are *naturally* bright, and those that are *naturally* dark.

These exercises can be valuable if they are regularly included in the routine of vocalizing warm-ups before each rehearsal. This vowel formation concept will soon become entrenched in the minds of the singers and will carry over into the singing of the repertoire.

Summary

We have now completed the *basic* techniques of producing a truly great choral sound. From "A Soloistic Approach to Ensemble Singing" to "Unified Vowel Formation," we have shown the pathway to truly great choral singing. It is the basic pathway to *all* singing. There are very few differences between fine ensemble singing and fine solo singing—so few that the two are basically the same if done well.

The following chapters will support and reinforce these concepts as we continue to enhance the sound of the chorus. But for now, it will suffice to say that we have laid a solid foundation for great singing.

Each section of the chorus has its own characteristics; learn them and serve each section to the best of your ability. As choral conductor, you must be a *voice teacher* in every rehearsal:

- Teach sopranos to sing lyrically, naturally, and beautifully, compromising both volume and diction above the staff.

- Teach altos to avoid the break in the mid-range by bringing their top voices down throughout the entire range. Altos must be taught and encouraged to sing musically and expressively with a beautifully warm tone quality.

- Teach young tenors to substitute vitality for volume, singing with a very natural, free (unforced) quality, tapering dynamics both at the top and bottom of the range. It is insufficient to simply sing softer. *Vitality* is crucial.

- Encourage all male singers over the age of seventeen to develop the male head tone fully to replace the falsetto they used in younger years. This will increase their range and allow the beginning of full volume and consistency in the upper range.

- Encourage basses to think of themselves as lyric baritones, trombones, or French horns, *not* as "bassos" or tubas. Basses should place the tone forward, keeping it up in their heads rather than in their throats and chests.

- Teach young basses (like young tenors) to avoid forcing with too much volume in the upper and lower ranges.

- Teach that unifying the formation of vowels, and therefore, vowel sounds, greatly enhances the sound, diction, and true intonation.

As conductors, our job is to teach that the "color" of choral singing is directly related to the uniqueness of both bright and dark vowels:

- Naturally bright vowels, formed vertically, and with the upper edge of the lower teeth and the lower edge of the upper teeth slightly visible, are *ee, eh,* and *ah.*

- Naturally dark vowels, formed with rounded, circular lips (with no teeth showing) are *oo, oh,* and *aw,* thought of as the size of a dime, nickel, and quarter.

- All vowels are formed in either a vertical or rounded shape, *never horizontal.*

- A well-produced *ee* will always have some of the rounded "warmth" of an *oo* within it. All vowels should have a bit of this "*oo*-warmth" in them. As long as it is not overdone, the result is sheer beauty.

Vocalizing and Warm-Ups

5

*C*onductors handle vocalizing and warm-up exercises in a variety of ways, from none at all to extensive. Some use them only when a vocal problem arises within the context of the rehearsal, whereas others have a strict regimen that they use to begin every rehearsal.

Over the years, I have observed methods used by many singers, voice teachers, and conductors (of elementary, middle, and high school and collegiate groups), as well as those used by Robert Shaw. I have combined these experiences with my own convictions to formulate the material presented in this chapter. In the following pages, I describe warm-up exercises that I have found valuable and *why* they are valuable.

I have eliminated exercises that seemed a bit silly, useless, or even somewhat embarrassing to the singers and those that *appear* to have value but actually have little or none at all. In this category I would place the rapid-fire of consonants— kuh, kuh, kuh, kuh, kuh, buh, buh, buh, buh, buh, and so on. Granted they activate the tongue and lips; I'm just not sure that it is necessary. Rehearsal time is precious. Not even one minute should be spent on something unnecessary or of minimal value.

I have also eliminated those exercises that repeat a meaningless, repetitive pattern. This would include such exercises as singing four-part harmonic progressions such as I-IV-V-I, then up a half-step, repeating it, and so on. Although the chorus can do them, I have found that these exercises accomplish very little. For one thing, they are usually done so fast that the singers don't have time to focus on the potential value.

Conductors rarely teach singers to really *listen* to the vocalises they are singing or specifically what to *focus* on while listening. I do not mean to negate the value of other exercises. I only remind us to examine carefully our vocalizing and warm-up exercises; let's make sure they effectively teach voice, musicianship, and musicality.

Using Vocalizing and Warm-Ups Productively

Teach the singers to completely understand the reason for the vocalise, then sing it slowly enough to allow them to think and focus on the potential benefit of the exercise. Vocalizing exercises must be done in a tempo that will allow singers to think, execute well, and constantly *evaluate the success of the process*. Never sing a vocalise quickly except in the advanced stages of individual vocal development when rapidity is the goal. Vocalizing should be a focused and thoughtful process—not a mindless, mechanical routine.

When vocalizing, the chorus members should think as individuals and consider this time their own personal practice moments, completely unaware of those around them, even the conductor. They do not sing to the conductor. Each member should sing as though alone in a practice room or in the studio of a voice teacher, *focusing totally on his or her own voice and its progress through each particular vocalise.*

Conductors should sit at the piano, accompanying the vocalizing and removed from the center of attention. Instruct the singers to look straight ahead, not toward the conductor, and sing as though they were *performing* to someone (as they would do in the practice room or vocal studio). We should not separate the singing of exercises from the conscious act of performing. It should all be one. During a performance, the singer is consumed with the text and melody. While vocalizing, the mental focus will be on the technique of singing. But in both activities, the singer should be in a *performance mode*. Always perform, every moment of every rehearsal, even when singing quietly, learning the notes of a new song.

Structure the warm-up sessions around basic concepts of fine singing.
Determine those vocal concepts you believe are most important, then sequentially structure your warm-up and vocalizing sessions around these concepts. First priorities must come first, second priorities second, and so on. Have a definite purpose and plan for vocalizing, then execute it.

As we follow our plan, some exercises might seem routine. That's fine. Don't vary simply for the sake of varying. Do what works, what you believe in, and do it consistently. Routine warm-ups need not be monotonous, boring, or thoughtless. With the responsibility for inspiring an energetic mental focus, the conductor needs to remind the chorus, again and again, to be aware of the technical aspects, benefits, and goals of the vocalise. Guide their thoughts. Stimulate their thinking and concentration.

Discipline in the rehearsal atmosphere must be rock-solid or the singers will not take these exercises seriously. The result will be humorous, chaotic, or boring (especially with younger singers). Establish credibility for what you are doing. Explain the reasons for doing the various exercises and mention that professional singers do the same warm-ups before their rehearsals and concerts. *Discipline is the foundation of any successful team-effort.* Every aspect of the rehearsal must be disciplined, serious, and based on a goal of achieving excellence in all things. Personal fulfillment comes as a result of hard work and artistic accomplishment, not from immature behavior and an undisciplined rehearsal atmosphere.

Structuring Warm-Up Sessions

The following list of objectives has worked well with every chorus I've conducted. It is structured on the first-things-first basis, with each new exercise building on the foundation of the previous one.

1. Loosening up physically

2. Having awareness of mental and vocal unity

3. Establishing the placement of the upper head tone

4. Projecting personal vitality and animation

5. Using a legato line with forward motion phrasing

6. Developing a full, mature vocal sound while increasing the top range

7. Creating melodic flexibility

8. Teaching pitch awareness

We will discuss each item in turn.

1. Loosening Up Physically

Singers bring varying degrees of stress, created by previous daily activities, to the rehearsal. This stress directly affects the muscles and tendons throughout the body, specifically the voice and the area surrounding vocal production. Our first priority is to help bring relaxation to the singer's "instrument," the body; the singer's voice must have the potential to function at its optimum level of proficiency.

1. Ask the chorus to stand, face the right, and begin "chopping" the shoulders of the person in front of them with the edges of their hands. Don't overdo the strength of this, which could be painful to some, but do exert sufficient energy, so a loosening-up process will effectively begin.

2. After approximately 15 to 20 seconds, ask that they turn, face the opposite direction, and repeat the process to the person now in front of them.

3. Next, ask them to face the right again, and, this time, deeply massage the shoulders of the person in front of them.

4. Now direct them to turn again, facing the opposite direction, and repeat the massaging process one more time.

5. Ask them to return to their original positions and begin stretching: arms go up in the air, above their heads, with fingers clasped and palms toward the ceiling, reaching as high as possible and stretching the arm and shoulder muscles.

6. In this same position, direct them to twist *slowly* to the right, as far as possible, feeling the pulling sensation in the arm, shoulder, and back muscles.

7. Now ask them to return to the forward position, reaching for the ceiling, and then slowly turn back to the right again.

8. After this second time to the right, ask them to return to the forward position again, and then twist to the left (always slowly). Do this twice, as we previously did to the right.

9. Now ask them to stand tall, centered, with their arms still up, and lean slowly backwards as far as possible, and return upright.

10. Have the singers (with their arms at their sides) slowly rotate their shoulders in a circular motion, both at the same time. Tell them to begin by raising their shoulders as though they were trying to touch their ears with them; then bring their shoulders forward, down, back, and up toward their ears again, ending in their normal positions.

11. Last, ask your singers to massage their own necks and shoulders.

If you choose to do breathing exercises, either as a regular part of the warm-up routine, or as a beginning to the teaching process, this would be the time to insert them.

The time element. At 10 to 20 seconds each, this process could take longer than the time you wish to allot to it. This will also be true regarding recommended vocal warm-ups. We can't do them all. We would have little time left to rehearse. Simply select those most appropriate, those you wish to do in any given rehearsal, and omit the rest. Plan carefully, consider the music to be rehearsed, and make the decisions. Productive choices will become quite clear. However, physically loosening up is a must!

When the chorus does these physical warm-ups properly, they are invaluable. We should not omit them. Warm-ups are not a waste of time. All that follows will be better and more productive if based on this foundation. In fact, singers will often complain if, on occasion, we choose to omit them.

2. Having Awareness of Mental and Vocal Unity

A quiet, perfectly in-tune, unison pitch can be a very unifying moment at the beginning of a chorus rehearsal. It will unify both minds and voices. The room is still, and all the minds are focused on only one thing: a perfect unison. The rest of the world goes away. The room, the singers, the instant—all become *one* in a very special way.

1. Begin with the same pitch each time—A-natural (top-line bass clef, and second-space treble clef). The singers may eventually develop a near perfect-pitch recognition of A-natural. Have the singers focus intensely on *exactly the right pitch,* with no scooping, accenting, or other distortions. *Loo* is a good sound to use for this because the singers must refrain from sliding up on the *L* (this minimal challenge is good). The *oo* is a pure sound, making it easier to hear the perfect unison.

2. Give singers the pitch from the piano and have them think it for an instant, then direct them to let their voices softly join the pitch that their minds had already established.

3. Then give singers another pitch from the piano, continuing the process for five to six different pitches, all within the span of the octave from D to D (thus, eliminating unnecessary vocal effort).

The conductor must listen carefully. Don't accept anything but perfection, and, in the process, train the singers to do likewise.

3. Establishing the Placement of the Upper Head Tone

Ask the entire chorus to randomly select a comfortable high note (approximately high G, with the singers using a relaxed, light, falsetto-type voice). Ask them to *quietly* and *slowly* glissando downward to the bottom of the singer's range on *nah* or *yah* (see Example 5.1). The sound/tone *must remain in the upper head,* as the pitch descends. Repeat. Firmly establish the feeling of the tone well placed in the head, even though the pitch is descending to the singer's lowest singable pitch.

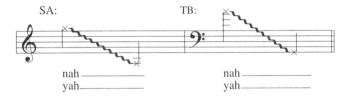

Example 5.1

Exercise 5.1. We will now do a series of five-tone descending scale passages. Descending is more effective than ascending for establishing head tone. Begin with D major, 5-4-3-2-1, using an opened-teeth, lips relaxed but closed hum (see Example 5.2). The hum is very effective in producing head-tone resonance. (There should always be at least one finger's-width opening between the teeth—teeth should never be tightly closed for *any sound.*) Relax the lips. Don't let them become tense. Do this exercise, *mp/mf,* ascending by half steps, until reaching A♭ major.

Example 5.2

Exercise 5.2. Then immediately begin descending, by half steps, from A♭ major down to D major. On the lower note (the tonic), allow the hum to open now into a warm and resonant *ee* (see Example 5.3), as developed in the vowel unification concepts (mm, mm, mm, mm, *mee*).

Example 5.3

Exercise 5.3.

1. Now ascend again, completely on *nee,* with the recently established warm *ee* vowel (see Example 5.4).

Example 5.4

2. Now descend, retaining the warmth of the *ee* vowel into *nee-ay-ah* (see Example 5.5). Employ the three jaw formations of the bright vowel concepts. Ascend, by half steps, to B♭ major. Instruct only tenors and sopranos to continue, taking them up to D♭ major, inviting the altos and basses to join back in, at A♭ major, when descending.

Example 5.5

nee - ay - ah   nee - ay - ah   nee - ay - ah

Exercise 5.4.   Begin the ascension again, if you wish, using *mah-ah, may-ay, mee* (see Example 5.6); you might prefer to ascend alternating bright and dark vowels with each new raised half step.

Example 5.6

mah - may - mee   mah - may - mee   mah - may - mee

4. Projecting Personal Vitality and Animation

These exercises are for the energy, animation and overall spirit of the singer's *entire being,* with special emphasis on *facial animation* and *physical assertiveness.* Basically, the chorus needs energy, and we must create it! *After establishing the head tone, energy is the most important aspect of singing.* In fact, it is *the* most important, but it must be done with the tone *properly placed* or it could be counterproductive. That is why we began with head tone.

When beginning to sing, a person should really come alive—facially reflecting the message to be sung and allowing the body to move *minimally* in and out of each phrase. Singing is an *assertive act,* not a passive one. The feeling should be one of *exhilaration and positivity.* When vocalizing without text, practice with an emphasis and facial expression that would be appropriate for a positive message.

> ✐ You will not have time to do each exercise suggested. Plan accordingly. Do those that will effectively develop your singers' vocal technique, that will enhance the productivity of the rehearsal, and that time will permit.

Exercise 5.5

- Sing 1-3-5-3-1, on *yah-ha-ha-ah-ah,* with the first two notes *staccato,* the third held for an extra beat, and the descending notes *legato* (see Example 5.7). The beginning feels and sounds almost like laughter. The face should be animated and thoroughly communicating. The dynamic is *mp/mf* to correct the misconception that energy is related only to *forte* singing. Sing the exercise with *great spirit* and *facial animation.* (We cannot over-emphasize facial animation!)

Example 5.7

yah - ha - ha_____   ya ha ha_____

ya ha ha_____   ya ha ha_____

Have the singers lean slightly forward, into their singing, as though they are telling someone something very important. The jaw should be in the extended position (for ah). Give a slight forward motion feeling to the eighth note following the tied eighth (also in Exercise 5.8).

Exercise 5.6. Sing 1-3-5-8-5-3-1, on *yah-ha-ha-ha-ah-ah-ah* (see Example 5.8), with the ascending notes staccato, the top note held an extra beat, and the descending notes legato. This spans the range of an entire octave, so sing it very lightly (*mp*), skimming over the ascending notes like a flat stone skipping over the water. Be sure to do it all in the top head voice; don't grab the first note with a lower chest sound. The total emphasis should be on animation, not on depth of sound (that will come later). Facial expression is paramount—not a broad smile that could distort the vowel sound but, rather, with expressive *eyes*, an overall positive *feeling*, and the *joy* of singing. Sing it lightly, but with the same spirit as in Exercise 5.5.

As you progress from one category to the next, be sure the singers retain what has been previously established. In this case, do not forsake placement, head tone, and personal vitality (the overall buoyant, uplifting "alive" approach) when singing the legato exercise. The members of our choruses need to be *complete singers who do it all.*

Example 5.8

yah - ha - ha - ha_____

yah - ha - ha - ha_____

yah - ha - ha - ha_____

yah - ha - ha - ha_____

Exercise 5.7. Next, sing these same exercises completely *legato*, but with the same degree of energy, *each note having an up-lifting quality about it.* We now want to create a concept of singing with abundant energy without the aid of the staccato approach. This buoyant, living sound will support all successful singing.

5. Using a Legato Line with Forward Motion Phrasing

Legato exercises are helpful when you will be rehearsing music in *legato* style. Legato exercises will also enhance the singer's purity of tone and awareness of melodic line. Singing *mp,* on the sound *loo* or *doo* (with a very soft and relaxed L or D) or simply a sustained *oo,* can be very effective.

In the following exercises, you will find phrase markings that place notes in melodic groups. Follow these indications carefully so that the chorus sings *melodically* rather than simply mechanically. At the beginning of each new note grouping or phrase, you will find an arrow. The arrow is an indication that you should give that note (musical moment) a bit of *forward motion emphasis*, creating even greater musicality in the phrasing. The conductor should implant this concept of note groupings, phrasing, and forward motion in the singers' conscious thinking. Employ it with *all the music you perform* and instruct the chorus where to place these phrase marks in their copies of the music. (We will discuss this further in Chapter 6.)

Do the following scale-step exercises softly, in a relaxed tempo. Remember, all exercises should be sung in a moderate tempo, or nothing of value will be accomplished. Focus on purity of sound and a flowing melodic line.

Exercise 5.8. Emphasize (1) vowel formation, (2) forward motion, and (3) a legato line (see Example 5.9).

Example 5.9

Exercise 5.9. See Example 5.10.

Example 5.10

Exercise 5.10. See Example 5.11.

Example 5.11

6. Developing a Full, Mature, Vocal Sound While Increasing the Top Range

We previously discussed two major kinds of tonal production, one for casual conversation and the other for great singing. The tonal production of great singing encompasses *solid tonal depth and resonance.* Casual conversation does not. All legitimate singing must be based on this tonal depth, no matter what the age of the singer might be. All singers can sing with a full-bodied *natural* tone quality—even young children and, yes, senior citizens.

Natural tone quality is simply a matter of (1) producing the best tone possible and (2) shaping the vowels properly. Together, these two concepts produce fine vocal tone quality. Without either, minimal results will be achieved.

Singers will only truly progress if they rehearse and perform with an ideal sound in their minds—a sound that directly affects the sound they are about to produce.

That is, they need to hear two things: the ideal sound they would like to produce and the sound they are actually producing. If your singers try continually to bring the latter toward the former, they will sound better with every rehearsal.

Without this process, the singers learn more songs but sound exactly the same as they did last week, last month, and last year. This equates to additional repertoire without vocal progress. Without the proper *image*, and conscious attempt to match it, vocal techniques piled on more vocal techniques will achieve nothing.

The image of fine singing. Remember the admonition, *any good idea taken to extreme immediately becomes a bad idea.* Therefore, I recommend the following: elementary school singers should try to emulate middle school singers in their overall quality of tonal depth; middle school singers should aim for a high school sound; high school singers should aim for college, and college, church, and other adult choral singers should aim for professional tonal depth. This is closely related to the exercise in singing beautifully suggested previously, in which the singers were asked to do impressions of gradually more mature singers—not emphasizing volume, just very fine singing. *A singer can strive for a slightly more professional maturity without manufacturing a false older sound.*

In all walks of life, people who succeed do so partly because they modeled their efforts after older, talented, successful professionals in their fields. This is as true in singing as it is in athletics, business, science, and all other areas of endeavor.

I must quickly say, once again, that this does not, repeat *not*, mean that young singers should sing with the power and volume of older ones. Nor does it mean that young singers should falsely darken their tones to sound older. What it does mean is that singers of any age can successfully attempt to sing *as well* as older, more experienced singers do. Singers should *produce tone,* albeit appropriate for their age—consciously *produce* it, not just let the tones come out. They must also consistently and consciously form vowels vertically or rounded.

Fine singing is not a natural phenomenon. It takes knowledge and hard work to sing well. Fine singing is not an accident. It results from singers being well taught, *thinking* about what they intend to do, and then *doing* it. The teacher/conductor must instill this knowledge and these thoughts in the minds of the chorus members, then insist that they discipline themselves to think and use the knowledge. In an ongoing process, singers of all ages must learn and relearn how to sing well. The choral conductor is a voice teacher in absolutely every rehearsal.

I recommend the following exercises. Do them at a moderate tempo, at all dynamic levels from *pp* to *ff*. Instruct the singers to sing softly especially at the lower (and sometimes upper) extremes of the range. Throughout the exercise, you could give oral instructions on dynamics as they progress by ascending half-step key centers. Call for the basses and altos to drop out above high D or F (depending on the maturity of the chorus), then bring them back in at that same point when descending. This precaution guards against their singing higher than they should, that is, higher than they can sing well.

Ask the singers to sing the following exercises with greater tonal strength and dynamic levels than they sang the exercises earlier in the chapter. You want them to produce *real tone,* that is, a sound that can make a *positive impact on the listener*. This is the sound that combines all that we have put together so far about energy, beauty, and placement. To these basic concepts, we will now try to add greater *depth* and *maturity*.

Exercise 5.11

1. Sing *nee-ay-ah-ay-ee* (bright vowels) on one sustained pitch, then ascend by half-step intervals (see Example 5.12). Use a well-focused tone placed in the upper head, and concentrate on a solid ringing quality, coming out of the forehead beginning at the hairline and descending to the tip-of-the-nose area.

Example 5.12

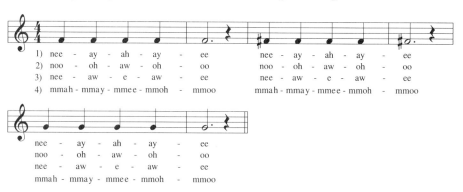

2. Similarly, sing *noo-oh-aw-oh-oo* (dark vowels), but with a naturally deeper and naturally darker tone quality.

3. Sing *nee-aw-ee-aw-ee* (contrasting bright and dark, with minimum and maximum opening), being very aware of the contrasting elements of color, jaw openings, and lip formations.

4. Sing *mmah-mmay-mmee-mmoh-mmoo*, sung similarly to the above, with an emphasis on the different vowel formations, and the intensity of the *mm* resonance being consciously carried into the following vowel sound.

Exercise 5.12.   Descend on scale-steps 5-4-3-2-1, sung on *mm*-ah, *mm*-ah, *mm*-ah, *mm*-ah, *mm*-ah, *mm*-ah (see Example 5.13). Highly intensify the *mm* each time, again capitalizing on the potential resonance achieved through the humming quality of the *mm*, and *carrying that resonance into the following vowel*. The *mm* can be either on the beat, or the preceding off beat.

Example 5.13

The goal is to establish resonance, and then continue that intense resonance throughout the following vowel. The point is that the *intensified* resonant hu*mm* is to be the underlying foundation of *all vowels*. It never ceases. The humming resonance is always present in great singing—nonstop. It's as though there is a generator in the head, creating resonance, and it does so without interruption. (You may substitute or rotate other vowels for the *ah,* such as *mm*ee, *mm*oo, *mm*oh, or *mm*ay.)

Exercise 5.13

- Scale-tones 5-8-5-3-1, sung in a legato manner, on *yah . . . nee-ah . . . ,* or any other desired vowel sounds (see Example 5.14). Hold the high note for an extra beat so the singer actually *sings* on that higher pitch. It is with this exercise that we begin consciously to employ the *entire body*. This is crucial to great singing, for all singers of any age. The person must sing from the arch of the foot to the top of the head, with every cell and fiber participating in the production and performance of the sound. The singer literally feels the singing take place throughout the entire body. All great performers feel this, whether they are instrumentalists or vocalists. Since, however, the voice is the only human instrument, it is especially important that singers include their entire being in the production of singing/performing. Remember to observe the phrase and dynamic markings.

Example 5.14

- To accomplish this fully, have the singers stand with one foot slightly in front of the other (as *always* when standing), allowing the body the opportunity to move slightly forward and back with musical phrases. Place the body-weight on the back heel to begin. As you ascend from the fifth to the eighth tone, let the body-weight shift to the ball of the front foot. Actually lean into the top tone with the entire being, physically and emotionally, as though you were truly performing these notes dramatically to a live audience. Slightly *raise* the body, and expressively stretch the hands *downward* (past your waist) as you ascend to the top note. The body rises while the hands are moving downward, not outward, creating an up-and-down *stretching* feeling.

- Enjoy it! *Perform it*—as though you were on a stage, singing a great role in a grand opera. The feeling should be exhilarating! Continue the exercises, ascending at half-step intervals. Begin with A♭ or B♭ major, and ascend to E♭ or F major, continue without altos and basses up to A♭ or B♭ major, with only the tenors and sopranos. Descend, inviting the altos and basses to join back in at E♭.

- Ask the singers to drop their jaw slightly as they ascend to the top note, as in a gentle yawn. Suggest a relaxed, open feeling at the back of the throat, with the soft pallet slightly raised. All of this will assure a pleasant, open, relaxed, free, and beautiful sound on the top notes.

Exercise 5.14

- Singers need to learn to crescendo without causing strain in the throat muscles. Teach this by crescendoing, on a sustained pitch, over eight counts (see Example 5.15). Start piano and arrive at forte on count eight, then (without interruption) decrescendo over eight counts, ending with piano on the next

Example 5.15

count of eight. Nee is a good vowel to use, as long as the lips and jaw are free and relaxed. Allow the jaw to drop slightly during the process of the crescendo, keeping the tone free and beautiful.

- While singing, place your hands at your forehead. As you crescendo, let the hands and arms extend outward throughout the eight counts of the crescendo. As you decrescendo, bring the hands back to their original position with the fingertips touching the forehead. The point is that the crescendo and decrescendo took place in the *head* not the throat and neck area. The throat and neck remain perfectly relaxed.

As with basic tonal placement, think of the tone and its crescendo as emanating solely from the area of the forehead. Imagine that you can see and feel the tone coming out of the area from the hairline through the cheekbones to the tip of the nose. (Remember: always include the *cheekbones* as part of this upper resonance area.)

- Do this exercise ascending at half-step intervals, but be careful not to extend it too high in the singers' range, which may become too vocally demanding— especially for untrained singers. (B♭ or C for altos and basses, and E♭ or F for tenors and sopranos is high enough.)

Exercise 5.15

- This exercise (see Example 5.16) is particularly effective in building the upper range, both in extension and quality. It spans the range of a ninth (an octave plus one), thus necessitating head tone placement *at the very beginning,* and staying in it throughout the exercise. (Do not allow the singer to begin in a low chest voice and then change into head voice for the upper notes.)

Example 5.16

- As with *all* exercises, begin the exercise *mp*. As the exercise progresses, crescendo to a climactic moment on the highest note. Sing that note and the following one (2 and 8) with poco rubato and espressivo. Sing the exercise with passion! Get the entire body involved. Again, with one foot slightly in front of the other, start with the weight of the body on the heel of the back foot, and gradually shift the weight to the ball of the front foot as you progress to the climactic point described above. Relax the body-weight back, to where it was in the beginning, as you end the exercise. Observe the phrasing, forward motion arrows, and occasional tenuto expressive markings in all the following exercises, and sing with *convincing expression.*

Exercise 5.15 uses the following scale tones and harmonic chords:

135	468	572	835	1
I	IV	V	I	I

Exercise 5.16

• Do this exercise twice (see Example 5.17), once full voiced, and then repeated softly, without taking a breath. This will ensure that the singer sings as beautifully softly as forte. (That is a good practice for many vocal exercises.) It is important to remember that the expression while singing softly should be as expressive, outwardly and inwardly, as when singing forte. The *entire human being* sings, always! Begin *mp,* crescendo to the high note, then diminuendo while descending.

Example 5.17

Exercise 5.17

• This is another exercise designed to build the top range (see Example 5.18). It covers the range of an octave and a half. It is now *especially important* to begin in the upper head voice, allowing the entire exercise to be sung in *one voice*—the head voice. The suggestions of the previous exercise also apply to this

Exercise 5.17 uses the following scale tones and harmonic chords:

135	135	427	542	1
I	I	V	V	I

one. Do it twice without interruption, once full, once softly. Begin *mp,* and crescendo to the top, employ an espressivo poco rubato on the top climactic moment, then decrescendo gradually as you descend.

Example 5.18a

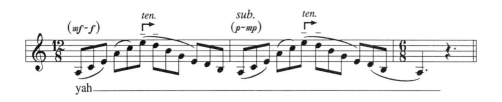

Example 5.18b

> Always phrase and arrange the note-groupings musically as you sing.

We have established a physically loosened-up instrument (the body), mental focus, a well-placed head tone, vitality and animation, a legato line, and building substantial sound and resonance throughout the full (and especially the top) range. Now we'll add the category of *flexibility,* one of the main factors in the quality of any great singer.

The best way to develop flexibility is through the use of rapid scale passages (sixteenth notes). We will do this with five-tone scales, nine-tone scales and combinations of both, and then we'll add another scale passage exercise. Finally we will consider combining them all.

Begin patiently, softly, and slowly.   This is most effectively done with the use of a metronome. Begin at the tempo of a quarter note equaling 76. Most amateur singers can comfortably perform sixteenth notes at this tempo. Progress faster by only one degree each rehearsal, or possibly, each week. Eventually, weeks or months later, the singers will be singing scale passages quite rapidly without really knowing how they got there. The process was so gradual that they were unaware of any difficulty. Each new metronomic degree faster was as easy as the previous one, the difference actually being imperceptible.

The dynamic level in either songs or exercises with rapid scale passages is usually mezzo piano to mezzo forte. The best dynamic for flexibility development is *mp.* Begin slowly (76), and softly.

Our examples will show the manner in which awareness of note-groupings results in a *musical* exercise as opposed to a mechanical one. The next chapter will address phrasing in greater detail, but, for now, just remember that we want to sing melodically, with note-groupings that make musical sense. Pay particular attention to the phrase markings in the exercises below. When you sing them, make sure that the listener will be aware that you are, in fact, *phrasing,* and not singing all notes with equal (mechanical) emphasis. The melodic line should have beauty, forward motion, and musical common sense. As before, begin softly, crescendo to the top of the phrase, then decrescendo to finish.

Place a slight fermata (one extra pulse) on the high note of *each exercise* to insure that the ensemble (or singer) is actually *singing for a moment* on that high note. Anyone can simply peck at it. It must be really *sung.*

Exercise 5.18

- Sing a five-tone scale on *nee-ee-ay-ay-ah,* remembering the three formations of the jaw opening for these three bright vowels (see Example 5.19). You may also use the dark vowels: *noo-oo, oh-oh, aw.* And finally, you may alternate them (bright – dark) at ascending half steps as you progress through the exercise.

- The decrescendo over the quarter tied to a following sixteenth-note, is actually a "lift" at the point of the sixteenth, rather than a gradual decrescendo throughout the quarter-note. This will enhance the beginning of the new phrase. *Crescendo* (moderately) *when ascending, and diminuendo when descending.*

Example 5.19

nee - ay - ah_____   nee - ay - ah_____

nee - ay - ah_____

Exercise 5.19

- Sing this nine-tone scale, using the syllable *yah.* Begin *mp,* and crescendo as you ascend, diminuendo as you descend (see Example 5.20).

Example 5.20

yah_____

yah_____

yah_____

Exercise 5.20

- Combine the five and nine-tone scales, sung as before, but one after the other without interruption (that is, both in one breath). See Example 5.21.

Example 5.21

nee - ay - ah_____

nee - ay - ah_____

nee - ay - ah_____

Exercise 5.21

- Ascending on *yah,* the scale steps: 123, 1234, 2345, 3456, 4567, 5678, 6789, 78 . . . (eventually, no breath here). Then descend: 321, 3217, 2176, 1765, 7654, 6543, 5432, 31. Sing it as though there were forward motion arrows at the beginning of each new 4-note phrase (see Example 5.22).

Example 5.22

Exercise 5.22

- Combine exercises 5.18, 5.19, 5.20, and 5.21 in one breath—if breath control has been worked on regularly and it is possible. If not, breathe at the top of the phrase of Example 5.22, singing uninterrupted with one breath to that point (refer to previous discussion of breath control). See Example 5.23.

Example 5.23

8. Teaching Pitch Awareness

It is difficult to teach consistent pitch awareness to singers. The reason? For years their *ears* have taken them "close enough," especially when singing in the midst of many others of the same voice category. To really zero in on the exact pitch of every single note may not have been asked for, seemed necessary, or wasn't a priority.

Remember our discussion of Robert Shaw's approach to pitch in Chapter 1? The only reason many of the rest of us don't achieve the same results is that we're not willing to work as hard or as relentlessly as Robert Shaw did. First, the conductor needs to make the commitment, then live it, day in and day out. If that means performing less music, then so be it. Fewer songs done well will always be better than more songs done poorly. (Audiences seldom complain about a concert being too short.) Let us all commit to Robert Shaw's ideal of absolute excellence—every note, every song.

There is one specific place for a pitch to be. Train your singers to know exactly where that is by developing sensitive, musical listening. Pitch awareness in musicians ranges from the keyboardists and mallet instrumentalists (whose intonation is set before playing) to string players and singers whose instruments are extremely sensitive to pitch variance. Singers have incredible potential for pitch sensitivity. They also have an unusual potential for pitch *inaccuracy*. They can sing very flat, or very sharp, intentionally or (usually) unintentionally. The first thing we must do is to make the singer *aware* of this variance potential.

Half-step slide exercise

- Ask your singers to sing *loo,* softly, on a sustained pitch of F natural. Continue to hold the tone at that pitch through staggered breathing. Now instruct them to gradually raise the pitch to F sharp. Then ask them to gradually lower the pitch back to F natural. Have them slide, or slur the pitch *evenly, slowly,* and *softly.* (This is for *ear training,* not vocal development.) Tell them to listen very carefully to themselves, actually hearing the several pitches in between the two established pitches.

- Next, ask them to slide (glissando) up from F natural to F sharp, slowly and gradually over eight counts. I repeat, slowly, evenly, and softly. Follow this by descending from F sharp back to F natural over a similar slow, soft, eight counts. This will be difficult at first, but any choir can master it with practice.

- Do this exercise frequently. They will soon become comfortable with it, consistently singing it accurately. Then ask them to switch: men begin on F sharp and slowly descend to F natural over the eight counts, while the women simultaneously begin on F natural and slowly ascend to F sharp over the eight counts. The sound will be very interesting to them, and it should also result in the *unique pitch of a unison quartertone* on beats four or five. They will hear it happening.

Obviously this will begin to develop a well-tuned ear. It also demonstrates to the singers that if they begin on F natural on beat one, and end up on F sharp with beat eight, they actually sang *six* other pitches in-between. You can then make the point that every time a singer moves from one pitch to another (an interval) in a given melody, there are actually six chances of singing the wrong pitch. This exercise will do much to help singers become aware of the significance of accurate pitch.

Interval exercise. The next exercise will help develop the knowledge of interval intonation. We will begin by singing half-steps, then whole steps, minor thirds, major thirds, perfect fourths, and so on. These are notated below in Exercise 5.23.

Exercise 5.23

- Remember, singing half steps and whole steps in tune is our *very first intonation priority*. They are often far more difficult to sing well than larger intervals. Do not take them for granted. (See Example 5.24.)

Example 5.24

(half-step)

loo _____ loo _____ loo _____

(whole step)

loo _____ loo _____ loo _____

(minor third)

loo _____ loo _____ loo _____

(major third)

loo _____ loo _____ loo _____

(perfect fourth)

loo _____ loo _____ loo _____

- When singing ascending half steps, the singer must mentally reach very high for the second of the two notes (not accenting it, just reaching for the highest possible accurate pitch).

- When singing descending half steps, singers should feel they are skimming down, ever so slightly, from the upper note. (The singer might think of singing from A natural down to A flat, rather than to G sharp, or from F natural to F flat, rather than to E natural.) In any case, relate the lower note very closely to the upper note.

- In singing whole steps, ask the singers to feel as though they are reaching in *both* directions, up when ascending, and down when descending. This is similar to the ascending half step, but the opposite of the descending half step.

- When singing minor thirds, think a bit low for the ascending interval, and very high for the descending one.

- For major thirds and perfect fourths, think high for the ascending interval and low for the descending one. From a practical point of view, this may be as far as you wish to take this exercise.

- Sing these mental exercises very softly. They are not voice builders. They are mind developers. Listen *intensely* as you sing *quietly*.

- You may wish to develop a chord progression from a beginning unison pitch. This is done by directing each section (soprano, alto, tenor, bass), one at a time, to continually change intervals in a sequential manner, resulting in a desired chord progression, or simply some interesting a-tonal sounds, finally arriving back at the original unison pitch. Check to see if the chorus has retained the original pitch.

These exercises and others you may develop will stimulate pitch awareness and musical ear training. They are particularly useful (1) in pitch development in general, and (2) if the chorus is about to work on either Renaissance or Contemporary music, in which pitch problems and challenges are abundant.

Reminder about setting a vocalizing agenda for each rehearsal.   We quite obviously cannot do all these exercises prior to each rehearsal. We wouldn't have time to complete them nor get to the music to be rehearsed. But it is an absolute necessity to begin every rehearsal with some appropriate warm-up vocal exercises. Do not yield to the temptation to "get right to the music." To eliminate the warm-up period is as unfair to singers as asking a runner to begin a race without first stretching-out the joints, muscles, and tendons of the body. The vocal chords deserve the same consideration.

Equally important, warm-ups are the time for each chorus member to make the transition from talker to *singer*. One of the basic challenges of the choral conductor is to teach the singers that there is a specific sound, consciously produced in a special manner, for singing. *It is in no way related to the anemic vocal production (or lack of vocal production) used in casual conversation.* Effective vocal warm-ups should enable the singer to make this transition comfortably *prior* to facing the vocal challenges of the music.

Plan the warm-up period well, economically and effectively. Each day select the categories you will use, and which exercises from those categories you will specifically use. I would suggest that you always begin with category 1 and consistently use categories 3 and 6. Next on my priority list would be category 7. For beginning groups, or choruses that you have not worked with before (new job or guest conducting with ensembles that have not been solidly trained) I would strongly suggest using category 4 early on to establish that all-important ingredient, energy!

Do as you wish, of course, in developing your own set of categories and exercises. The main thing is that your categories and specific exercises make good common sense. They should not sound silly or be impractical. The chorus should make vocal and/or musical progress during each moment of every exercise, which should be of true substance. Choose wisely and carefully, but do use them. Many of our singers do not take private voice lessons. We are their *only* voice teachers. During the warm-ups we often have our most productive moments of really *teaching voice.*

Summary

- Singers should not look at the conductor while vocalizing. The conductor should be at the piano, playing and *controlling* the exercises. Ask singers to sing as though performing to an audience, or in a solo practice room, *consciously thinking* about what they're doing, while listening to and evaluating themselves as they progress through the exercises. Guide their thinking prior to (and sometimes during) the exercise. Do this through spontaneous oral commands, and/or by writing significant

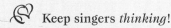 Keep singers *thinking*!

thoughts and diagrams on the chalkboard that will directly draw their attention to those techniques on which they are to focus (head-tone placement, vowel formation, energy, and so on). *Keep them thinking!* Do not let warm-ups become a mindless routine.

- Use vocalizing exercises to begin each rehearsal!
- Teach the singers to understand the reasoning behind every exercise and focus on that while vocalizing.
- Structure the warm-up session around basic concepts of fine singing. Develop a basic outline for this structure built on the following categories:
  1. Loosening up physically
  2. Awareness of mental and vocal unity
  3. Establishing the placement of the upper head tone
  4. Projecting personal vitality and animation
  5. Using a legato line with forward motion phrasing
  6. Developing a substantial, full, and mature sound
  7. Creating melodic flexibility
  8. Teaching pitch awareness
- Understand that the *conductor* creates a great chorus. It will not happen automatically. We must make it happen!
- Keep the singers *thinking*! Succeed because of intelligent thinking, not luck.
- Organize and predetermine warm-ups.
- Do not accept bad or offensive sounds. Teach beautiful singing and accept nothing less.
- Great singing is *produced*. It is not a natural phenomenon.

Rhythmic Interest, Forward Motion, and Phrasing

In this chapter, we will look at musical notes and their functions. We will study each note in depth, microscopically, to determine its function and its relationship to the note(s) both before it and after it. We will determine its role in the phrase, whether it is part of a crescendo, the actual stressed note following the crescendo, or part of a diminuendo following the stressed note. All notes, syllables, and words should fall within the pattern of this natural and continuous crescendo-stress-diminuendo. This can best be shown in the phrase structure diagram in Figure 6.1 in which several smaller phrases are contained within a larger phrase.

The notes in the beginning crescendo or the ending diminuendo may number from one to many. They may begin with only a single upbeat or several lead-in notes. They may end with a single eighth note or several notes. It doesn't matter. What does matter is that

- The lead-in note or notes significantly represent the area of forward motion and rhythmic interest
- The main note, word, or syllable effectively represents the proper stress-feeling
- Those notes that are a part of the falling-away diminuendo are handled with sensitivity.

We use rhythmic interest, forward motion, and phrasing to create interest in music. We use ***rhythmic interest*** to take a fundamental accurate rhythm and bring it

Figure 6.1
Phrases within a phrase

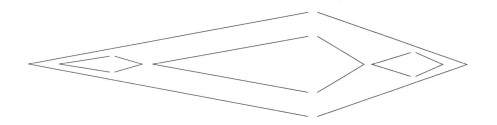

> Never perform two consecutive notes, words, or syllables with equal emphasis.

to life with the off-beat emphasis normally related to fine jazz. **Forward motion** allows us to use rhythmic interest to move the music forward, to the right, taking the listener to the end of the phrase with lively motion. We use **phrasing** to transcend the mathematical mechanics of accurate pitches and rhythms into the realm of artistic music, or *musicality*, by creating

- Note-groupings in which every note has a specific melodic function in relationship to every other note
- Melodic rise and fall emphasis
- Crescendo-stress-diminuendo patterns

Rhythmic Interest Results from Off-Beat Emphasis

Rhythmic interest means a *slight* emphasis on off-beats, or those beats that are normally de-emphasized. That would be beats 2 and/or 4 in a 4-beat measure, beats 2 or 3 in a 3-beat measure, beats 3 and 6, or 2 and 5, in a measure of 6, and beat 2 in a measure of 2. This can be recognized as the *basic rhythmic element of jazz*.

The world-renowned Handel scholar, Jens Peter Larsen of Copenhagen, Denmark, at age 84, said that "fine Handel is just like fine jazz." We, of course, will not attempt to transform classical music into jazz, but we will try to instill within our performance of classical music that wonderful rhythmic vitality so basic to fine jazz. The *rhythmic spirit* of fine jazz is what we want to feel in classical music, thus bringing it to life.

Notice that Larsen was referring to "fine jazz," not pop, rock, gospel, or Broadway. One basic element of fine jazz is a subtle, driving rhythm. The word *subtle* is paramount to the success of this concept. Restrained subtlety will keep us from overdoing it. We will strive to *serve* and *enhance* the music, but hope never to draw attention away from the composition itself.

By the time we have finished, you will find that the concept of rhythmic interest applies to the music of all composers and stylistic periods. Common sense will dictate the manner and extent to which it should be employed. For example, off-beat emphasis might be considered in the following ways:

1. Much more obvious and spirited in allegro than in slower tempi.

2. Extremely subtle in music of the Renaissance and earlier periods.

3. Less subtle, very spirited, a bit jazzy and dance-like in music of the Baroque period, intended basically for the tempi of allegro, and faster, but also present in andante and slower tempi, with greater degrees of subtlety.

4. More obvious and pronounced in the Classic period of Haydn, Mozart, and early Beethoven and Schubert.

5. Often very physical and much more obvious in the forte allegros of later Beethoven, actually amounting to "driving accents" at times.

6. Less percussive subtlety by romantic composers, somewhat similar to that of the Renaissance, but with a greater intensity, appropriate for the depth of Romantic expressive passion.

7. Incorporating all these for the variety of styles found in contemporary music, depending on the composer and the composition.

Forward Motion

Forward motion is just that, consciously moving the feeling of the music forward, to the right. Forward motion and rhythmic interest are closely related. The off-beat emphasis that creates rhythmic interest actually moves the music to the right. Emphasizing an off beat automatically takes you to the next note or beat. In 4/4 time, emphasis on beat 2 takes you to beat 3, and emphasis on beat 4 takes you to beat 1.

Consistent forward motion picks up the listeners when the phrase or song begins and doesn't set them down until it ends. Without it, the motionless music sets the listeners down in a continual stopping manner, over and over throughout the entire piece. The resulting effect seems monotonous and endless. Truly alive rhythm and sparkling off-beat emphases take the music, performer, and listener forward. Rhythmic interest is the vehicle with which forward motion becomes possible.

Defining and Indicating Forward Motion

What is this emphasis we're talking about? What musical sign are we going to place on these off-beats? Is it an accent (<)? Is it a stress (—)? Actually, there is no mark or musical sign that adequately describes what we want to do.

What we really want is a lifting, rhythmically interesting, forward motion in our music. That is, rhythm that is not merely accurate but vitally interesting rhythm that really speaks and moves forward. How do we mark or indicate that? Let's invent a new sign for it:

1. We might think of it as a slight crescendo, with a whirlwind inside it, moving to the right in an uplifting manner (⟪⟫) over one or more notes.

2. We could also use an arrow, aiming to the right, *above* the note(s) to be energized (⌐). You will find many of these in the vocalizing exercises of Chapter 5, especially in those dealing with flexibility (5- and 9-tone scale passages).

3. Or, we could place a curved arrow *under* a *word* or *syllable*, to indicate the same kind of rhythmic/forward feeling (↳). In which case, that *word* is to move forward, with real momentum, into the following word(s).

That's what it should look and feel like, but there would not be time nor space for us (or our singers) to place the crescendo-whirlwind sign in the music. Instead, I recommend either of the arrows. If you prefer use an accent. Use a regular accent when you want it fully employed, and an accent-in-parentheses when you want it done in a more subtle manner.

If you select accents, be sure the singers realize the *difference* between a normal hammered accent, and the rhythmic interest and forward motion feeling we want to achieve with these accents. These accents may at times be similar to regular accents, especially in Beethoven fortes. For most of our purposes, however, the efforts to stimulate rhythmic interest and indicate forward motion are best expressed with the arrow symbols.

Retaining Significant Word Emphasis and Melodic Stress on Primary Beats

The energy we are now giving to up-beats does *not* negate the logical stress placed on normally emphasized words and syllables found on primary beats. This energy is *added to* and *combined with the logical stress*. The energy will *not* detract from the stress.

For example, in the word "divided," "di" (the up beat) is energized for forward motion, *vi* (the primary beat) is stressed, and "ded" is de-emphasized. In the word "education," "ed-u" is the energized up beat, "ca" (the primary beat) is the normally stressed syllable, and "tion" is the de-emphasized (diminuendo) syllable. We will refer to this process as *energy-stress-diminuendo*. Yet another example is in the word "rudimentary,": "ru-di" is the energized up beat, "men" is the stressed syllable, and "ta-ry" is the de-emphasized diminuendo.

In an example using more than one word, "The Lord our God is great!," "The," "our," and "is" are all forward motion or rhythmic interest words. "Lord," "God," and "great" are all primary beat *stressed* words. In "The music is lovely," "The" and "is" are the rhythmic interest or forward motion words, "mu" and "love" are the primary emphasis syllables, and "ic" and "ly" are the de-emphasized (diminuendo) syllables. I recommend marking the score as shown in Figure 6.2.

Figure 6.2

Text emphasis and forward motion

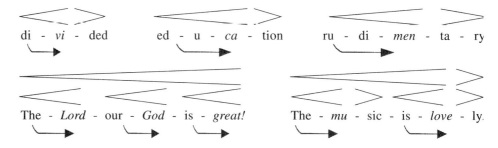

Rhythmic Interest, Forward Motion, and Phrasing

Phrasing is the grouping of notes that musically relate to each other. The phrase is artistically enhanced with the crescendo-stress-diminuendo process described earlier.

4/4 Time

In 4/4 time, the energy emphasis will be on either beat 2 or 4, depending on the melody. If the primary emphasis is the second beat, then the fourth will get a somewhat slighter emphasis. If it is on the fourth beat, then the second will get the slighter emphasis. If using accents, we might think of the main emphasis as an accent, and the lesser one, an accent-in-parentheses. (Remember that we use the term "accent" to represent an energizing of the note, sending it forward, with a lifting feeling.) Example 6.1 illustrates the main emphasis on two, then on four, with secondary emphases in parentheses.

Example 6.1

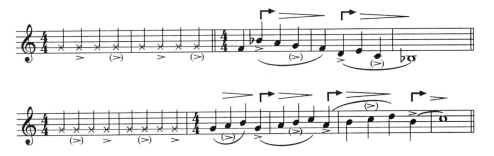

Pairs of Eighth Notes

Pairs of eighth notes usually fall on beats 2 or 4, for the purpose of forward motion. There are really three kinds of eighth-note pairs (from left to right in Example 6.2):

1. Those that are called a "sigh" motive

2. Those that *both* move forward

3. Those in which the first belongs to the previous note(s), and the second of the pair moves forward, belonging to the following note(s)

Example 6.2

The sigh motive.   Example 6.3 illustrates the sigh motive, with a stress on the first eighth and a softening of the second. This is usually used in slower tempi, especially in the Baroque period. When considering the overall use of pairs of eighth-notes, the sigh motive would be the least common and is *not* related to our forward motion concept. (Sigh motives have a rather halting and somewhat haunting feeling.)

Example 6.3

Two eighths moving forward.   Example 6.4 shows *both* eighth notes moving forward, into either beat 3, or beat 1. Dynamics have been included because we want to emphasize that melodies should always be sung musically, rather than mechanically without feeling or expression. We also want to establish the concept that forward motion begins with an energized crescendo (even if it is very short), which is followed by a stressed primary note and then by a tapering or softening (diminuendo) throughout the following note or notes. Arrows indicate points of forward motion.

Example 6.4

Splitting the function of eighth notes.   Example 6.5 demonstrates a pair of eighth notes in which the first belongs to the previous note(s), tapering a bit, and the second is the forward motion note, belonging to the following note or notes. The arrows show the direction of emphasis on each eighth note, and the dynamics indicate the crescendo-stress-diminuendo concept.

Example 6.5

Dealing with Dotted Rhythms

The term *dotted rhythm* is a misnomer. The actual dotted rhythm is the note after the dotted note and the following note. That is, in the instance of a dotted quarter note, a following eighth, and a following quarter note, the dotted rhythm is actually the eighth note and the following quarter note. The preceding dotted quarter note is simply an *introduction* to the dotted rhythm, or the last note of a previous phrase. Example 6.6 shows three kinds of dotted notes.

Example 6.6

The shorter notes of dotted rhythms start the phrase.   Example 6.7 shows a melody using the dotted quarter and eighth, in which the eighth always begins the next phrase. The first dotted quarter simply begins the melody, and thereafter ends each brief phrase.

Example 6.7

The melody in Example 6.8 demonstrates a dotted eighth followed by a sixteenth note. In each case, the sixteenth note begins a new phrase, and the dotted eighth ends one.

Example 6.8

The Difference between ♩. ♪ and ♪. ♬

There is a major difference between a performer's approach to an eighth following a dotted quarter and the approach to a sixteenth following a dotted eighth. Singers usually sing the eighth after a dotted quarter late and the sixteenth after a dotted eighth early, thus confusing true accuracy with that of a triplet figure. Therefore, we will establish a concept of bringing the eighth after a dotted quarter to the left, seemingly singing it a bit early and staying on it a moment (singing its full duration). And we'll do just the opposite with the sixteenth after a dotted eighth. We'll wait until the last split second, moving it slightly to the right. This wouldn't work in slower tempi. The sixteenth needs to be exactly one fourth of the slower beat. Placing it far to the right, in *faster* tempi, does, however, usually put it right on the final fourth of the beat.

Example 6.9 will demonstrate these two ideas. The arrows *above* the notes still refer to *forward motion*. The arrows *under* the quarter notes are a reminder to sing them (seemingly) early. The arrows under the sixteenth notes remind us to wait, placing them further to the right. Understand both very clearly.

Example 6.9

Example 6.10 demonstrates these concepts combined in a single melody.

Example 6.10

Example 6.11 demonstrates the forward motion of three eighth notes following an eighth-rest, usually at the end (but occasionally at the beginning) of a measure. In each case, the first and third of the three notes are the second half of a beat. Therefore, they function as forward motion notes. The conductor will determine which of the two is primary, and which is secondary, as with beats 2 and 4 in 4/4.

Example 6.11

Various Functions of Eighths and Sixteenths

Example 6.12 demonstrates the forward motion of two sixteenths following an eighth, in which they actually are a part of the next eighth, not the preceding eighth (as the misleading bar line would seem to indicate).

Example 6.13 shows an instance in which sixteenth notes are used as a method of momentarily halting, purposely negating forward motion. Placing them *on the*

Example 6.12

Example 6.13

beat completely emphasizes each pulse unto itself, giving a stopping feeling at each beat. The same effect would be accomplished by placing pairs of eighth notes on primary beats (1 and 3 in 4/4).

Forward Motion in Triple Meter

We now begin forward motion with *triple meter*. In a three-beat measure, forward emphasis will be either on beat two or three, again depending on the melody. Let the melody speak to you, and the decision will be simple. Example 6.14 shows each, the first on two, and the second on three.

Example 6.14

Example 6.15 melodically demonstrates emphasis on two, and Example 6.16 demonstrates emphasis on three (the dotted eighth notes and sixteenth rests are written for phrase clarity).

Example 6.15

Example 6.16

Variations of Emphasis in 6/8 Time

The following two examples demonstrate the difference between 6/8 measures when the emphasis is on beats 3 and 6, and when it is on 2 and 5. This is a very important musical difference. They are completely unalike. A three-and-six emphasis consists of continuous crescendo-stress-diminuendo patterns (in which beats 2 and 5 are minimized). A two-and-five emphasis consists of either continuous crescendi or continuous diminuendi, but not both (similar to Examples 6.15 and 6.16).

Emphasis on 3 and 6. Examples 6.17 and 6.18 demonstrate emphasis on beats 6 and 3 (6 and 3, rather than 3 and 6, because this forward pattern usually begins with the up-beat 6).

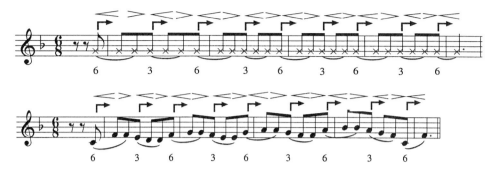

Example 6.17

Example 6.18

Emphasis on 2 and 5. Example 6.19 shows the opposite, emphasis on *2 and 5*. Notice that in each case, the pattern is in either a crescendo or diminuendo. The conductor, in studying both the text and the melody, may determine whether it will be a crescendo or diminuendo. This will usually be consistent but occasionally will interchange throughout the phrase or song.

Example 6.19

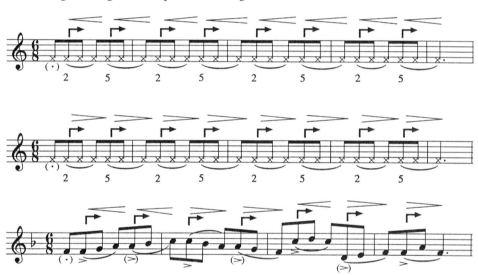

If taken to extreme, however, these concepts can easily become distracting to the composition. Our goal is to enhance the piece, not detract from it. To incorporate these ideas appropriately, use common sense, good taste, and sensitivity.

The Scores: The Source of These Techniques

Without rhythmic interest, forward motion, and phrasing, there is no *music,* only the *mechanical mathematics* of accurate pitches and rhythms. Granted, there will be occasional markings by the composer (crescendi, diminuendi, accents, stresses, accellerandi, ritards, fermati, and so on), but early composers included few or none of these. Later composers gave us more. But no composer gives us enough to truly bring

> Learn the style of the piece to ensure the best possible interpretation and then work relentlessly to bring out all of its potential musical and textual beauty.

the music to its greatest potential. Randall Thompson came the closest with abundant, and very effective, markings. But even his music needs additional markings for beauty and nuance (see Examples 6.40, 6.41, and 6.42).

Upon hearing the Robert Shaw Chorale recording of *Symphony of Psalms*, composer Igor Stravinsky reportedly said, "I did not know my work was that beautiful." Robert Shaw was able to hear and produce potential musical and textual beauty that the composer was unable to imagine, even a truly great composer. (See Example 6.39.)

I do not mean to suggest that conductors have a special license to make changes or additions to the music because of their own individual thinking or feelings about a composition. I have always felt that composers are somewhere between God and people. They are in a special category with authors, poets, and others who *create*. It is our job and responsibility to *recreate* with *honesty and integrity* to those who create.

We must remember, however, that interpretation, based on a study of the style and intent of composers is the *creative responsibility of the conductor*. Always keep in mind, though, that I said, "based on a study of the style and intent of composers." Conductors should not base their interpretations on feelings alone. That is never sufficient. Creditable feelings must rest securely on a foundation of serious study.

Advice from Musicologists and Composers

The surest way to know (as much as we can know) how to approach a score and its interpretation is to contact a musicologist who specializes in the music of the composer we're about to perform. Musicologists should be the conductor's best musical friends because they spend entire careers learning the significant aspects of musical style and performance that we conductors would never have the time to do. Furthermore, they are eagerly waiting for us to ask their advice. They have all this valuable knowledge. We need it. Ask them for it. Pay them for it. Invite them to come to your rehearsals to make suggestions based on their reactions to your work.

I have found it an incredibly positive experience to invite (to *many* rehearsals) a musicologist who feels free to interrupt, at any time, to make a suggestion (or constructive criticism) to the chorus, orchestra, soloists, or me, regarding anything at all that will better serve the piece. Everyone learns, grows, and appreciates this wonderful opportunity. Admittedly, the conductor needs to have a significant amount of security, patience, and humility, but it is well worth the effort, believe me.

If you are doing the music of a living composer, invite the composer to your rehearsal. If this is not possible, contact the composer and get as many ideas from the source as you can. If neither is a possibility, seek advice from another contemporary composer (as you might have done with a musicologist regarding composers of the past).

The main point is that we gain substantial knowledge concerning the composition we are about to perform. This, of course, pertains to music of substantial difficulty, or about which we might know very little. Simpler songs do not fall into this category. However, if we don't *really know* how a piece (even a simpler one) should be interpreted, we must seek help. Don't just venture out into unknown waters. *Know the music.*

Wise Advice

Let me pass on the good advice of three great musicians.

Musicologist/pianist Julius Herford told me that after first studying with a scholar, I was to trust myself and go forth with confidence. I was not to worry about pleasing the teacher (or anybody else). I should become consumed with the music and, as a conductor, believe in myself and lead effectively.

The great American tenor, Seth McCoy, took for granted that we would study the music with knowledgeable teachers and scholars. But then, he admonished conductors, "do what you do with confidence and make a definite statement in doing so." He went on to say, "It makes no difference whether others think you are right or wrong; do that in which you firmly believe—and do it with conviction!"

Alex Tregger, concertmaster of the Los Angeles Philharmonic Orchestra, described to my choral-conducting students those qualities an orchestra expects of a conductor. He said, "We want you to know the music, know how you want it to be performed, and approach it with confidence. In turn, we will respect and follow you, even if we are used to doing it another way, or even prefer another way. If you know what you are doing, and are not egotistical about it, we will be receptive and go with you."

> ✆ Many considered Seth McCoy the "king of oratorio," the finest oratorio singer of the twentieth century. Seth admonished choral conductors to do what they do with 100 percent conviction—significantly affecting the performers and listeners. That's the way he sang. He didn't try to please everybody or do as others did. He simply studied to learn all he could, then did those things in which he believed completely. This is great advice from a performing legend.

Examples from the Literature

In this section we will look at musical examples that illustrate the foundation from which the preceding discussion of rhythmic interest (off-beat emphasis), forward motion, and phrasing derives. These concepts come from the *compositions themselves,* not from a conductor's imagination. I will use many musical fragments to emphasize different aspects of the concepts. The first examples come from Handel's *Messiah.*

Chorus no. 25, "And with His stripes we are healed." Example 6.20 is written in true Renaissance style, with each section (soprano, alto, tenor, and bass) having independent melodic lines, and the accompaniment doubling the voice parts. Handel begins on beat two and gives us the first ascending leap to beat four, thus establishing our "jazz" element of emphasizing beats two and four—even within the conservative Renaissance style. Extremely subtle emphasis on these off-beats, and conducting it in two *with the whole note getting the beat,* enhances both the rhythmic interest and the flow of the Renaissance linear quality. (In the Alfred Mann edition, in which Mann used the original two half notes per measure, conduct in *one.*) This enhances the linear flow of the Renaissance style. Notice that in measure four, Handel chooses to begin the phrase on the second half of a beat, further establishing

Example 6.20

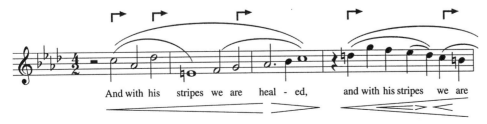

And with his stripes we are heal - ed, and with his stripes we are

rhythmic interest. You could place the third forward motion arrow before the F natural, thereby moving both "we" and "are" forward. If so, I would still recommend that the word "are" be given a little more motion than "we."

Chorus no. 51, "But thanks be to God."   The little thanksgiving chorus shown in Example 6.21 is composed in a madrigal style, and almost every phrase begins on the second half of a beat. If we slightly emphasize these many upbeats, the forward motion is continuous, and the song floats along in a most delightful manner. That is, *two thoughts of forward motion: "thanks* be" and *"to* God," within one longer line, incorporating it all in a linear or flowing manner, aiming for "*God.*"

* Every upbeat eighth-note should be ♪ ♩, but the final ones in "to God" are especially important.

**Each case of "thanks be to God" should be thought of as "thanks be" — "to God", two thoughts in one, and articulated as such:

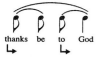

Example 6.21

Chorus no. 28 ("Turba"), "He trusted in God."   In Example, 6.22, we see again that Handel elects to begin each phrase with an upbeat eighth note, his way of telling us to "get the piece moving, and keep it rhythmically interesting." The upbeats are there for a very good reason. Take advantage of them. *Emphasize them.* (Remember, however, never emphasize to extreme, which would draw attention to the concept and away from the piece itself.)

In this case, "let," "de-," "-er," "if," "in," "he," "that," and "would" are all more *musically* significant than the primary words and syllables such as "Him," "-liv," "trust," "him," "-light," and "God." Accents now replace arrows.

Chorus no. 53, "Worthy is the Lamb."   In the excerpt in Example 6.23, Handel once again chose to begin each new note grouping with an upbeat. Thus,

Example 6.22

the words "for" and "and" are more *actively* significant than "ever". Emphasize them and de-emphasize "ever" (remember: not to extreme, and always within the realm of good taste and common sense).

Example 6.23

Chorus no. 9 "O Thou that tellest good tidings to Zion." In this triple-meter example (Example 6.24), the forward motion emphases are on beats 6 and 3, thus creating an accent-stress-diminuendo effect with consecutive eighth notes beginning on either 6 or 3. This is also an automatic indication of the need for accented (energized) upbeats in all cases beginning on 6, 3, or both.

O   thou   that   tell-est   good   ti-dings   to   Si-on,   good   ti   -   dings___   to   Je -

Example 6.24

Chorus no. 4, "And the glory of the Lord."   In this excerpt in triple meter (Example 6.25), Handel begins each new phrase on beat two ("*and* the"), the second half of two ("-*ry* the glory of" and –"*re*-vealed") or beat three ("*shall* be"). Slightly emphasizing all three, and approaching them just a bit early, will continuously propel the song forward with a natural triple meter "lilt." Conducting it in one will help establish that lilt (quarter note = 132–138; dotted half-note = 44–46).

"Glo-ry of" sung in the rhythm of a dotted eighth and sixteenth note will also heighten rhythmic interest. In which case the syllable "ry" actually belongs to "of," not "glo," "ry–the", and "ry of the Lord" becomes the new phrase, after an introductory "and the glo," or "the glo": *And the glo–ry the glo–ry of the Lord.*"

Example 6.25

And   the   glo - ry,   the   glo - ry of   the   Lord

the   glo - ry of   the   Lord

And   the   glo - ry,   the   glo - ry of   the   Lord   shall   be   re -

And   the   glo - ry,   the   glo - ry of   the   Lord

* Sung in a very uplifting one-beat per measure, with added energy at the beginning of each new small phrase (>)! (Suggest ♩. = 44–46)

** Tenor phrasing is different because of the extension of their phrase.

*** A slight feeling of rushing forward should be felt with each third beat "shall", and each group of three eighth-notes at the end of a measure ("re" of "re-veal-ed").

Chorus no. 53, "Worthy is the Lamb."   In the final twenty-three measures of the chorus shown in Example 6.26a and b, I circled instances when Handel took advantage of beats 2 or 4, or the second half of a beat, to accentuate the potential for

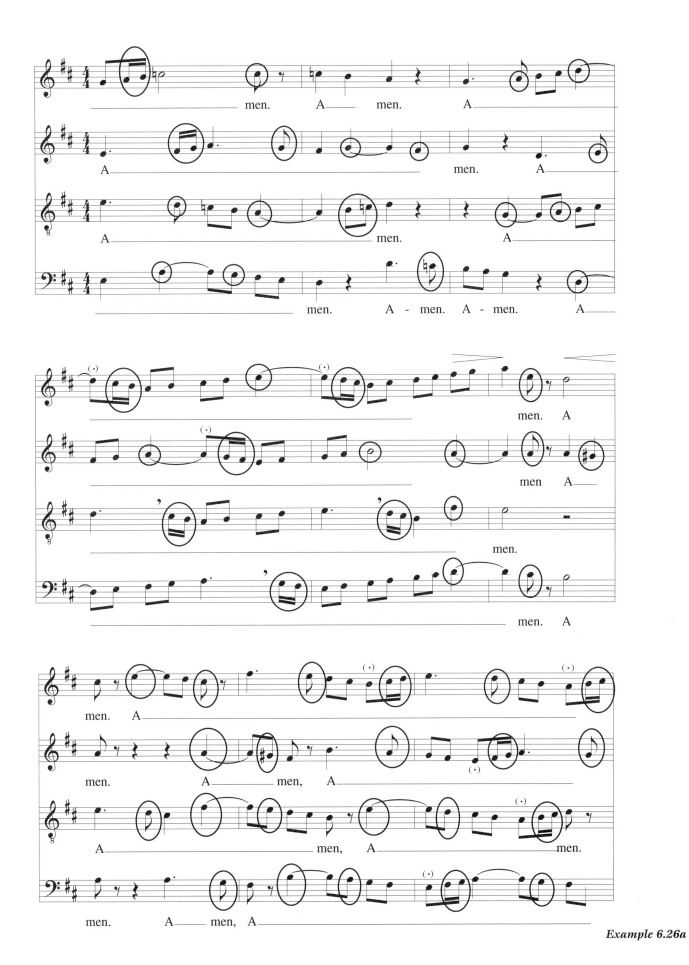

Example 6.26a

Example 6.26b

rhythmic interest. There are often three or four in each measure! This demonstrates how these concepts arise from the *composition*, rather than from the conductor. The *poco ritard, poco meno mosso,* and *ritard* in the final eleven measures are my editorial markings (after consulting with Julius Herford and Alfred Mann—an example of seeking advice). These markings seem to bring the oratorio to a grand and glorious conclusion. (Some quarter notes on "men" have been changed to eighth notes.)

> In the allegro tempi of Bach to Beethoven, the music usually takes precedence over the text. This places phrasing, forward motion, and rhythmic interest at a higher priority than the normally emphasized primary beats, words, and syllables. These primary beats may still be emphasized, but the *upbeats* are literally the life of the music.

Mendelssohn, *St. Paul* Oratorio, "How lovely are the messengers." Example 6.27 is another example of triple meter, in which beats 6 and 3 move the piece forward, and in which accent (energy)-stress-diminuendo takes place during consecutive eighth notes.

Example 6.27

* Along with forward motion/rhythmic interest emphasis, we must also always keep in mind the presence of *long-line* melodic direction.

J. S. Bach, *Magnificat*, "Sicut locutus est." The eighteen measures shown in Example 6.28 are from the bass part of this piece. The purpose of this example is to show its note-groupings (phrasing) and suggested dynamics.

- Note that groupings (phrases) usually end and begin anew when the melodic line changes directions or scale passages are interrupted by an interval of a minor or major third.

- The dynamics are based on the concept that even short phrases *frequently* begin with the energy of a crescendo, move to a climactic moment, then diminuendo at the conclusion of the phrase.

Consider the following items in the first four-and-one-half measure phrase:

1. The first two notes (D and E) belong to each other because the third note, which is beat *4*, must belong to the following beat (1). Remember, in 4/4 time, beat 2 takes us to 3, and beat 4 takes us to 1. (Although this piece should be taken in 2, we'll *discuss* it in 4.)

2. The fourth beat of measure one, therefore, belongs to the following note or notes—in this case, the following three because the consecutive eighths change direction with the fourth.

Example 6.28

* Staccato quarter notes are for the purpose of singing them in a slightly shorter manner similar to instrumental articulation of this period. (in 2, ♩= 78–84)

3. The fourth eighth note of measure two begins a note grouping that includes the downbeat of measure three. That is because the eighths ascend to beat 4, which must belong to the following beat 1.

4. The second beat of measure three belongs to beat 3, and the fourth to beat 1 of measure four. The motion here is two-three, and four-one.

5. The fourth beat of measure three takes us to the half note beginning measure four, and the second half note of measure four takes us to the downbeat of measure five (G♯ to A).

6. Dynamics: The overall phrase crescendos slightly to the downbeat of measure four. Measure four will then diminuendo throughout to the downbeat of measure five. Within that, however, each small note grouping will employ its own slight crescendo-diminuendo (there are potentially six). The first two notes will simply be a stress-diminuendo. The final three may be one gradual diminuendo (B-G♯-A), or emphasize C♯, which diminuendos to B, then emphasize G♯, which diminuendos to the final A (totaling 6 groupings). What you do is up to you. The main point is that you do *something*. The only really bad interpretation is no interpretation at all!

Beethoven, *Missa Solemnis*, "Gloria." The next three examples are all from the "Gloria." Example 6.29 shows the melismatic phrasing of consecutive eighth notes, in which the first phrase ends and a new phrase begins with the *interruptive interval of a minor third*. The point of interest is that Beethoven chose to do this on the second half of beat 4, which highlights rhythmic interest. He is consistent in the

Example 6.29

following measure with the C natural beginning the final note grouping also on the second half of beat 4. Dynamically, each phrase or note grouping would slightly crescendo, then diminuendo toward its ending.

Tenor Part from Beethoven, *Missa Solemnis*, "Gloria."   This thirteen-measure tenor part (Example 6.30) illustrates nine phrases. The first contains seven notes; the second begins with the eighth (C natural) on the rhythmically interesting second half of beat 4. The third phrase musically begins on the second half of beat 4 also, but we have a conflict with *text* at that point. The text begins with the *entire* fourth beat (B-E). Musically that is not good. Rhythmically it's not as alive as the second half of beat 4, and melodically speaking, to end with an interval of a fifth is not pleasing to the ear. The final E of this measure does, however, melodically line up well with the following C natural creating a new phrase with the pleasant sound of a sixth.

What do we do with this dilemma? Simply move the word "in" one note to the right. We have consistent phrase beginnings on the second half of each fourth beat, including the fourth phrase, which begins with the last note of measure three. (Not that it is necessary; it just happens to be true.)

Example 6.30

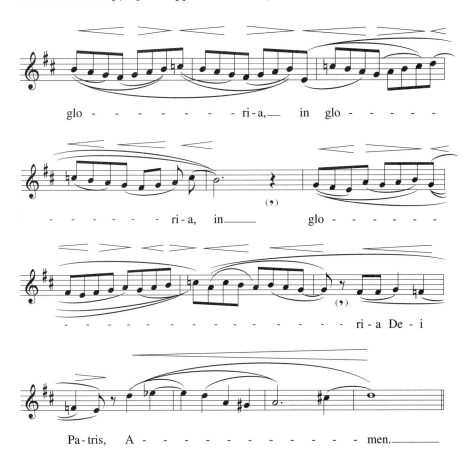

The fifth phrase is a seven-note phrase (3 + 4), the sixth is a ten-note phrase (6 + 4), the seventh, an eight-note phrase (4 + 4), the eighth is six (3 + 3), and the final is nine notes (3 + 4 + 2).

Soprano Part, Beethoven, *Missa Solemnis*, "Gloria." This nine-measure soprano melody (Example 6.31) is basically the same as the tenor melismatic phrases, except that it is only half as fast. We now have seven (or eight) quarter-note phrases instead of seven or eight eighth-note phrases. Let's make several changes to enhance both the soprano sound, and clarify the phrase structure.

Example 6.31

1. Shorten the final note of each phrase to an eighth note followed by an eighth rest, for greater clarity in defining the end of one musical phrase and the beginning of another.

2. Ask the sopranos to add a diminuendo as they ascend to the final high notes (for beauty of sound).

3. Change the syllable "tris" on each high note to "ah," again for beauty of tone ("in gloria dei pa---). Many sopranos singing "tris" on a high A can be quite ear-shattering (even many *very fine* sopranos).

4. Add forward motion arrows to the fourth beat of each measure. (The diminuendi placed on the fourth beats of measures two and four are for the purpose of softening the approach of the high A, A♯, and B, to help ensure a more beautiful tone.)

I would not attempt to change Beethoven's music in a noticeable manner. That is, I should do nothing of which the audience would be aware. The conceptual changes should only enhance the music, not detract from it. If a composer were to be in the audience listening to his or her composition, these kinds of changes should be *imperceptible.* The composer should simply like the performance, maybe more than ever, and not really know why.

Handel, *Messiah*, "Since by man came death." In Example 6.32, notice that even in grave a cappella singing, Handel begins the chorus on beat *2*, and moves next on beat *4*. Forward motion is always paramount.

In the allegro section, Handel begins the chorus not only on the second beat, but the *second half* of the second beat. How jazzy can you get? This first allegro phrase has three parts to it: "By man came also—the resurrection—of the dead." Does the second third of the phrase begin with "the" or the second half of "also"? Is

Example 6.32

it "By man came al—*so the resurrection*—of the dead," or is it "By man came also—*the resurrection*—of the dead? It's your decision. The point is you have to make the decision, and you need to base it on something musically or textually solid.

My choice is to begin the second third of the phrase with the syllable "so" of "also" because the phrase actually begins with the first violin, on the second half of the downbeat. The second violins, violas, celli, and basses also begin on the second beat. These two factors tend to influence my decision to bring the chorus phrase *back to the left* toward the beginning established by the first violin, followed by the other strings. Either way would work. The important thing is that you find one and employ it. (Remember: Bach-Beethoven, allegro tempo, music is primary and text is secondary.)

The third part of the phrase begins with the syllable "tion" of "resurrection." Thus, the full phrase: "By man came al—so the resurrec—tion of the dead" with emphasis placed at the beginning of each: "by", "so", and "tion", moving the phrase forward with great momentum each time. Again, the text is secondary to the music.

Handel, *Messiah,* "For unto us a child is born."   "For unto us a child is born" is a very difficult phrase to sing beautifully. It needs to sound somewhat like a lullaby. Yet the melody does not lend itself to that. It begins with a high note, seemingly inappropriate for the word "for" (see Example 6.33). Next, we find an awkward ascending leap to the word "us."

Example 6.33

* Two thoughts (clearly expressed) in one:
   "a child" — "is born"

and

   "a son" — "is given"

The problem is that Handel is using music that he originally wrote for a secular love duet for tenor and soprano. The Tenor is angry because the Soprano no longer loves him and adamantly declares, "*No,* I shall *never* love again!" This original text works much better than "for unto us." We have to come up with some musical nuances to make this melody seem appropriate for these new words, for example, the following:

1. Employ a slight lift on the word "for" and sing it gently.

2. Begin "un" with a somewhat full sound, then diminuendo "to us," singing "us" as gently and carefully as possible.

3. Energize "a" forward into "child," with a slight emphasis on "child."

4. Energize "is" forward into "born," with a slight emphasis on the first eighth of "born," and then softening the second eighth.

5. Crescendo, with feeling, the following "unto us" with a special emphasis on "us."

6. Crescendo the phrase "a son is given," by energizing "a" into an emphasized "son," and then an energized "is" into an emphasized "giv," with a softened "en."

You have now developed a musical phrase in which *no two consecutive notes, words, or syllables are given equal emphasis*. It is filled with musicality, gentleness, and meaning. Approach every phrase in the same manner. The conductor will often be able to add appropriate beauty, effectiveness, or excitement to a melodic phrase that the composer did not indicate or even think about. If done cautiously and with utmost care for the composition, this is a part of our normal routine as conductors.

Reminder. When two smaller phrases are expressed in one longer one, be sure to emphasize not only the forward motion of the two smaller ones, but also the linear quality of the long phrase. *Both are crucial to total musicality.*

Melody in melisma.   Example 6.34 is an example of finding the true melody within a melisma. The bar line over the four sixteenth notes is misleading. The melody (of a fine composer) is seldom defined within the sequence of the repetition of those four notes. It is usually 12341, *2341, 2341, 2341,* and so on, or 123, *4123, 4123, 4123,* and so on, but not *1234, 1234, 1234.*

In this example, the melodic pattern is 123456, 7812345, then continuing, 678123456, 7812345, then again, 678123456, 7812345, and again, 678123456, 7812345, and so on. Here again, sing this with the feeling of a forward motion arrow at the beginning of each new phrase.

Example 6.34

Every melismatic passage will have a well-defined melody within it. Search for it and you will find it. Have your score well marked indicating this melody and ask your singers to mark theirs accordingly. Teach it melodically, on "doo, doo, doo," then with soft "D's" *on the vowel to be sung* (daw, daw, daw or dee, dee, dee). The word "born," sung on *eight sixteenth notes* and a following quarter note, might eventually be as follows:

"baw, daw, daw, daw, daw, — daw, daw, daw, dorn."
(1   2   3   4   5   6   7   8   9)

That sixteenth note pattern would be five plus three, and then the following quarter note. To sing the passage as rapidly as an appropriate tempo might demand, leave these (soft—legato) Ds in, even for the performance. If you feel that the listeners might hear the Ds, sing them in a more legato style, or have only one fourth, one third or one half of the singers employ them, with the balance of the ensemble *not* using them. The result will be most satisfactory.

Handel, *Messiah,* **"And the government shall be."**   Example 6.35 emphasizes the techniques used for singing continuous dotted rhythms. Sing the dotted eighth note, extending the vowel "to the right" as far (long) as possible. Then accent the sixteenth note. We would like the sixteenth to be exactly one fourth of the beat, but in allegro tempi it is very safe (within the tempo-pulse/beat) to think of really extending the vowel, and then energetically accenting the sixteenth into a solid relationship *with the following note.*

Example 6.35

The lift off the eighth note preceding the two sixteenth notes is for the sake of clarity of both the sixteenths. Without it, the first of the two would probably be partially obliterated by the tone of the eighth and its slight *echo*. This lift can be a definite break in the melodic line, or in most instances, just a pulling-back of the *volume* of the eighth note.

Haydn, *Lord Nelson Mass,* **"Kyrie."**   Example 6.36 gives us the opportunity to discuss several concepts:

- Accent the first and third eighth notes at the end of a measure.
- Relate these three eighth notes to the following notes, *not* to the prior dotted quarter note.
- Place a crescendo on these three eighth notes, then a stress (–) on the following note and a diminuendo on the final two notes.
- Treat the repeated "e-lei-son"s with an energized forward motion feeling (accent?) on the "e," a stress (–) on "le," and a diminuendo on "i-son." (In measures 7–9, the tenor and bass parts would be sung in the same manner as the women's parts have been marked.)

*All final ♩'s should be performed in the classic style of ♪. ⅞

Example 6.36

- Recognize the jazz-like, syncopated feeling in measure 10, with the obvious division of six eighth notes into groups of 3 + 3, instead of 2 + 2 + 2 (which we would normally find in 3/4 time). Therefore, capitalize on the situation, and energetically accent the fourth eighth note (in the case of the alto, the first eighth after the dotted quarter note).

- Change most of the final quarter notes (at the ends of phrases) to dotted eighths followed by a sixteenth rest, in keeping with the stylistic period. Also, shorten the bass upbeat to measure seven, for clarity of the octave leap (followed by a stress and diminuendo per the women's parts).

- Refrain from breathing in measures seven and eight. Shorten the dotted quarter note in measure nine to a quarter note followed by an eighth rest.

- Place a staccato on the downbeat of measure thirteen to clarify an accurate leap in the soprano part and set up the syncopation of the half note in the alto, tenor, and bass parts.

- If you wish, allow the final quarter note (downbeat of measure sixteen) to be full length, released in the following rest, because the basses and orchestra have a dotted quarter note.

Bass part, Mozart, *Requiem*, "Kyrie."   See Example 6.37.

Example 6.37

Ky - ri - e   e - le - i - son.   e - le - - - - i - son, e - le - i - son,

1. Energize (accent) the eighth notes following the dotted quarter notes.

2. Lift, buoyantly, the quarter note on beat four.

3. Accent the eighth following the next dotted quarter note, and sustain the quarter note that follows (simply a matter of preference)

4. Slightly break the flow of tone before the two sixteenths in measure three for the sake of sixteenth clarity.

5. Unite each pair of sixteenth notes with the *following* eighth note, and then slightly shorten the eighth to prepare for the next set of two sixteenths.

6. The first eighth note of measure four belongs to the *preceding* notes; the second begins a new phrase grouping, so slightly accent it.

7. Shorten the final two eighth notes of measure four and the downbeat of measure five, to coincide with the manner in which the bassoon and celli/bass will play their similar parts.

8. Divide the final six sixteenth notes into groupings of 3 + 3 (not 2 + 2 + 2) grouping the notes *melodically,* moving the third syllable of E-le-*i*-son back one sixteenth note to be placed with the last three sixteenths. This, of course, will be inaudible to the listener but will help clarify the musical phrase.

Alto part, Mozart, *Requiem*, "Kyrie."   See Example 6.38. The phrase analysis of the opening alto melody is as follows:

Example 6.38

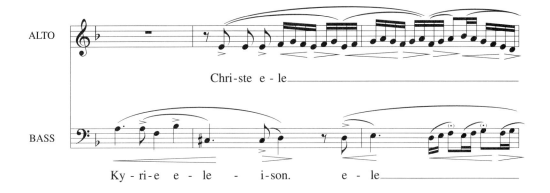

1. Accent the first and third eighth notes beginning the phrase.

2. Group the sixteenths in the melisma 6 + 8 + 3, ending with the eighth note, beat three of the second full measure.

3. Shorten that eighth note (with a staccato) to help clarify the following sixteenths.

4. Proceed with six sixteenth notes into a shortened eighth note C♯ on the downbeat of the following measure, which melodically ends that part of the phrase.

5. Place the next four eighth notes in a phrase, then two sixteenths, and finally the remaining four sixteenths in to the final quarter note.

These two parts (bass and alto) should be taught individually, then together, in a light "cool jazz" style, on a neutral syllable such as "doo-doo-doo." Have the entire choir learn both tutti. Next, have all men on the bass part and all women on the alto part. It will sound like (*mp*) cool jazz. In fact, teach the entire movement—all four parts—in that same manner. Then introduce the text, still lightly and "jazzy." Last, have the choir sing in the same style, but now with the appropriate dynamics: (1) main theme (bass, mm. 1–7) forte, and (2) the secondary theme (alto, mm. 2–5) mezzo forte.

A vast amount of contemporary music is seldom fully appreciated by singers, players, and especially audience because conductors have not realized that *feelings* can and should be found and emphasized in this music as in any other. The majority of performances of this music seem to be presented with no thought to phrasing, crescendo-stress-diminuendo, syllable inflection, word meaning, rise and fall emphasis in melodic lines, and other nuances. Its musical complexity can make it more difficult to be aware of these feelings, in addition to accomplishing the challenging task of accurately executing the often-difficult mechanics. These feelings are there, however. Take the time to search for them and bring them to life. Our rule that "no two consecutive notes, words, or syllables should receive equal emphasis" applies to *all music*.

Stravinsky, "Ave Maria."   In the soprano part for the first eighteen measures of Example 6.39, the composer indicated no interpretative or dynamic markings at all. If we were to perform it exactly as it is, it would have no communicative beauty whatsoever. It would simply be mechanical, meaningless notes sung accurately, but with unrealized beauty. All markings are those I have added when performing the piece. I would also add occasional *poco tenuti* and *atempi*, almost in the style of relaxed Gregorian chant. With these additions, *performed with subtlety,* I feel that the composition has enormous beauty. Again, it must be done subtly and in good taste. Note: Some quarter notes have a dual dynamic function: first half diminuendo and second half crescendo. This is a very effective technique.

Example 6.39

Randall Thompson, "Last Words of David."   No composer more thoroughly marks a score with interpretative indications than Randall Thompson did. In the "Last words of David," however, there are portions in which even more can be added (see Example 6.40). "And he shall be as the light of the morning" might be considered as three short phrases:

- "And he shall be," with a *very slight* crescendo through it all, and the word "and" energetically leading to the word "*he,*" and the same with "shall" into "*be*"

- "as the light," again, with a slight crescendo from "as" through "light," with "the" energetically leading into "light"

Example 6.40

- "of the morning," with a crescendo through "of the morn," a stress on "*morn*" and a softening on "ing"
- Forward motion arrows could have been placed to include "And he shall", "as the", and "of that".

In considering the entire phrase (of the three mini-phrases) I would place a *very slight* crescendo throughout until the softening of the final "ing," all within the basic dynamic range (*p*) indicated by the composer.

Randall Thompson, "Last Words of David."   The phrase "as the tender grass springing out of the earth by clear shining" (Example 6.41) needs extra help.

- "as the" needs a slight forward motion feeling (slight crescendo) progressing into the very delicate word "tender"
- "tender" necessitates a slight stress (emphasis) on the syllable "*ten,*" in a gentle caressing feeling, and then a softening for "der"
- The word "springing" must reflect the very word, with a buoyant lifting feeling on the syllable "spring" and a softening on the "ing" (remember: never overdone!)

Example 6.41

clouds;——— as the (ten) - der   grass   (spring)-ing   out   of   the

* *ten*-der must actually sound expressively *tender,* and *spring*-ing must have a real *springing-upward* quality to the first syllable; all, however, done very subtly, within the dynamic level of piano.

Randall Thompson, "Last Words of David."   Page nine, measure five, of the "alleluia" section needs to be renotated as shown in Example 6.42 to allow the singers to breathe, and do so in a disciplined uniform manner, ending one phrase and beginning another.

The tenor "alleluias" on the final page (Example 6.43) are indicated to be sung *mp* and legato. That is insufficient. There needs to be a slight but meaningful crescendo through "al-le" into a stressed "*lu,*" followed by a softening for "ia."

Mendelssohn, *Elijah*, "He watching over Israel."   The first phrase in Example 6.44 has no marking except piano (*p*). Consider the following suggestions. The composer indicated none of this, yet all are absolutely necessary for a truly artistic approach to the beauty of the phrase.

- "watching" belongs to the first syllable of "over," thereby necessitating a slight crescendo through "watching" into "o" of "over," continuing the concept of forward motion; "ver" belongs to the first syllable of "Israel," and "ra" belongs to "el." In each case, "watching," "ver" and "ra" all need the energy of rhythmic interest and forward motion, *albeit in a subtle manner*. This should *not* disturb the linear beauty of the melody (line). Yes, textually, we are emphasizing the wrong syllable. In this case, however, the music again takes precedence over the text. This text is repeated—nearly twenty times throughout the piece.

Example 6.42

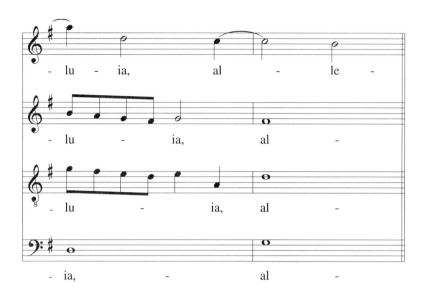

Example 6.43

Example 6.44

As with Baroque composers (whom Mendelssohn admired, especially J. S. Bach) repetition of text is a signal that *text is secondary to music.*

- "slumbers" needs a very slight stress or emphasis on "slum" and a softening on both "bers" and "not."

- "nor" is another forward motion moment taking us to "sleeps."

- There should be no breath between "Israel" and "slumbers." Even though there is a comma, the musical (melodic) line takes precedence.

- The final whole note might be changed to a dotted-half note and a quarter rest for clarity of its completion and the following tenor entrance.

> ℘ Renotating final phrase notes, or any notes before a breath, is one of the choral conductor's major responsibilities. That is, change a final quarter note to an eighth and an eighth rest or dotted eighth and sixteenth rest, a half note to a quarter and quarter rest or a dotted quarter and eighth rest, a whole note to a half note and half rest or dotted half note and a quarter rest, and so on. The ensemble thereby consistently breathes in a uniform, disciplined, rhythmic manner.

Verdi, Requiem.   Consider the following suggestions for the opening of the Requiem (Examples 6.45–6.48).

- The opening "requiem" needs a slight stress on "*re,*" the slightest energy emphasis on "qui," and then a softening for "em." All this needs to be on a foundation of a slight lifting feeling.

Example 6.45

- "requiem aeternam" calls for the same treatment of "requiem," and then forward motion emphasis on "ae," a stress on "ter," and softening for "nam." All this is on a foundation of a slight crescendo from the beginning to "ter," then diminishing to "nam." Thus, "re" and "ter" are emphasized, "qui" and "ae" are forward motion vehicles, and "em" and "nam" are de-emphasized.

Example 6.46

- "et lux" will need a slight crescendo from "et" through "lux." It's marked *ppp*; therefore, the crescendo is almost only a feeling, rather than actually getting louder.

- "per" has a forward motion minimal crescendo into "pet," which is slightly emphasized, then we diminuendo through "tu-a."

- In the continuous phrase "et lux perpetua," we will slightly crescendo throughout "et lux per" (with the slightest accent on the eighth note of "per" for clarity and rhythmic interest), then emphasize "pe," and articulate clearly the eighth note on "tu" while softening it and "a."

- "luceat Eis" will have a very minimal crescendo from "lu" through "E" of "Eis" and will then soften for the final syllable, "is." The eighth note of "at" must, again, have great clarity, through the slightest accent.

Example 6.47

et lux per - pe - tu - a

Example 6.48

lu - ce - at E - is

Brahms, German Requiem.   In Examples 6.49 and 6.50, we will consider the new and very beautiful English translation by Lara Hoggard, published by Hinshaw Music, Inc. Brahms scholar Ralph Locke and fellow musicologists Alfred Mann and Robert Freeman all agreed that this glorious work should be done, as intended, in the language of the performers and listeners. That is the reason Brahms wrote the *Requiem* in German rather than in the usual Latin.

Brahms knew as much or more than the clergy of his time about the Holy Bible. He carefully selected those passages that best describe the concepts of peace, comfort, and joy surrounding death, and eternal life with God the Heavenly Father. His intention was that every person involved would directly receive the work's message. The intensely significant mission of the work is, to varying degrees, lost when it is done in German, by a non-German speaking chorus, for a non-German speaking audience. Brahms himself authorized its performance in languages other than German. The full edition of conductor's score (in both German and English), orchestra parts and vocal scores are available through Hinshaw Publishing. This is a marvelous edition that includes never-before-published revisions by Brahms and highly effective string bowings. I heartily recommend it.

In addition to the dynamics scored by Brahms, I have added a few more to enhance textual meaning and emphasis with crescendi/diminuendi (measures 4–10):

- The two consecutive crescendi/diminuendi for "de*sire*th" and "*long*eth" should be enclosed within a larger crescendo from "de" to "long." Therefore, "long" has greater emphasis than "sire."

- I have changed some quarter notes to eighth notes followed by eighth rests to facilitate phrase endings and strengthen phrase beginnings.

- I have slightly shortened the soprano upbeat to the high A♭ for the sake of clarity (bottom of score).

In this next segment (Examples 6.50a, b, and c), I have added our "arrow system" to indicate points of rhythmic interest and forward motion. This entire segment must be incredibly alive, but not rushed. Rather, it should be very stately.

- In Example 6.50a, arrows appear on quarter notes (and significant pairs of eighth notes) falling on either beats 2 or 3, and on single eighth notes that begin a phrase on the second half of a beat. Remember that this is *in addition* to the normal emphasis on primary beat 1. This does *not replace* the normal emphasis, but simply adds rhythmic vitality, energy and interest to the total phrase.

- An occasional eighth note has been shortened with a staccato, thereby adding clarity to the beginning of the next phrase.

Example 6.49

- Some final quarter notes have been changed to eighth notes followed by eighth rests, for uniformity of the phrase ending and breathing (men and altos on the first page; basses and altos on the second page; and women on the third page).

- Two bass notes are changed to dotted eighths for clarity (m. 7 and m. 25).

CHAPTER 6 ⌣ RHYTHMIC INTEREST, FORWARD MOTION, AND PHRASING ⌣ 109

Example 6.50a

Example 6.50b

- Add an uplifting, buoyant approach to the main quarter and half note phrase "They praise Thy name evermore" and, similarly, the women's half notes and tied quarter notes on page three (caret accents would be appropriate).

- In addition to forward motion, the word "Thee" in the men's parts on page three should be stressed in contrast to the previous energy arrow.

Example 6.50c

My Own Markings

Figure 6.3 shows my own markings—done with pencil, not specially printed—on a typical vocal score. It shows exactly what I write and ask my singers to write in their own scores. I have marked all four parts, but it is often sufficient to mark only the soprano part when all are similar.

If there are singers in the ensemble who do not read music and who have little or no knowledge of notation, giving them extensive markings obviously won't work. If the chorus includes somewhat advanced musicians, then I strongly encourage giving an abundance of markings. That is the only way to consistently achieve the desired interpretive ideas of the conductor.

The amount of time spent giving markings also depends on the musical maturity of the ensemble. An advanced chorus can take markings for eight to ten minutes, and then sing the portion marked. With a less advanced group, the time-span for marking will need to be reduced to approximately three to five minutes before we rehearse that portion.

If an ensemble doesn't read at all, then markings are almost impossible, other than underlining or circling words for special emphasis. But, if this is the case, then it is the conductor's responsibility to teach them to read music, either as part of each rehearsal, or during extra sessions (Saturday or Sunday afternoons, and/or an evening per week, for seven or eight weeks). Whatever it takes, teach the singers to read.

An explanation of specific markings

- Arrows to the right for *forward motion,* in which case we really want the singers to feel the forward movement of the indicated notes and words/syllables.

- The letters F and M (F.M.) indicate *forward motion* over several notes/words, followed by the letters E and Z (E-Z), which indicate a "relaxing" of the tempo back to the original (particularly appropriate for romantic and expressive music).

- Words circled for special meaning and emphasis.

- Added crescendi and diminuendi (in addition to those the composer may have indicated). These will be for two reasons: melodic rise and fall, and syllable and word inflection.

- Renotated breathing indications (changing quarter notes to an eighth note followed by an eighth rest, a whole note to a dotted half note followed by a quarter rest, for example).

- Interpretive directions that may not have been indicated by the composer, such as: mysterioso, animato, sostenuto, hold back, molto espressivo, no breath, tenuto, rallentando, and so forth.

The May Night
Die Mainacht
SATB and Piano

Duration: 3 min.

Original Text by Ludwig Hölty
English Text by Richard Griffith

Johannes Brahms Op. 43, No. 2
arranged by Arthur Frackenpohl

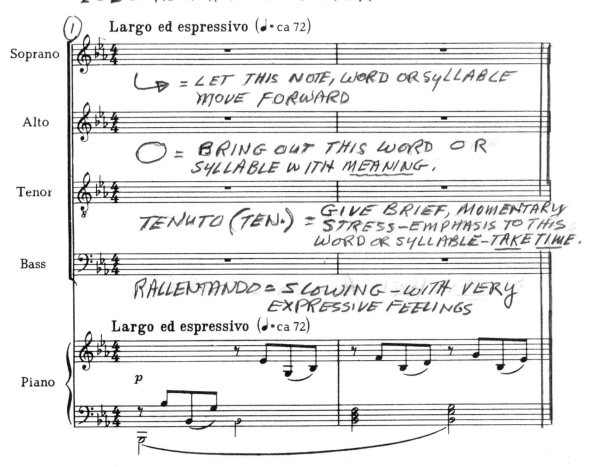

Figure 6.3a

Figure 6.3b

3

Figure 6.3c

Figure 6.3d

5

Figure 6.3e

Figure 6.3f

Figure 6.3g

Honor the Composer

We know that composers seldom if ever place sufficient markings in the score to bring forth the full potential of its beauty and communication. We must be careful to honor the composer, however, and not change the song to become our own.

- Never do anything that will draw attention to itself, and thereby away from the composition. That includes a technique, interpretation, and the extent to which it is done. Subtlety is frequently a quality to be desired.

- Be acutely aware that composers might not be fully conscious of the potential beauty of their compositions. The conductor must be! The composers do not place sufficient indications of necessary nuance markings in the score. The conductor must! We must be able to hear creatively the potential of every piece we conduct, and see beyond the notes and words to the ultimate beauty and communication of the composition.

- Study each piece *microscopically*, one measure (each note, word, and syllable) at a time, missing absolutely nothing. Do not be in a hurry. Take your time and find the beauty awaiting you. If we must do fewer songs to really do them effectively, so be it. We are artists. Our singers and players are artists. We therefore commit to doing all things artistically, with beauty, excitement, and the communication of our deepest feelings.

- The music must come alive through our teaching and conducting, and then, through the performance of our forces. The music must make an appreciable impact on the listener and the performers. We must really *say something* and say it with conviction. That means every note, word, and syllable of every song, every concert, every year! What we do can truly make a difference in people's lives, a very positive and meaningful difference. The arts exist to express feelings in a manner that will stimulate the human spirit, in ways that nothing else but love and God can do.

Summary

- The golden rule of musicality: *There shall never be two consecutive notes, words, or syllables, performed with equal emphasis.* Each will function within the crescendo before the main stressed note, word, or syllable; or actually be the stressed note, word or syllable; or function within the diminuendo following it.

- Several small crescendo-stress-diminuendo phrases can occur within one larger phrase.

- Rhythmic interest and forward motion are created by slightly energizing off-beats; that is, two and/or four in 4/4 time, two and/or three in triple meter, or six-three or two-five in 6/8, for example. In doing so, the music, singer, and listener are all taken forward with an animated energy-flow within each phrase.

- None of this interpretation is to be overdone, thus drawing attention to itself and away from the composition. The interpretation must enhance the music, not detract from it.

- The notes in melodic note groupings actually relate to each other. These notes that make musical sense with each other become a phrase. Phrases begin with energy, head for a stressed point, and then usually (but not always) relax and taper at the end.

- Determining these phrase structures is paramount in analyzing the score and determining the eventual interpretation. These concepts come from compositions; they have not been superimposed on compositions. Great composers write in this manner. Conductors must recognize these qualities and bring them to life. The *composition* itself is the basis for appropriate interpretation.

- All this effort, however, must rest on the sure foundation of the knowledge of
    1. Voice
    2. Musicianship
    3. Expressive musicality
    4. Textual communication
    5. Score
    6. Stylistic interpretation
    7. Organization and rehearsal planning
    8. Effective and inspiring teaching
    9. Conducting artistry

    —and a solid commitment to *excellence!*

English Diction, Dramatic Communication of Text, and Latin Pronunciation

7

*M*ost American singers, voice teachers, choruses, and choral conductors take English diction for granted. Seldom can the audience understand the words in English, and rarely does the ensemble present the "color" potential necessary to make the language exciting and meaningful. Even in the performances of the finest choruses and soloists with advanced training, the English songs are the hardest to understand. The German, French, Italian, and Latin songs are usually much better pronounced, enunciated, and projected than the English songs are—perhaps because we make a greater effort with a foreign language.

In addition to the *understandability* of the words, the *depth of meaning* underlying each word helps an audience more thoroughly enjoy the singer's presentation. Words that are clearly understood but have no passion in their delivery are meaningless to the listener.

The third element (after understandability and meaning) of our discussion about diction is *color*. A symphony orchestra is filled with a wide spectrum of color. This is produced by a wide range of instruments, from piccolo to tuba, violin to timpani, finger cymbals to harp, English and French horns to trumpets and bassoons. They all combine for a truly exciting array of color for the listener.

Our chorus has only the human voice; the four categories (soprano, alto, tenor, and bass) are comparable to only a string orchestra: violin I and II, viola, cello, and bass. The string orchestra is not nearly as interesting to hear as the full orchestra. Compared with orchestras and bands, our mere chorus may sound a bit less interesting.

With the full color spectrum of an entire language, performed as effectively as great actors would speak, however, we can create a range of color wide enough to successfully captivate any audience. We simply have to incorporate the enunciation, projection, and passion of these great actors, thereby succeeding in making a significant impact on the minds and hearts of the audience! We make that impact with

- Professional sound of our instrument, the voice

- Beautiful music
- Language's understanding, meaning, and color

The Addition of Text to the Musical Spectrum

Instrumental ensembles have only their instruments and the music. They cannot speak *directly* to anyone. They have no direct language. Their listeners can only *imagine* possible meaning in the music. Our chorus, however, can communicate with a *direct* affect on the hearts and minds of the listeners.

The chorus actually has more to offer an audience. An instrumentalist is half musician and half instrumental technician. The singer, on the other hand, is one-third musician, one-third vocal technician, and one-third *actor, theatre, and drama.* This full third of our potential must be realized before we can become complete artistic performers.

This element of *dramatic presentation of text* is the area that is least consistently taught. Yet, this aspect sets us apart from all other musicians. Potentially, dramatic presentation sets us on the very top of the world of art. We can do it all: music, drama, and, at times, movement. Ours just may be *the* art. Instrumentalists and dancers have no direct dramatic communication (theirs is an indirect, imaginative communication), and the dramatists have little or no music. If we do it right, we have it all!

The Power of Words

I would like to expand on the discussion we began in Chapter 6 about my decision to use the Lara Hoggard English translation by describing my experience after a combined rehearsal of chorus and orchestra in preparation for a performance of Brahms' *German Requiem*. Scholars had agreed that Brahms—contrary to the practice of the time, and writing in German—carefully chose biblical passages dealing specifically with peace and comfort at the time of death. His contemporaries used text from the Requiem Mass, in Latin, which represented a theology fearful of hell. Brahms used the German language, the language of his people, because he wanted each singer and listener to understand the meaning of every single word. He was on a musical mission of peace and comfort, and he was intent on communicating it successfully.

Therefore, to do this great composition in a language other than the native language of the performers and audience would totally ignore the intent of the composer. It is titled *German Requiem* simply because it was originally written for the German audience—not to ensure that ensembles around the world would perform it in German.

After my first combined rehearsal of Brahms' *Requiem* by the chorus and orchestra, the young man who had been playing principal cello came up to talk to me. He said, "After hearing the words of the chorus during this rehearsal, I am, for the first time, at peace with the death of my father who died of cancer this past summer."

After the performance, a very elderly white-haired gentleman came backstage to say, with a warm smile, "Thank you for that wonderful message. I am now ready

> Take the language seriously. It sets us apart from all other musicians. It allows us to speak directly to an audience and make an indescribable impact on their hearts, minds, and lives. The language, however, must be (1) understood, (2) projected, and (3) filled with the substance of emotional expression.

to meet my maker." He really meant it. He was at peace, the peace that Brahms intended.

This kind of language success can only take place if the language is understood and makes an impact on the listener. That means the choral conductor must become as proficient in the dramatic elements of presenting language as is a professor of theater, or a professional actor on live stage. This is a huge responsibility, yet a necessity for total choral success. This element actually brings the choral art to its highest level of personal fulfillment. Without it, we are only doing ⅔ of our job, and people would probably rather hear an orchestra.

> The purpose of this discussion is to encourage you to confidently perform music in the language of the country in which it is being performed. This is especially true if it tells a story (passions, opera, and so on), or if the message, such as the monumentally meaningful Brahms *Requiem*, has great significance.

The Percussion of Our Language: Consonants

Singers sustain the life of their sound through the vocal production of *vowels*. But the physicality of *percussive consonants* not only adds to the color of our sound; it is absolutely necessary if we are to be understood. Consonants should be done in a manner that to most singers seems exaggerated, especially when compared with the way they speak conversationally.

To illustrate the necessity of oversinging the percussive aspect of consonant production, consider the following. The vowel sound that precedes a middle or final consonant is much louder than a consonant could ever be. In addition, the reverberating echo of the vowel lasts anywhere from one to two or three seconds (or more, depending on the acoustics of the performance hall). The consonant lasts but a fraction of that duration. The consonant, therefore, has little or no chance of being heard throughout an audience, especially in a large hall or sanctuary. Consider magnifying this problem with an organ or orchestral accompaniment. Now the consonants have even less chance to be heard or understood.

Singers, therefore, must articulate and project consonants with the same effort and intensity as the fine professional on-stage actor. If you've ever seen professional theater, you've noticed that these actors articulate with such effort that you can often actually see, over the footlights, a fine spray coming from their mouths as they very physically deliver their lines. In this process of hard-work-articulation, they succeed at having every single word understood by every person in the audience. These professionals should be our role models when it comes to fine diction. Their livelihood depends on it. Ours should also!

Voiced and Corresponding Voiceless Consonants

Many consonants have corresponding partners. That is, a voiced consonant such as **B,** which has a slight, brief pitch to it, has a corresponding voiceless, or pitchless partner, **P,** which has no tone, only air as its vehicle for making sound (purely

Table 7.1 Voiced and Corresponding Voiceless Consonants

Voiced Consonants	Corresponding Voiceless Consonants
B	P
D	T
V	F
G (girl)	K
J	CH
S (measure)	SH
Z	S
W	WH
TH (they)	TH (think)

Table 7.2 Consonants with No Corresponding Partner

	Voiced	Voiceless
	—	H
	L	—
	M	—
	N	—
	R	—

percussive). These corresponding partners are produced in exactly the same part of the mouth (lips, tongue, and teeth), and in the same manner, except for the quality of either tone or air.

Try saying the consonants listed in Tables 7.1 and 7.2.

Explosive Consonants

Certain consonants have the potential to be "explosive." They are B, P, and T, and to a lesser extent, D, G, K, and CH.

B, as pronounced in "better," would be handled in a somewhat normal manner. The same B in "battle" might need to be expressively "exploded" by tucking your lips between your teeth, increasing the air pressure against the lips, and then letting the lips "explode" in the sound of a very percussive B(!). The difference between the letter P in "people" and in "power" would be executed similarly.

D in a forte "Domine" might be "exploded" by the same intensified air pressure against the *tongue,* as it touches the roof of the mouth.

G and K follow the same procedure with the tongue now touching the area in the very back of the mouth (where G and K are naturally produced).

An "explosive" CH is produced in the same manner, but the tongue is placed in its natural "CH position," which is just a little further back from the D position.

Substituting Voiceless for Voiced Consonants for Extra Percussion

A percussive voiceless consonant can be substituted for its corresponding voiced partner, if a more percussive quality is needed. If, in a forte or fortissimo passage, the word "Gloria" seems lacking in power, try "Kloria." If it seems overdone, you might have only ⅓ to ⅔ of your chorus sing the K, with the remaining singers singing G. In a similar manner, if you need more power on the word "battle," have a portion of your singers sing "Pattle."

On occasions in which you use a full orchestra, you could have *all* singers use the voiceless substitute. Do whatever you feel gets the job done and makes the most sense. The audience will not be aware of your substitution if you do it sensibly, and this does have the potential to make a far greater impact when needed and appropriate.

Consonants That Require Special Consideration

R. There are three kinds of articulations for the sound of R: Roll it in opera (other than English), "flip it" in Latin, and simply sing the American R in English.

Some advocate leaving the R sound out because they think it is an unpleasant sound (example: "chahm" instead of charm). This is an unnecessary crutch. The consonant sound of R is no less beautiful than CH, SH, G, K, or many others. The answer is not to omit it, but to sing it properly. That is, do not approach an R too early, nor prolong it after it is once articulated.

The way to sing R inoffensively is to keep the tongue in the formation of the previous vowel, and then let it move to the back of the mouth, between the back teeth, as is natural for it to do when producing the RRR sound. It shouldn't last any longer than a T (or any other consonant).

Try singing RRR. Notice that the tongue must be placed between the back teeth to produce the sound. Try the same thing again, this time keeping the tongue relaxed, flat, and slightly touching the bottom teeth. The result: you can't produce the RRR sound (unless the tongue goes back).

Now try it on a word. Sing "we're." Sustain the vowel sound of *ee* until you are ready to finish the word. At that exact instant, allow the tongue to slip back to produce a very brief RR sound. That's it. You've done it, and done it appropriately, without the help of gimmicks or crutches. The American R is a fine legitimate sound, just like all the other sounds of our language. Don't modify or eliminate it. Use it properly.

> **Important:** You need not be overly concerned about the placement of the tongue. It "knows" where to go. If we focus on it, we could cause counterproductive tension. Let the tongue do its job; we'll simply extend the air pressure.

L, S, SH, and V. L, S, SH, and V also fall into this same problem category, except the results aren't quite as offensive as the prolonged RRR. These consonants can be demonstrated in words such as "willll," "thissss," "wissssh," and "lovvvve." Treat them all as I recommended for R, and the problem will disappear. That is, keep the tongue in the formation of the previous vowel, and then, at the last instant, allow it to briefly form the L, S, SH, or V.

D, T, B, and P. Some final consonants have a hard percussive sound. Consonants such as D, T, B, P (especially D), and occasionally the somewhat softer consonants V, M, and N need to be clarified in their release by doing the following:

* Articulating a dotted rhythm, or
* A grace-note effect between the word ending with this consonant and the beginning of following word.

See Example 7.1.

Intensifying TH. TH can be either voiced (they) or voiceless (think). In either case, the TH needs to be greatly intensified to be heard and understood. When TH is voiced, place the tongue between the teeth and draw it back through the teeth as you produce tone. This tone is actually part hum and part breath. The understandability of TH is in direct proportion to the intensity used in producing the TH *tone*.

TH is particularly difficult to enunciate clearly when preceded by a word ending with S, such as "was the" or "is Thy." Without an intensified TH, the resulting sound is usually "wuzzuh," or "izzeye." I would venture a guess that in 90 to 95 percent of such instances, that is the erroneous result. (The dotted rhythm mentioned earlier will work here: wuz-za-the and iz-zuh-thy.)

Example 7.1

Consonants That Present
Unique Problems

A. AND THEY = AN - DUH THEY * OR: AN - D'THEY **

B. THAT DAY = THA - TUH DAY * OR: THA - T'DAY **

C. IN THE = IH - NUH THE * OR: IH - N'THE **

D. LIVE NOW = LI - VUH NOW OR: LI - V'NOW **

* In Slower Tempi:

** D', T', N', AND V' = DUH, TUH, NUH, AND VUH

The *voiceless* TH in words such as "<u>th</u>ink" and "<u>th</u>rough" needs air flowing through the area in which the TH is being produced, the space between the tongue and the upper teeth. The amount of air, however, should be more than needed for ordinary speaking. Remember, an entire audience needs to hear it, sometimes over an organ or orchestra.

W and WH. There is a significant difference between W and WH. However, they are spoken and usually sung as though they are both W. A word beginning with W actually begins with oo—"<u>oo</u>We ; <u>oo</u>will; <u>oo</u>win". Although done very quickly, the *oo* needs to be sung with intensity. WH, on the other hand, needs the same airflow that the voiceless TH needed. It is similar to the air used to blow out a candle: <u>wh</u>at, <u>wh</u>y, <u>wh</u>en, <u>wh</u>ere.

Ms and Ns. These are the least audible consonants. They can barely be heard when accompanied by an organ or orchestra unless they are greatly intensified. They really have to be produced with energy: <u>N</u>now, <u>nn</u>ever, <u>nn</u>o<u>nn</u>e, <u>nn</u>atus, <u>mm</u>agnu<u>mm</u>, <u>mm</u>i<u>nn</u>e, <u>mm</u>e, a<u>mm</u>e<u>nn</u>, and so on.

This does not mean that the M or N sound is to be prolonged: ame<u>nnnnnn</u>. It means that the M and N must resonate with sufficient strength to be effectively heard. (Occasionally it is impressive to hear the sound prolonged, but we must remember that it is an effect, a gimmick; we must use the idea very, very sparingly.)

Ending one word and beginning the next with the same consonant. This necessitates repeating the consonant if done in classical English, "classical" being anything other than "pop," ethnic, and other types of music in which we want to sing the same way we casually speak. In those cases, we employ the "stop-consonant." We sing only one, stopping on it for an *instant*, then proceeding: nigh<u>T</u>o (instead of nigh-<u>t</u>uh-<u>t</u>o).

In all serious or classical music, we would pronounce both: nigh<u>t</u>-<u>t</u>o, sa<u>d</u>-<u>d</u>ay, ha<u>ve</u>-<u>v</u>ictory, mi<u>ne</u>—<u>n</u>ow, sai<u>d</u>—<u>D</u>an, and so on. The sound usually needs to be night<u>uh</u>to, sad<u>uh</u>day, ha<u>vuh</u>victory, mi<u>nuh</u>now, said<u>uh</u>Dan. The same grace note effect, or dotted rhythm approach we recommended for final Ds and other consonants would also be appropriate here.

The Five Most Important Rules of English Diction

The following five rules of English diction are listed *in order of importance*. I have found that if choruses consistently adhere to these five principles, their diction will be effectively understood and meaningful to hear. They are not gimmicks, they are techniques, and *will not fail*. They are not extreme in any way. They are logical, unaffected rules for excellent enunciation of the English language. They are suitable when singing a cappella or with piano, organ, or orchestra. They will cut through the orchestra if done with sufficient intensity, and they will not be obtrusive when singing a cappella if done with common sense and good taste.

Entire books are written on the subject of English diction. Most of what is written is fine. As a matter of practicality, though, neither the chorus members nor the conductor can remember and implement all that is written. The chorus certainly cannot keep it all in mind. I have tried to establish a procedure of five steps that can be easily remembered, and that, if employed with consistency, will produce very effective and understandable diction. These five rules will serve you, the chorus, and the audience well. The audience, by the way, should never have to work or strain to understand our words. Audiences should be able to relax, enjoy the great singing, and understand everything that we intend them to understand. They deserve that.

Effective diction will require as much daily work as correct pitches, rhythms, phrasing, and tone quality do. Diction needs to be patiently taught and re-taught, just like everything else. Don't take the language for granted. Proper diction is difficult to establish firmly because people (our singers) never speak the way we want them to sing. It's a re-learning process. They must *learn to sing*, and they must also *learn to enunciate*.

Rule 1. Vowel Articulation

The *single most important rule* in effective English diction is *never elide the last consonant (or vowel) of one word onto the beginning of the following word*. Table 7.3 provides examples of proper and improper pronunciation.

You can do this in a manner that is totally unobtrusive. You do not have to negate or disturb a desired line in the musical phrase to accomplish this concept. *Caution:* Do not overemphasize the beginning of the new word or allow extra space between the first and second word for the purpose of preparing a slight attack on the second word.

The attack at the beginning of the second word is a very, very slight glottal attack. I said *very, very slight* because that is all that is necessary. Overdoing the attack will result in two negatives: (1) the music will reflect unintended accents, and (2) heavy glottal attacks can be hard on the vocal chords.

Table 7.3 Recommended Vowel Articulation

Sing This	Not This
it is	ih-tis
come all	co-mahl
those I	thos-zye
God of	Gaw-duv
I always am	I-yal-weh-zam
way over	way-yover

Try the following exercise to understand this concept fully. Repeatedly sing a legato "circle of vowels" on a sustained pitch—A, E, I, O, U; A, E, I, O, U; and so on. Place that *very, very, slight* glottal attack on the beginning of each vowel. You will notice that you easily sustained a beautifully legato line, and there were no exaggerated accents at each beginning or any spaces between vowels. There are only slight articulations of each new vowel.

This manner of articulation, within a legato style (or any other style) of singing, is what I recommend. There are no negative aspects resulting from the implementation of this concept. I consulted with an otolaryngologist who was also a professional oratorio soloist about glottal attacks being harmful to the voice. I asked him directly: "Will *slight* glottal attacks, at the beginning of words that start with a vowel, done consistently over a lifetime of singing, be harmful to the voice in any possible way?" He said, "Absolutely not."

Because people do not speak this way, however, it is difficult to discipline a chorus to sing this way consistently. As difficult as it may be, I firmly recommend it as the singularly most important aspect of English diction.

Actually, there are benefits achieved *in addition to diction-understandability*. This recommended vowel articulation will also enhance *rhythmic clarity* and *pitch accuracy* (avoiding scooping to pitches). So, diction, rhythm, and pitch are all improved with this one concept.

Rule 2. Final Ds (and Similar Consonants)

Final consonants that have a hard percussive sound, such as D, T, B, and P, and occasionally those with somewhat softer sounds, such as V, M, and N, should be clarified in their release by articulating a dotted rhythm or a grace-note effect between the word ending and the following word (see Example 7.1 on page 128). This is the second most important aspect of productive English diction. Singers will, at best, willingly sing DH, or DIH after a final D. In most cases, however, DUH is needed. Allow both the dynamics and the type of accompaniment of the music (a cappella or with piano, organ, or orchestra) to dictate the degree of physicality and percussiveness. With the exception of pop, ethnic, and other music in which you wish to sing as we speak, this is a must!

Rule 3. Voiced TH (and V)

Whether voiced or voiceless, the TH needs to be greatly intensified to be heard and understood (see Consonants That Require Special Consideration on page 126).

Rule 4. W versus WH

Both W and WH are spoken and sung as though they are both W (see Consonants That Require Special Consideration on page 128).

Rule 5. Diphthongs

Diphthongs have uniquely brilliant, colorful sounds. Take advantage of those sounds. There are actually two ways to "sound" the second vowel sound in a diphthong: (1) passively neutral, and (2) colorfully affective. These alternatives are listed in Table 7.4.

The sounds in the "passively neutral" column are very relaxed, easily blended, and passively boring. Those in the second column are colorful and exciting to hear. They add to the impact being made on the listener, add color to the sound, and add to the effort made by the singers to be understood.

When thinking about the difference of the two sounds within a diphthong, review the appropriate jaw and lip formations to produce them properly. The second sound of the diphthong should be placed as far to the right as possible. That is, approximately where a final consonant, such as T, would be articulated, and no earlier. Be sure, however, to give real intensity to this second vowel sound. Let it be truly *sung*. Take advantage of the opportunity to make an additional colorful sound!

Table 7.4 Neutral and Colorful Diphthongs

Diphthong	Passively Neutral	Colorfully Affective
thy	thah-ih	thah-ee
they	theh-ih	theh-ee
thou	thah-u	thah-oo
though	tho-uh	tho-oo
joy	jaw-ih	jaw-ee

> ℘ Language is the heart of the reason a chorus exists. We *must* exaggerate, *must* overstate, *must* be physically percussive, *must* project, *must* work hard at it, *must* teach, re-teach, and re-teach, 100 percent of the time!

The triphthong *our*. I must make reference to one triphthong: "our," because it is usually sung as though it were "are." Make a definite difference between our (ah-oo-wur) and are (ahr).

This is as far as we will go in the area of English diction. If your singers use these recommended techniques with consistency, your ensemble (or any soloist) will be understood when they sing, and their sound will be filled with the full potential of color available in the English language.

Textual Communication

It is one thing to enunciate clearly, producing fine diction. It is quite another to deliver the text in an *expressive manner*. That is, to communicate the *meaning* of the text in a way that reaches the fullest possible potential of *making an impact on the listener*, one that will make a difference in their feelings (the reason for the arts), their thinking, and their lives.

This is not only possible but should be the rule rather than the exception. Audiences should consistently be moved by the singing they hear. That includes quality areas of popular, ethnic, country or Broadway music, classical songs, sacred anthems, oratorio, or opera. If the song has true value, then there is meaning to be communicated. A great singer communicates that meaning and does it with conviction! Our chorus is not an exception.

We are now dealing with the *meaning* of words, and how to communicate them directly to an audience. We will begin by singing them in a manner that allows this communication to become a possibility. That means, begin with (1) logical syllable inflection, (2) word inflection, and (3) word meaning emphasis.

Syllable Inflection

There are always emphasized and de-emphasized syllables in words with more than one syllable. Everyone speaks that way quite naturally. Singers, however, seldom sing in that natural manner; they usually emphasize every syllable equally. They do this because they consciously attempt to execute each note, syllable, and word accurately on an individual note-by-note basis. In so doing, singers emphasize each one in exactly the same manner as every other. The result: mechanical, robot-like singing. It happens in most choruses and with many soloists.

If the chorus sings with consistent attention to logical syllable inflection, they will *immediately* achieve a more professional sound. It is amazing that this is so rarely done, especially because we all talk that way. This is *one instance* in which we would like our singers to sing the way they speak! Some simple examples appear in Table 7.5.

Table 7.5   Examples of Logical Syllable Inflection

1st syllable stressed >	Crescendo into 2nd syllable <	Either < > or >	< >
di-stant	sup-port	di-vi-ded	e-du-ca-tion
su-per	an-nounce	be-got-ten	e-nun-ci-ate
so-lo	be-fore	de-struc-tion	de-em-pha-size
dra-ma	con-tain	con-tin-ue	e-num-er-ate
an-guish	for-get	fab-ri-cate	em-bar-ca-tion
do-nate	sur-vive	per-se-cute	pon-ti-fi-cate
for-tune	re-mind	em-u-late	ex-ca-va-tion

These lists are simply for the purpose of drawing our attention to the necessity of singing in a manner similar to that in which we normally speak. In the first column, the first syllable is emphasized and the second is de-emphasized. The *de-emphasis* is actually more important (from a conductor's point of view) than the emphasis on the first syllable. The reason: the first syllable will usually be placed on an important beat or melodic note. The singer may *automatically* emphasize it. The singer, however, will *not* de-emphasize the second syllable *unless we ask for it.*

Both are important. The singer must lean slightly into the emphasized syllable with feeling, and consciously lighten-up on the de-emphasized one. This is a definite mental and physical action by the singer—a conscious act of communicative, professional artistry in singing.

The words in the second column necessitate a crescendo of forward motion throughout the first syllable into the second, on which the main emphasis takes place.

In the third column, we either (1) forward-motion-crescendo the first syllable into the second, stress the second, then de-emphasize the third, or (2) stress the first syllable, then diminuendo throughout the second and third syllables.

With those in the fourth column, we will either forward-motion-crescendo the first two syllables into a stressed third, followed by a de-emphasized fourth, or forward-motion-crescendo the first syllable into a stressed second, followed by a diminuendo throughout the third and fourth syllables.

Reminder: No two consecutive notes, syllables, or words should receive equal emphasis! This is a matter of *dynamics*: (1) crescendo-stress-diminuendo, (2) stress-diminuendo, or, (3) crescendo-stress. This pattern goes on unceasingly with each phrase throughout each song. We must not ignore this. It is a crucial aspect of great singing—in an ensemble or *as a soloist.*

Word Inflection

All words are not equally important. Some, obviously, are much more important than others are. There actually can be several degrees of importance and therefore, several degrees of emphasis *all within a single dynamic level.*

Just as a fine actor discovers more than one way to interpret a line in a play, we can analyze a textual phrase in many ways. We should try several different ways and then determine which one best fits the melody.

In the following example, our analysis shows that there are five levels of emphasis within one dynamic level. The numbers under the words indicate the intensity of emphasis that I decided each word will receive. Five is the greatest and one the least.

"From all false-ness, set me free"

1   4   5   1   3   2   5

- Most significant words are "false" and "free"
- Next, "all"
- Next, "set"
- Next, "me"
- Least significant, "from" and "ness"

Within these seven words and syllables, we have five intensities of emphasis, all within one given dynamic level. Now let's take that thought, write it out, and analyze it with our crescendo-stress-diminuendo concept in a three-step process.

1. We will determine the small groupings of crescendo-stress-diminuendo, and place those markings directly below the words.

2. We will determine the next step of combining these short phrases into somewhat longer ones, and place these markings at the top.

3. We will determine the long-line full phrase marking and place it at the very bottom.

Practice the following sentence.

With-in a giv-en dy-nam-ic le-vel, we find five in-ten-si-ties of em-pha-sis.

When performing this example, be sure to include every nuance in steps one, two, and three. One or two, alone, would lack line. Three, alone, would lack syllable and word inflection and forward motion. *Syllable and word inflection, word meaning emphasis, forward motion and rhythmic interest,* and *line* all work together to complete musicality and communicate expressively.

Word Meaning Emphasis

Each word, other than articles and prepositions, is very unique, having a very special meaning, message, and color. Conductors must become as proficient at delivering words as a great actor in a dramatic role. We must be totally without inhibitions and completely consumed by the meaning of the word, phrase, and song. We study the text the way an actor prepares for an audition or rehearsal. After sufficient study, we determine the interpretation we prefer, and master it to the point that we can *demonstrate it effectively* to our chorus members and successfully teach them to do it.

In the study of each word, we determine whether it is (1) a forward-motion-word (or words), connecting one significant word to another or, simply, (2) a single word of special importance. At this point, we are concerned with those special important words. "Love" should not sound like "fire." "Anger" should not sound like "peace." "God" should not sound like "touch." And, of course, none of these important words should sound like "the" or "it."

The singer should sing important words with *true feelings*, really singing those feelings into the words in a manner that is convincing to the listener. This is not only a mental and emotional effort but a physical one as well.

> Nuances are all concerned with musicality, expression, communication, and true artistry. Without these qualities, we would reduce our efforts to simple mathematics: accurate pitches and rhythms—a necessary foundation but, unto itself, *boring.*

Facial expression is an absolute must! The full body must feel these words, and the facial expression is a true reflection of them. Few things are as boring as a chorus of expressionless singers.

Next, speak the words of the *first column* in the following list with dramatic expression sufficient to convey their meaning to someone who doesn't know the language, but might know what was meant simply by the way the word sounded. Then sing them in that same manner. They are very different, and should sound and *feel* very different. They should sound exactly like their meaning. Remember, the facial expression must come to life as a true reflection of the meaning of each word.

Song	*Sing*
Touch	*Caress*
Move	*Force*
Happiness	*Joy*
Fire	*Burn*
Light	*Shine*
Anger	*Fight*
Peace	*Love*

Now, say, then sing, the words in the first column, followed by their corresponding words in the second column (song—sing). The second word is similar, but not exactly the same. Make the difference clearly understood. Until this ability becomes second nature to the *choral conductor*, it will be difficult to communicate it effectively to the *chorus. The conductor must be the example, the role model, for everything.*

> ℘ Reminder. Singers are ⅓ musician, ⅓ vocal technician, and ⅓ dramatic actor. Be sure you are capable of teaching each third successfully. *Stay in the music, stay in the drama, stay focused.*

Focus on the Song and the Singers

Focus on, and be consumed with, the song and singers—with the same intensity that a terrific voice teacher would use to focus on the aria and the individual student being taught. The emotional and mental intensity is almost overwhelming. *The focus never waivers.*

Soloists or actors can consistently maintain such a relentless focus because they *stay* inside a role. They stay *in character*. A conductor and teacher must frequently step out of the role—to correct mistakes, teach techniques and interpretation—and then step back into character, once again being consumed by the role. This is not easy. And the transition must be done with lightening-like speed and pacing, without losing basic focus.

To give you an example of doing both successfully, consider this. Hold your hand up in front of your face, about 12 inches from your nose. Stare, with great intensity, at a spot in the center of your palm. Don't lose the focus of staring at that spot. As you do, you will also be able to see peripherally many other things around you without losing your intense focus on the spot on your hand.

This is an example of a conductor staying within the focus of a song, yet able peripherally to stop, correct, and teach, then continue with the song without losing focus or letting the rehearsal pacing, intensity, and ensemble interest drop for even a moment.

Liturgical Pronunciation of Latin

There are several sources of Latin pronunciation, including the manner in which French and Germans pronounce it. I will present what I believe to be the most commonly accepted Italianized pronunciation.

As for the German or French pronunciation of Latin, if you find it interesting and want to use it, fine. I much prefer to accept Italianized Latin, which is based on the actual pronunciation of the Clergy of the Province of Rome. I am not in the least concerned that Haydn, Mozart, Schubert, and Beethoven masses would have been originally heard in a Germanic form of Latin (and similarly the French composers with their masses). Carried to its logical conclusion, if the rest of the world followed suit, there would be dozens of Latin pronunciations (Swedish Latin, Korean Latin, Hispanic Latin, American Latin, and so forth). My recommendations for the basic Italianized Latin sounds are as follows.

Vowels

A   ah, as in Father

E   eh, as in red (not ay)

I   ee, as in seen (not ih)

O   o, as in for, or glory; aw is acceptable but not o as in go

U   oo, as in soon (not you)

AE and **OE**   eh, as in red (see E)

AU   ah-oo, as in house; when sustained in singing, extend the first sound until the release, and then sing the second

EI, EU, and **EO**   pronounced as two separate vowels. The same rule holds for **UI** (cu-i, hu-ic) except when preceded by q (qui, which would be pronounced kwee).

Consonants

C   before e, i, y, ae, oe, as ch, in church; in all other cases C is as K

G   before e, i, y, ae, oe, is soft, as in gentle; in all other cases G is hard, as in go

H   is mute, except in the words *mihi* and *nihl,* then it is pronounced as K (mi-ki, and ni-kil)

J   y, as in yes (Jesus = Yeh-sus)

S   s, as in sanctus, spiritus, Jesus, and hostias, not as Z (miserere, not mezerere)

R   flipped, by slightly jarring the tongue against the palate (*not* an American RR, and not rolled)

X   ks, as in *lux, Rex, dixit* (di-ksit), and *dexteram* (de-kste-ram)

Z   as dz, (not ds); Nazareth = Na-dza-reth

EX   alone, is pronounced eks. If ex is the beginning of a word, combined with a vowel, it is pronounced egs, (exaudi = egs-au-di); when combined with a consonant, it is pronounced eks, (exspecto = eks-pec-to, excelsis = eks-chel-sis, not ek-shel-sis)

TI   when followed by a vowel, is like tsi (etiam = e-tsi-am, potentio = po-ten-tsi-o); except when the ti is preceded by s (hostias = os-ti-as, and hostium = os-ti-um); in all other cases, TI is pronounced simply as TI (petitionem = pe-ti-tsi-o-nem)

TH   as T, because the H is mute (Catholicam = Ca-to-li-cam)

CH   always as K (chorus-korus, cherubim = ker-u-bim)

GN   has a liquid sound similar to that of the ni in *dominions* (agnus = ah-nyus, magnum = mah-nyum)

SC   before e, i, y, ae, as sh in *shell* (descendit = de-shen dit, suscipe = su-shi-pe, sciat = shi-at); in all other cases, SC is pronounced as sk (scriptura = skrip-tu-ra, schola = sko-la); **SCH**—always SK as in scholar

PH   always as F (prophetas = pro-fe-tas)

Q   as K (qui = kwee)

Double consonants are supposed to actually be doubled in their intensity; thus, to_ll_is, pe_cc_ata, hosa_nn_a, a_ll_eluia; not tolis, pecata, hosana, and haleluia. However, this "correctness" will often negate the full, healthy vocal sound of the chorus. A_ll_eluia or ha_ll_eluyah will "dull" the sound of the chorus if they sing the double ll. In this case, we might compromise a bit and use only one consonant: a-le-lu-ia, or ha-leh-lu-jah. I feel similarly about tollis (to-lis). I would recommend a stop-consonant for peccata (pe_C_ata, in which there is a slight staccato feeling on the first syllable, pec). An intensified double nn in hosanna is often effective.

There are more extensive lists, but I believe that this one will suffice in most instances. We should not, however, take it for granted that we know Latin. It is best to check a pronunciation guide regularly when performing a work in Latin.

A Practice Exercise with Latin Text

The following pages contain the full text of the Latin mass with English translation. Use it to practice pronunciation and to become better acquainted with the translation.

I. Kyrie

Kyrie eleison,	Lord, have mercy upon us,
Christe eleison,	Christ, have mercy upon us,
Kyrie eleison.	Lord, have mercy upon us.

II. Gloria

Gloria in excelsis Deo,	Glory be to God on high,
et in terra pax hominibus	and on earth, peace to men
bonae voluntatis,	of good will,
Laudamus te, benedicimus te,	We praise thee, we bless thee, we adore thee
adoramus te, glorificamus te,	we glorify thee,
Gratias agimus tibi	We give thanks to thee
propter magnam gloriam tuam,	for thy great glory,
Domine Deus, Rex coelestis,	Lord God, heavenly king,
Pater omnipotens. Domine Fili	Father almighty, Lord
unigenite, Jesu Christe,	the only-begotten son, Jesus Christ,
Domine Deus, Agnus Dei,	Lord God, Lamb of God,
filius Patris,	Son of the Father,
Qui tollis peccata mundi,	Who takest away the sins of the world,
miserere nobis,	have mercy upon us,
suscipe deprecationem nostram,	receive our prayer,
Qui sedes ad dexteram Patris,	Who sitteth at the right hand of the
miserere nobis,	Father, have mercy on us,
Quoniam tu solus sanctus,	For thou only art holy,
tu solus Dominus,	thou only art the Lord,
tu solus altissimus, Jesu Christe	thou only are the most high, Jesus Christ,
cum sancto spiritu in gloria	with the Holy Ghost in
Dei Patris, Amen.	the glory of God the Father, Amen.

III. Credo

Credo in unum Deum,	I believe in one God,
Patrem omnipotentem,	Father Almighty,
factorem coeli et terrae,	maker of heaven and earth,

visibilium omnium
et invisibilium,
Et in unum Dominum, Jesum Christum,
Filium Dei unigenitum,
et ex Patre natum,
ante omnia saecula,
Deum de Deo, lumen de lumine,
Deum verum de Deo vero,
genitum non factum,
con substantialem Patri,
per quem omnia facta sunt,
Qui propter nos homines
et propter nostram salutem
descendit de coelis.
Et incarnatus est
de spiritu sancto
ex Maria Virgine
et homa factus est,
Crucifixus etiam pro nobis
sub Pontio Pilato,
passus et sepultus est,
Et resurrexit tertia die
secundum scripturas,
et ascendit in coelum,
sedet ad dexteram Patris,
et iterum venturus est
cum gloria
judicare vivos et mortuos,
cojus regni non erit finis.
Et in spiritum sanctum,
Dominum et vivificantem,
qui ex Patre Filioque procedit,
qui cum Patre et Filio
simul adoratur et conglorificatur,
qui locutus est per prophetas,
Et unam sanctam catholicam
et apostolicam ecclesiam,
Confiteor unum baptisma
in remissionem peccatorum,
Et expecto resurrectionem
mortuorum,
et vitam venturi saeculi,
Amen.

and of all things visible
and invisible,
And in one Lord, Jesus Christ,
the only-begotten Son of God,
born of the Father
before all ages,
God of God, light of light,
Very God of Very God,
begotten, not made,
of one substance with the Father,
by whom all things were made,
Who for us men
and for our salvation
came down from heaven.
And became incarnate
by the Holy Ghost
of the Virgin Mary
and was made man,
And was crucified also for us
under Pontius Pilate,
suffered and was buried,
And the third day he rose again,
according to the scriptures,
and ascended into heaven,
and sitteth on the right hand of the Father,
and he shall come again
with glory
to judge the living and the dead,
whose kingdom shall have no end.
And in the Holy Ghost,
the lord and life-giver,
who proceedeth from the Father and the Son,
who with the Father and the Son
together is adored and glorified,
who spake by the prophets,
And in one holy catholic
and apostolic Church,
I acknowledge one baptism
for the remission of sins,
And I expect the resurrection
of the dead,
and the life of the world to come,
Amen.

IV. Sanctus et Benedictus

Sanctus, sanctus, sanctus,
Dominus Deus Sabaoth,
pleni sunt coeli et terra
gloria tua.
Osanna in excelsis.

Holy, Holy, holy,
Lord God of hosts,
heaven and earth are full
of Thy glory.
Hosanna in the highest.

Benedictus qui venit
in nomine Domini.
Osanna in excelsis.

Blessed is he who cometh
in the name of the Lord.
Hosanna in the highest.

V. Agnus Dei

Agnus Dei,	Lamb of God,
qui tollis peccata mundi,	who takest away the sins of the world,
miserere nobis,	have mercy upon us,
dona nobis pacem.	give us peace.

Summary

The language is the sole vehicle with which the singer makes vocal sound. It is a musical method of direct communication from artist to listener. The singer's language must be filled with color (vowels), percussion (consonants), inflection of syllables and words, word-meaning emphasis, and projections. *Deliver the text in a manner that energetically makes an impact!*

Score Preparation and Analysis

*T*his chapter will deal with the conductor's complete preparation of the score. We are responsible for knowing as much as possible about the musical composition with which we are working. We should take it one step at a time, attempting to study the music *microscopically,* one detail, note, word, syllable, or phrase at a time. We want to know the function of every aspect of the music, and each aspect's relation to every other. This takes time, patience, perseverance, and a desire to know and serve the score in great depth. Our reward will be the ability to interpret thoroughly, teach, and conduct with honest confidence. In this chapter, topics will range from style, text, and tempo to structural analysis, cues, composer's and conductor's markings, and conducting problems.

Style

The first thing to be determined is the style of the song or work. All further study will rest on this foundation. This includes not only such obvious categorical decisions as renaissance, baroque, classic, romantic, and contemporary stylistic periods, but also further considerations such as

- Italian renaissance versus German, French or others
- Early versus late within a stylistic period
- Differences among composers and compositional styles within a given period (the many varied styles within 20th century music, or the nine different styles of choral writing within Handel's *Messiah*).
- Different compositional periods within a single composer's lifetime (early Haydn versus later Haydn).

- Appropriate approaches to the great variety of ethnic music (folk songs, spirituals, nationalistic music, and so forth).

- The differences in lighter music, such as Broadway, jazz, pop, "top forty," Dixieland, country music, rock, and music representing particular decades (1930s, 1940s, and so on).

- Church and temple music in general, traditional or contemporary, and seasonal and regular service music.

- Oratorios, masses, cantatas, and other major works for chorus and orchestra.

- A cappella traditions from early to contemporary music.

There are as many considerations as there are composers and varieties of music. We will not attempt to discuss the interpretive elements that would be appropriate for a text specifically on interpretation. At this point, our purpose is simply to make ourselves aware of the wide spectrum of potential stylistic decisions that must be made intelligently when approaching *any* piece of music.

Musicologists should be the conductor's best friends. Such a friendship can be most valuable in determining the appropriate stylistic approach to compositions. If the music is not within the realm of a musicologist or ethnomusicologist, then seek an authority in that particular area (jazz, pop, avant-garde). The important thing is that we enable ourselves to interpret compositions with the kind of confidence that only comes through really knowing the music from every necessary perspective. Remember: someone, somewhere, is able and willing to help us. Ask.

Text

We have discussed in detail the manner by which we need to approach words and syllables. We are now interested in the analysis of the song's text. I recommend that we study the text as though it were for a class in interpretive literature, determining potential communication, line by line, thought by thought. We should know exactly what the song is trying to say through its text. Furthermore, we need to know how the text and music form a marriage to accomplish this and how we can best serve this union. Again the perspective needs to be that of a great actor who experiments with several different but appropriate interpretations until he discovers the most convincing one. In our case, we also need to know which one is most closely aligned with the composer's melodic material.

When studying the text, especially if it has dramatic potential, literally walk around your study area, imagining that you actually are an actor, and deliver the lines with dramatic depth. You will find great things to express in significant text, and you will look forward to teaching the chorus to deliver them. First, solidify it within yourself and then teach it convincingly to the chorus.

All this goes hand in hand with diction, syllable and word inflection, and word meaning emphasis discussed in Chapter 7. It all comes together to encompass the "one-third actor" that is a part of every successful singer and choral conductor. If you need help in the dramatic aspect of your role as a conductor and teacher, seek it from an actor, drama coach, or theatrical stage director. This, like everything else, is available to us.

Tempo

Determining the appropriate tempo of a song is paramount to serving the score and composer successfully. The elements of style and text that we've already discussed will help in determining tempo. Thus it becomes our third category. The following describes some further considerations in determining tempo.

> Occasionally, it is a good idea to introduce a particularly significant textual message to the audience or congregation before singing the song. Thirty to ninety seconds of dramatic presentation or explanation to the listeners will often greatly enhance their appreciation of the musical presentation. Make this decision based on the ability to look through the eyes of the listeners, thereby determining the value of such a moment and how to express it.

Follow specific tempo indications given by the composer.   Although contemporary composers are usually very flexible and generous of spirit when it comes to suggestions regarding the possibility of changing a tempo, I believe we should honor the wishes of the one who created that which we are about to re-create. Conductors do not have license to make the piece their own. We might have a unique interpretation that may bring out special beauty or excitement of a composition, but it is and always will be the *composer's work of art!*

A few metronomic degrees one way or the other are acceptable. More than that actually changes the piece. We should not do that. If we or our performing forces cannot perform the composition at the composer's indicated tempo, we should not perform it. It would be better to wait until we can do it as the composer intended it to be performed.

Granted, some composers are known for being inaccurate concerning their tempo indications and actually performed the pieces at tempi other than those they indicated. So be it. These are the exceptions to the admonition here, which is to *honor the tempo instructions set for us by composers.*

If an editor indicates the tempo, our obligation to abide by it may be lessened. The credibility of this tempo indication, of course, parallels that of the editor. This, however, necessitates our knowing the editor and publisher well enough to make an intelligent decision. I encourage you to accept the editor's suggestion unless you are able to dispute it based on prior scholarly study or as a result of discussion with your musicologist partner. In all of this, humility is an admirable quality.

Determine a specific tempo, even if the indication is general.   If the tempo indication is simply allegro, andante, grave, and so on, we have greater latitude and freedom of choice. We also have a greater responsibility and more work to do in justifying an appropriate tempo.

Let us establish firmly that a specific tempo *does* need to be determined. Once done, the conductor lives with it throughout the entire study and rehearsal process. This gives both the conductor and performing forces the optimum potential of consistently rehearsing and then performing the piece at the appropriate tempo. Daily mood changes and nervous performing conditions have less effect if the tempo is under control on a regular basis. I suggest working consistently with a metronome, both in personal study and in the rehearsal process.

These factors will help determine tempo:

- Style—that which is appropriate for a given musical style

- Text—whether it is stately, light-hearted, serious, joyful, powerfully dramatic, sorrowful, and so forth; what it *really means*; the potential impact intended for the listeners

- The most complex rhythmic figure—wherever that may be: in the vocal forces or the accompaniment, and how fast or slowly it can effectively be sung or played

- Acoustics—of the concert hall in which the music is to be performed. That is, you might wish to take a somewhat slower tempo in a very reverberant hall and a slightly faster tempo in a "dryer" hall

As an example, we will create a hypothetical situation of a baroque composition marked allegro. We should be aware of the following considerations:

- The outer extremes of baroque allegro are probably 90 to 96 at the slower end and 126 to 132 at the faster (for a quarter note).

- The text will be our next determining factor. We'll assume it is a *dignified* text with a message of *substance,* which would tend to send our tempo into the slower allegro range, somewhere between 90 and 114.

- That it is homophonic will further substantiate a stately tempo. The composition is one of great joy and positive faith, which will move it slightly toward 114 (96 to 114).

- In checking the most complex rhythmic figure, we find only an occasional eighth followed by two sixteenths, but nothing more.

- I will now *sing* the complex rhythm, with the above considerations, at several tempi between 96 and 114. Probably, one will feel just right. I will check the number of pulses (beats) in one minute, and that will be the tempo—perhaps 104.

- I will place the selected tempo indication on the music, set the metronome accordingly, and begin my further study with it turned on (softly). I will also take the metronome to rehearsals to confirm, on a regular basis, that I am rehearsing at the correct tempo. If, during the rehearsal process, I decide to slightly alter the selected tempo, that is fine—as long as I remain consistent.

Structural Analysis

Conductors use structural analysis to discover the phrase and basic harmonic structure of a composition. Our major emphasis here will be on the *phrase structure*. Each conductor will determine to what extent he or she wants to develop a *harmonic* analysis. Some prefer, and have the time, to do much more than others do. This is your decision. You *know what is essential* for your understanding of the piece and its potential, and its effective rehearsal.

Dissecting a Piece of Music

We will view a choral anthem as an entity to be dissected into *major sections*, *long phrases*, and *short phrases*. Major sections will be divided into long phrases, and long phrases will be divided into short phrases. We'll discuss their relationship to each other, and to the entire piece. These phrases and sections will be marked in the scores as follows.

Major sections. Major sections are (1) the introduction, (2) one, two, or possibly three truly significant portions of the piece, and (3) the coda (ending). Major sections are *indicated in the score by placing full-length parallel lines*, running down the regular bar lines, at the beginning of such a section.

Major sections, which often are 24 to 48 measures or more in length, do not *always* have to be that long. Introductions and codas can be as short as 6 to 12 measures. *Significance* alone, rather than length, may be the determining factor.

Long phrases. Long phrases are *indicated by a single, full-length bar line* running down the regular bar lines, at the beginning of each such phrase. Long phrases, comparatively speaking, are not always *long*. Again, *significance* can dictate shorter duration, but they can often be 8 to 16 measures long.

Short phrases. Short phrases are *indicated in the score by a partial bar line*, which will run down the regular bar lines, but only through the voice parts (not the accompaniment). When used in orchestral scores, the partial line may be drawn through only the string parts (or wind parts if they are more significant at the time).

Julius Herford, Knowledge and Energy

Julius Herford—the man responsible for developing this concept of structural analysis of music—laid the foundation for musical integrity in American choral music. That is, he taught the wealth of great music and how to perform it musically and stylistically. One of Herford's remarkable qualities was his extraordinary knowledge of the full range of repertoire. Many musicologists specialize in only one stylistic period. Herford understood how the music of all composers was to be performed—from Palestrina and Monteverdi to Stravinsky, Bartok, Britten, and Schoenberg—but he dearly loved Bach. My entire approach to structural analysis is based on Julius Herford's teaching.

During the sixteen years that I studied with him, Herford told me that European choral conductors possessed enormous musical knowledge and that American choral conductors possessed enormous energy. His life's mission was to bring about the marriage of European knowledge and American energy.

Most of the rhythmic interest, forward motion, and phrasing concepts discussed in this book are also based on Herford's teachings.

Suggestions for marking a score using this system

1. *Before placing the bar lines in the music*, place a checkmark at the bottom of the score at the point at which the *long* phrase begins, and a checkmark in parentheses at each point at which a *short* phrase begins. The reason for this: if you change your mind during the process of analyzing the entire piece, you don't have to erase an entire line, only a check. Place the bar lines in the music, with a ruler for neatness, after you have *definitely decided on them*.

2. When lead-in notes are involved (which is often the case), consider them as such, and place the check, and eventually the bar lines, at the point of the *following* regular bar lines. Do not place structural bar lines *within* a measure. This looks confusing, especially when quickly glancing at the score in rehearsal or performance.

3. Place mathematical equations of the phrases at the bottom of the score, at each point where a check or single long bar line would be placed. This indicates the number of measures in the following *long phrase*, and those in each of the *shorter phrases* within the long one (there may be two or several). For example, a long phrase of 16 measures, with shorter phrases of 6, 4, 4, and 2 measures, would be equated as $16 (6 + 4 + 4 + 2)$.

4. An *introduction, special interlude,* or *coda* of 10 measures could be considered *both* a major section and a long phrase. The long phrase might be 10 measures, with two short phrases of 6 and 4. The parallel lines at its beginning or ending will serve both the major section and the long phrase. The mathematical equation at the bottom is $10 (6 + 4)$.

In his structural analysis, Julius Herford used only the checks and checks-in-parentheses. I added the concept of bar lines for three reasons:

- When looking down at your score, you will immediately and easily see an organized view of the musical ideas, set up as an architect would arrange rooms on a blue-print

- Your eyes will travel quickly to the beginning of a new phrase or musical idea

- You can ask your singers to place the bar lines in their own music to help them sing structurally, one *musical idea* after another, rather than singing one *note* after another

If done neatly, with a ruler, the score can actually look as though it was published with the bar lines in it. Make the lines heavy, with a soft lead pencil, so they can be seen easily. Don't make any marks with a pen. A pen negates the opportunity to change your mind. And, you *will* change your mind, frequently.

An Example of Structural Analysis: Haydn, The Creation, "Awake The Harp"

We will go through it step by step. Remember this is a "conductor's" analysis; we can do it any way that best serves our needs. Yours may differ from mine. Begin with the *choral material*.

Awake The Harp

Joseph Haydn
Edited by Donald Neuen

And the heav-en-ly host pro-claim'd the third__day. prais-ing God, and say-ing

Measures 1–10. The first 10 measures are an opening introductory statement. This introduction is both a major section and the first long phrase. The long phrase is divided into two short phrases, one of 6 and one of 4 measures. The latter decision is based on 6 measures of homophonic, block-style singing, followed by 3 measures of the upper three voices answered by the bass section (twice), and a final closing instrumental measure. The equation 10 (6 + 4) appears below measure 1. Also acceptable is 10 (6 + 3 + 1).

Measures 4–11. The partial bar line is placed at the beginning of measure 7, which begins the second short phrase.

Measures 11–22. Parallel lines are placed at the beginning of measure 11 to indicate both the end of the first major section and the beginning of the first long phrase. One 12-measure long phrase, consisting of two short phrases of 8 and 4 measures each. The equation for this, placed below measure 11, is 12 (8 + 4). This is based on four 2-measure entrances of bass, tenor, alto, and soprano, followed by the next 4 measures, in which the basses have it for two counts, the tenors for two counts, the altos for a full measure, and the sopranos return for the original two measures.

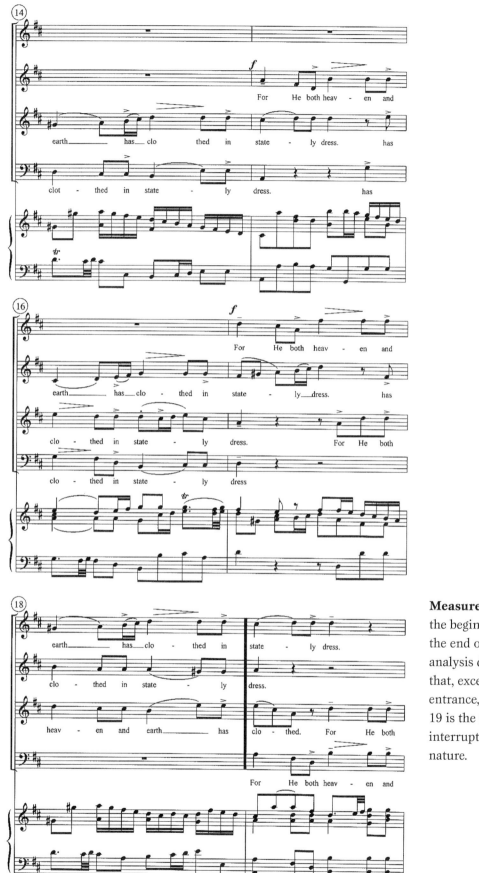

Measure 19. Place a partial bar line at the beginning of measure 19 to indicate the end of the first short phrase. The analysis draws our attention to the fact that, except for the opening bass entrance, the tenor entrance in measure 19 is the most important because of its interruptive and therefore percussive nature.

Measure 20. This structural analysis also shows that the altos' third and fourth beats in measure 20 may be more significant than beats one and two because of the elongation of their entrance compared with that of the bass and tenor. Similarly, the second measure of the soprano entrance may be more important than the first.

Measure 22. Place a full single line at the end of measure 22 indicating the end of the long phrase begun at measure 11.

Measures 23–36. These measures make up the next long phrase, which consists of a short phrase of 5 measures, another of 2½ (which we will call 3, because we don't want to get involved with *parts of measures*; in such cases, we will always go to the next bar line), and the final 6 measures. Partial bar lines are placed at measure 28 and 31, indicating the ends of *short phrases*. The next full-length line is at measure 37, beginning the next *long phrase*. The equation below measure 23 is 14 (8 + 6). We can further analyze the eight measures as 5 + 3 in *brackets* under the 8.

Measures 23–27. These measures include a major bass entrance, altos coming in three beats later, sopranos entering one beat later, and tenors picking up the fourth beat before the final two measures.

Measures 28–30. After this 2½–3 measure *transition*, the same sequence begins again (in measure 31). The basses have it for three counts, after their major entrance (this time on the leading tone C♯), followed by the altos again for only one count. This time, the tenors and basses follow with a significant duet, beginning on high D and F♯ ("significant" to the conductor, because male voices singing in that range produce an absolutely glorious vocal sound).

Measure 28. The soprano and alto entrances begin the transition from one short phrase (measures 23–27) to the next (measures 31–36) and needs to be very percussive, coming through clearly for rhythmic interest.

Measure 30. The bass entrance is a leading tone high in the bass's vocal range. "For" needs to be placed forward in the upper head and almost thought of as "far" to be sufficiently high in pitch and refreshingly brilliant in tonal color.

Measures 32–37. Sopranos enter at the end of measure 32, measure 35 contains the women's duet, and measure 36 contains the men's duet.

Measures 37–42. We now find a very short "long phrase." This is an example of significance overriding length. Measure 37 is a measure unto itself—four explosive entrances. Measures 38 and 39 are a two-measure unit of a short "baroque dance" (a sequence of an eighth note followed by two sixteenth notes). This is followed by three measures, the first (m. 40) containing two important high Es for the women, especially the altos. Measure 41 contains an interesting rhythmic and melodic figure in the tenor part, imitated by the sopranos in the last measure (42). This is a six-measure single idea. We're calling it a long phrase even though it's only six measures.

Measures 37 and 43. We place a full-length single line at the beginning of measure 37 to begin this "long" phrase. The next long phrase begins with measure 43. The equation 6 (1 + 2 + 3) appears below measure 37. Partial bar lines begin measures 38 and 40.

Remember, this is a *conductorial analysis*; it can be done in any manner that best serves our needs.

5 (3+2)

Measures 43–56 (the end). The piece is now returning, for the first time, to a homophonic, block-style, *tutti* manner of singing (as in the beginning). We might call the following passages a "semi-recapitulation and coda." Therefore, I feel it is significant enough to warrant the double bar lines, indicating a new section. That could be a 14-measure, long phrase, with 2 short phrases of 5 and 9 measures each. The equation beneath measure 43 would be 14 (5 + 9).

I recommend that you choose to make it a 5 (3 + 2) measure "long" phrase at measure 43, and another "long" phrase at measure 48, which is 9 (5 + 4). The justification for me was the approach to the fermata, then the 9 measure ending. Remember, it is always your analysis.

Measure 52. Notice the interesting difference between the melismatic material of the sopranos and the men. For the sopranos, each group of four sixteenth-notes is arranged as 1 + 3, the men's group is arranged as 3 + 1, giving the listener a continuous off-beat effect).

Analysis Worksheet and Markings

In addition to the work in the score itself, the structural analysis also includes a *worksheet*. The form of the worksheet is exactly as Julius Herford taught it. You can write your own descriptive notes under it that will serve you in your attempt to memorize portions of the analysis.

The point of forming and studying the worksheet is to solidify the piece's skeleton in your mind *before the first rehearsal*. The analysis and full score preparation should help a conductor to begin the first rehearsal completely prepared and confidently able to lead the chorus through a successful session.

The Analysis Worksheet

The worksheet shown in Figure 8.1 (page 158) is simply a display of the structural analysis through measure groupings, equations, abbreviated reminders, and a skeletal harmonic indication. We should have this worksheet clearly in our minds when we begin the first rehearsal. We do not have to completely memorize a composition, but we should *really know it* so that we can *look into the eyes of our singers*, and *inspire them* as they rehearse and perform. The analysis and worksheet will help us do this.

Additional Markings in the Score

Identify all potential conducting problems and work them out thoroughly before the first rehearsal. Never take a conducting problem to the rehearsal. Solve the problem and mark the score appropriately to remind yourself of the solution. I believe in marking everything in a score that we want brought to life in the rehearsal and performance process. That includes the following.

Cues. Cues in a choral score are most effective if written with a *red* pencil and ruler (for neatness). In an orchestral score, use a *green* pencil for woodwinds, a *red* for brass and percussion, and *blue* for strings. In combined choral-orchestral scores, I would suggest either a *black* or *red* pencil for the choral cues. If it's an important entrance, mark it, and cue it consistently. Consistency is very important to the members of the ensemble. If they are used to being cued, they will depend on it. If later the cue is not there, their entrance might be tentative.

The color-coding is for the convenience of the conductor when glancing quickly at the score. Again, it should be neatly done, as though printed that way by the publisher, and designed by an architect. A messy score can be confusing when glanced at quickly in rehearsal or concert.

Cues are necessary for performers who have been tacit then re-enter. Cues are equally important for significant entrances that the conductor wants to reinforce for their potential impact. Both need to be *predetermined* and executed with *consistency*. (We'll discuss cues more in Chapter 11.)

Interpretive markings. Draw attention to all interpretive indications of the composer and editor, and those that you wish to add to the score. These can be done with either black or red pencil. I suggest *black* so they won't be confused with red cue markings. These markings might include small circles for *pp, p,* and *mp,* squares for *mf, f, ff,* and circles around a ritard, tenuto, accellerando, accent, stress, and heavy commas for special breathing indications. It also might be helpful to color in with a red pencil a crescendo or decrescendo indication. These indicators are highlighted to ensure that they will be observed.

Special articulations and phrasing. Indicate with a black pencil all other markings you want to indicate, for example, phrasing, special articulations such as shortened or slightly lengthened notes, inflection of words and syllables, specially emphasized words, and re-notated final notes that involve a rest. This last category

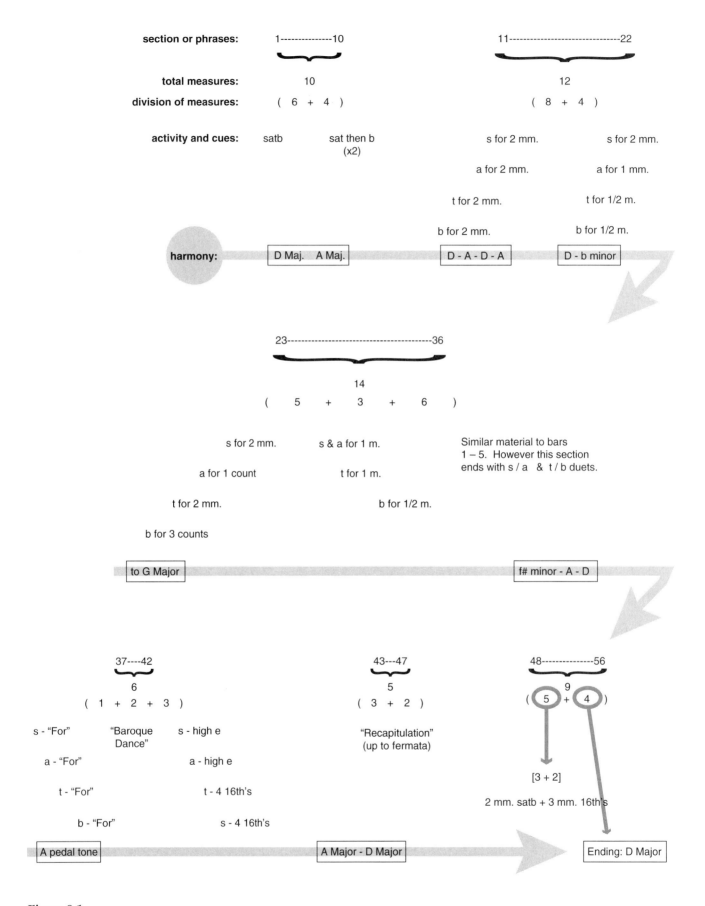

Figure 8.1

Structural Analysis Worksheet for "Awake The Harp"

will enable the ensemble to achieve releases and phrase-endings together and exactly as you want them done.

- If a phrase-ending note is a *half note*, do you want it to be sung as a half note tied to a staccato eighth, a dotted quarter-note followed by an eighth rest, or a quarter-note followed by a quarter rest? Each is an option. To varying degrees, *each* will be done by your ensemble members if you do not make it perfectly clear which one you prefer, and have them notate it in their score. Mark it in your score *before* the first rehearsal.

- If the final note is a *quarter note*, do you want it to be a quarter tied to a staccato eighth, a dotted eighth followed by a sixteenth rest, or an eighth note followed by an eighth rest? Again, you predetermine it, they mark it, and everyone does it.

- This same procedure takes place when two half notes (or quarter notes) are written with a comma in between them, indicating that a breath is to be taken. The first note is re-notated according to your predetermined plan for the phrase and the breath. *Every such instance should be thought through very carefully and notated in the score.* Then, give these markings to the chorus in the *first* rehearsal.

Conductor's Preparation

A conductor needs to study the score *microscopically* to achieve all the preceding steps: each note, syllable, word, measure, and phrase scrutinized until it is clearly known and understood, with all significant decisions solidly made *and notated.*

This type of preparation will begin to enable the conductor actually to *become* the music, be a true reflection of the score, and be able to communicate that successfully to the chorus. It is important to realize that this cannot happen on a foundation of "feelings" alone. Our feelings must rest securely on the foundation of complete knowledge of the fundamentals of the piece.

To do this, the conductor must prepare very patiently. Do not merely go through the piece. Study the individual notes, words, and syllables of one measure, and then one structural phrase at a time. Thoroughly dissect it. Don't go on until you know it. It is better to cover less material and cover it well than to skim though the entire piece really knowing none of it.

Give yourself realistic goals. Don't select more music or accept more concert engagements than you can comfortably handle. Score preparation takes an enormous amount of time. Schedule and program only those songs and concerts that can be done well. Less is often more.

Make constructive use of professional recordings to gain insight into a piece of music. Respect and learn from the experience, knowledge, and wisdom of others. Don't reinvent the wheel when it isn't necessary.

Do not, however, depend on repetitively listening to and conducting those recordings as a complete method of learning your score. Use the recording to acquaint yourself with the piece and its potential and to derive insight

> Prepare solidly, believe in yourself, know what you want, and then rehearse confidently to get it.

into possibilities of performance interpretation. You might also want to use a recording for *minimal* conducting practice. Then put the recording away. As you study, hear it in your head. Frequently sing the piece as you practice conducting (not casually, but in the manner you will eventually want to hear). Learn from others and incorporate as many of their ideas as you want, but the final interpretation must be yours.

Don't force score memorization. I do not demand that my conducting students memorize their scores. Conductors who memorize have a greater chance of making errors. The conductor also could be somewhat lacking in passion if he or she is too busy focusing on memorization. I do, however, suggest that the conductor know the worksheet before the first rehearsal, then continue learning as much as possible during the process of rehearsals to follow. All this should allow the conductor to look up—out of the music and into the eyes of the performers, 95 percent of the time, especially in the final rehearsals and the concert.

Focus on individual phrases. When studying the analysis, focus on one short phrase at a time. Thoroughly understand it and its relation to the phrases before and after it, before going on. You will thereby always know where you are in relation to where you've been and where you're going. Put the phrases together in your mind like the pieces of a puzzle. They will all make logical and musical sense. This will help you gain a confident feeling of the entire piece.

When rehearsing, teach one structural phrase at a time. Make the singers aware of these phrases. They should occasionally add the bar lines to their music as well, especially on more difficult songs or passages, to help them to see the piece from a structural point of view, thus enhancing the learning process.

Frequently refer to phrases or sections, not always to page and measure numbers. You can include roman numerals at the beginning of each long phrase, and add A, B and C at the beginning of some shorter phrases. Example: I, II, II-A, II-B, III, IV, IV-A, and so on. When beginning a rehearsal on a given piece of music, you might instruct the singers to "begin today at phrase II-B," instead of "page four, measure 21." This instruction will condition them to think structurally.

When stopping to correct something in the music, it is often effective to begin again at the nearest previous bar line. When rehearsing a predetermined number of minutes on a composition, work specifically on a structural section or long phrase(s). This also makes good musical sense. Don't end the rehearsal in the middle of a fragmented phrase.

Your analysis is just that, *your* analysis. If someone disagrees with you, that's okay. Your analysis is there to serve *you,* your understanding of the piece, your rehearsals, and your performance. Granted, there may often be one best way to analyze a composition, a conclusion at which most conductors who are well studied, would arrive. In fact, you will frequently change your mind concerning an analysis when re-doing it later. The point is to differ on an analysis is all right. This is not like a theory or harmonic analysis, in which there is only one correct way to do it.

You may see a musical idea as one long phrase of sixteen measures, with two short phrases within it of eight measures each. Someone else might see the same sixteen measures, as twelve plus four. No one is wrong. You might see a four-measure interlude as an independent four measures, not being a part of that which either preceded or follows. Someone else may see the same four measures as part of an eight plus four, twelve measure single idea (long phrase).

Summary

It is our responsibility as conductors to know all that can be known about the musical score regarding the following:

- Style
- Text
- Tempo
- Structural (and basic harmonic) analysis
- Interpretive indications
- Musical and dramatic potential

Reminder: Develop and use structural analysis as the *foundation* of learning, teaching, rehearsing, and conducting the piece.

Rehearsals and Auditions

9

Both general and specific concepts can positively affect a rehearsal. This chapter is concerned with those topics. Our goal is to create both an atmosphere, and a manner of teaching and conducting, that will result in 100 percent productivity within the context of a consistent, day-by-day routine. A conductor's success is not accidental. Rather, it is the result of consciously planned methods of working with a chorus (or instrumental ensemble) that *really work*.

I have found these techniques, methods, and related topics to work well in elementary, junior high, and high school choruses, church youth and adult choirs, university, symphony and opera choruses; chamber and show choirs; and with professional singers. My suggestions are also based on observing successful rehearsal procedures of other conductors.

Compile your own list according to your own preferences. Use the following items, add them to those you have gathered in your own experience, and make your own very special road map to rehearsal success. The all-important factor: *predetermine* your route to excellence. (It will never happen accidentally.)

Basic Necessities for the Conductor

Preparation.   Prepare incredibly well for every rehearsal. Never yield to the temptation to do less because you can easily stay one step ahead of the chorus. Don't fool yourself into thinking you can fool the singers. They know when we are well prepared, and they know when we are not.

Instructions.   Talk very little. The singers are there to sing. Be *brief* in giving instructions, and use *musical terminology* when it's appropriate. They'll learn,

> Everyone in the chorus, whether privately trained or not, *should be a leader*. There should be no followers, only leaders, unafraid to take risks and accepting of the occasional mistake. This philosophy is paramount in developing an aggressive, fast-learning, solid performing chorus.

absorb, get used to it, and appreciate it. Refrain from informal talking, reminiscing, stories, repeating yourself, and taking longer than necessary to say what needs to be said. We should regularly tape our rehearsals and listen (or better, yet, watch) to check on the effectiveness of our rehearsals, making sure we are specific, direct, clear, motivating, and *brief.*

Security. Do not sing with your chorus. First, when we sing, we can't hear the chorus accurately. We hear ourselves. Second, the more physically involved we become, the less discerningly we are able to *hear.* The conductor's goal should be to become a great listener, evaluator, and teacher *first,* and then an expressive conductor second.

We may think that our singing with the chorus helps singers learn faster or perform better, but this is seldom true. The negative results, however, outweigh any positive. Chorus members will become accustomed to hearing, following, and leaning on the conductor's voice for that which should be developed within themselves. Teach individual security and positive leadership and independence.

Do not mouth the words. Mouthing the words (like singing with the chorus) physically involves the conductor in the activity of *vocal performance*. That is the sole responsibility of the *chorus*. Participating with them in this manner distracts the conductor from listening effectively and teaches the singers to watch the conductor's mouth (which they will do) rather than *follow the conducting.*

Conductors frequently do this for *their own confidence*, thinking the chorus will do well (or better) with the help of spoon-fed words. Build your confidence in chorus members alone, not in their ability to lean on mouthed-words for a crutch. Let's keep our mouth shut, listen, teach, and conduct!

Positivity. Use positive energy. Inspire, motivate, encourage, and support the chorus. Do not become only a negative corrector. Here again, tape your rehearsals and listen to them. A conductor can easily become impatiently negative or actually angry with the singers for normal mistakes that need to be corrected. Anger, insults, berating, and demoralizing are all counterproductive and harmful. Be intense, demanding, businesslike, and relentless in your pursuit of excellence, but do it all in a *positive* and *encouraging* manner. The chorus needs to be encouraged to feel confident and that they *can do it.*

Rehearsal environment. The rehearsal atmosphere and facilities need to be inspiring and conducive to fine singing. If we want the singers to sing in a special manner, the surroundings should subliminally indicate clearly that we feel the singers are special, and we have created these *special* conditions *especially for them.*

- The room must be clean, neat, organized, and cheerful. If we are the only ones to clean it, and keep it clean, and even paint it (white, off-white or very light gray), then so be it. Whatever it takes to make it happen, do it. The room must be as special looking as we expect the singers to sing. The entire creative process should rest on *order*, not varying degrees of chaos.

- The rehearsal room should also be well lighted and properly ventilated. Find a way, even if it takes new lighting, to have a bright room that will help stimulate the energy level we desire from our singers. The room must not be dull, musty, stuffy, or too hot. No one can sing well under such conditions.

- Chairs should be adequately spaced. The chairs should be *at least* 4 to 6 inches apart for a "soloistic approach to ensemble singing." Singers cannot perform well under crowded conditions. Elevated risers are best and will greatly enhance the rehearsal conditions of the room. This is not always possible, but it certainly is beneficial.

- A grand piano (at least a five-foot grand), in tune and good condition, is necessary for a highly productive rehearsal. The chorus deserves to hear the accompaniment adequately and hear it with a true quality sound. If you must use an electronic keyboard, make it a great one. It should have a realistic piano sound and high quality speakers. In either case, you owe your ensemble a high-quality rehearsal instrument. If you need to initiate a fundraiser for this, do it.

Discipline.   Solid discipline is an absolute *must* for the choral rehearsal! A creative process cannot flourish in chaotic confusion. One creative person can behave in any manner he or she desires. Two or more, however, must employ varying degrees of teamwork and cooperation. That necessitates discipline. The conductor is responsible for instilling consistent, rock-solid discipline in an ensemble of any age or experience level.

- There is no reason for singers to talk to each other while rehearsing. In between songs, yes, but during the actual rehearsing, absolutely not—*even about the music.* The person being disturbed might have been concentrating on something much more important at that moment. In addition, it could disturb the conductor, in which case everyone loses. *The conductor must make it very clear that anyone, at any time, may raise his or her hand to ask a question.* The conductor will gladly stop immediately to answer it.

- The positive attitude, soloistic posture, 100 percent focus, and intense concentration that we have talked about are essential aspects of the overall discipline that the conductor needs to set solidly (and maintain day after day). *Discipline and productivity go together.* Singers should view a rehearsal as a joyous time. Singers (and conductor), however, must also see the rehearsal atmosphere as one of (1) extremely hard work, (2) intense focus and concentration, (3) learning and perfecting the techniques of great singing, musicianship, musicality, and personal expression. Enjoyment and personal fulfillment come from *achieving all this!*

- More experienced conductors might find it easier to establish and maintain discipline than the less experienced. Solid discipline is something we might have to *develop,* and experience will help in that development. Personal security and effective teaching, which come with knowledge gained through years of conducting and teaching, are major plus-factors in maintaining consistent discipline. The better and more knowledgeable teacher will produce better-paced and more substance-filled rehearsals. The singers' respect for that conductor will be at an optimum level, increasing their personal desire for *self-discipline,* hard work, and intense focus. Each conductor must develop an effective disciplinary process within him or herself, then find a way to make it work. Seek advice from well-established conductors whose discipline you admire.

Fair, firm, and friendly.   The successful conductor will adhere to the "3 Fs": fair, firm, and friendly: Be fair to each singer regarding everything; firm in enforcing rules you deem important; and *professionally* friendly. Make only those few rules you feel are absolutely necessary, then enforce them relentlessly.

Tools.   Each singer must have a pencil and write down every directive. *If the conductor says it, the singer writes it!* The experience-level of the singer does not matter, they *all* write when given a directive, *even the professionals*. No one can remember everything. Writing the directions does three positive things:

- Ensures that the singers think about what has just been said.

- Reinforces the point made.

- Increases the probability of success the next time the chorus sings that particular passage.

Energy first.   Before anything else of substance can be accomplished in choral singing, a foundation of abundant (but completely controlled) energy must first be established. I don't mean chaotic hyper behavior. I refer to a mind and body that is filled with mental and physical animated, positive, and productive spirit. The voice is the only living instrument, coming from within a living being. The singer must uninhibitedly bring the voice out from within. Remember, all this equates to life, and life is energy—the voice is energy! Thus, any choral conductor's first priority is to create energy within the mind, body, and spirit of every singer in the ensemble. Once this is successfully generated, all else can be added. First, the *conductor* must have the energy. The conductor is the living example of *everything needed by the chorus.* We are the source!

If there were such an instrument as an "energyometer" with a range of 1–100 indicating the energy level of choruses, I would estimate that 5 percent are in the 0–10 category, 15 percent in the 10–25 category, 40 percent in the 25–50 category, 20 percent in the 50–75 category, 10 percent in the 75–90 category, 8 percent in the 90–98 category, and finally, only 2 percent in the 98–100 category. Where do *we* fall in all this? Every chorus should be in the 98–100 category. Video your rehearsals regularly and be your own best teacher regarding energy and everything else.

Rehearse Efficiently

The following suggestions will help our rehearsals be efficient and productive.

Begin with a confidence builder.   Begin the rehearsal with a song (or part of a song) that the singers can do well, establishing their interest and self-confidence. The second song should be the most demanding, while they're confident and still fresh. The last song planned should be something they really enjoy, and on which they can succeed with ease, sending them on their way in a great positive spirit, looking forward to the next rehearsal.

Sing through a new song completely.   Do this even if the group falters a bit because they are sight-reading. Ask the pianist to give extra support. Singing through it can give the chorus a picture of where they're headed during the following slowing down, tearing-it-apart and putting-it-back-together-again process.

Work backwards.   Our normal routine, of going straight through a song to be rehearsed, necessitates continuously going into the unknown. That is fine, but the backwards-approach is sometimes a more effective process. That is, begin with the last phrase, then the next-to-the-last, then the one before that, and so on. Each time, sing a few measures (or more) into the following phrase that has just been rehearsed, to re-establish the connection and relationship between the two. Each time the chorus approaches the portion previously rehearsed there is a good and confident feeling of success associated with it.

Work through a piece from a structural approach.   Inform the singers of the structure, and frequently, if it will be helpful in difficult music, have them place bar lines and Roman numerals in the different sections and long and short phrases. Be sure that the chorus is aware of the relationship of one significant phrase or musical idea to another. The composition should make logical and musical sense to the singers, not appear to be a multitude of consecutive notes, words, and measures. Bar lines in *their music* will greatly aid this.

Place a new Roman numeral at the beginning of each new long phrase. Then write I-A, II-C, III-B and so on, at the beginning of each short phrase. Refer to the Roman numerals to indicate starting places, for example, "Today we will begin at Roman numeral V." It is both educational and productive to rehearse from a structural perspective.

Plan, in advance, the specific section or phrases you will rehearse each day. Accomplish the learning of complete musical ideas. Don't stop the rehearsal on a given song in the middle of a section or phrase. That is frustrating for the singers. Allow them to feel a sense of completion about that which they have just rehearsed—a complete musical thought or phrase.

Sing without the conductor.   Once the chorus is well on its way to knowing a song, have the chorus members all turn to the center, as though there were a microphone directly centered above the back row of the ensemble. (No one is now facing the conductor; the left side of the chorus faces the right side, and so on.) Ask them to sing the phrase, section, or entire song as though they were a chamber ensemble without conductor. Do not yield to the temptation to conduct. Just listen, interrupting as frequently as needed to teach or re-teach anything.

They are to focus their eye direction toward the imaginary microphone and *each other*. They *sensitively* become a *team*. Each person feels *leadership* (physically, mentally, and emotionally) as though it were his own responsibility to lead. Each singer minimally moves his or her music—as though each one were conducting.

They sing through every interpretive nuance that has been taught: ritards, accellerandi, tenuti, fermati, without conductor. They *can* do it. And when they do, they will gain a feeling of great security and confidence. If they can do it well *alone*, think how great it will be with our *artistic conducting*.

Rehearse only those passages that need it.   Refrain from going back to the beginning for no apparent reason. Don't stop the chorus, then start them again without teaching something of substance! The singers deserve to know *why* they are doing what they are doing. Without that information, they will make little or no progress, and become bored. Furthermore, we don't *always* have to start at the beginning when starting to work on a piece. Begin where it makes good sense, based on what is needed.

Practice moving into tricky spots called "seams" or "lead-ins."   Although it is important not to *overrehearse* the *simpler passages* while practicing the tougher sections, it is critical that an ensemble knows how to get *into* a tricky passage. Many times an ensemble will perfect the execution of a difficult passage only to foul it up when they approach it in the context of the piece as a whole. It is always easier to master a tough section when you start right on it; it is often a different story when approaching it from a few bars back. This concept also applies to rehearsing rhythms, pitches, and difficult text. Make sure you and the chorus are completely secure with the "seams" between musical ideas (tempo, meter, key and rhythmic changes).

Insist on accuracy.   When something is sung inaccurately or improperly, stop *immediately*, correct it, then go back to the nearest logical spot (bar line) and continue. If, for familiarity's sake, you want to go back further, do so, but explain why. Do not go over and over segments that are already sung well. This leads to extreme boredom of the singers. Focus your attention and time only on those phrases that still need work.

Correct one thing at a time.   Do not mention *several* potential mistakes that *might* arise. That insults the chorus. Begin. Let them sing. When the first mistake is made, *stop and correct it.* Don't sing through several mistakes, finally stopping in an effort to correct them all. The singers' attention can best retain one thing at a time. Furthermore, if you allow them to continue after having made mistakes, they subconsciously think it's okay to make them or they think you didn't hear or care about them.

Do, however, give advance warning for potential "disasters."   Although we don't want to insinuate that the chorus will make mistakes, we might want to pre-work a portion of the music that we know will not make it the first time through. Go to that spot, in advance, and work it out carefully and slowly. Clap or speak difficult rhythms, then sing them. Teach difficult intervals. Do what is needed, then go back and progress through this same portion with *first-time success.* If you head straight into it without this pre-work, it could be a disastrous failed attempt about which they might *always* feel insecure, even after they have learned it. Their minds will always see it as a potential failure.

Keep the rehearsal pace going lightning-fast!   Keep up the pace. I cannot over-estimate the value of a fast rehearsal pace. The conductor must be so mentally alert, completely knowledgeable about both the music and vocal techniques, and positively spirited *about it all* that he or she can produce a quick and continuous flow of teaching that will result in *motivated singers producing great results quickly, continuously, and effectively*!

If the chorus and accompanist can *comfortably* keep up, they're probably bored. The pace should not be chaotic or confusing, which is frustrating and unproductive, but it should be very, very fast. The musicians should have to work and concentrate to keep their brains alive and to keep up with us!

Instruct the accompanist.   The accompanist should be told that he or she must always be *thinking ahead* regarding where it is that the conductor might start again after we've stopped to teach or correct something. I rely on the pianist more than some conductors do, but I want the pitches given, from the bottom up, at almost the same moment that I'm telling the chorus where to begin again. No wasted time, and no bad starts that have to be re-done. If I stop four times for the same point, I want the pitches given quickly and solidly each time.

Keep your eyes in their eyes.   Except for early rehearsals, which consist mainly of note learning, keep your head out of the music and communicate personally with the individuals in the chorus. This is essential for all conducting, but especially for choral ensembles. Singers, because of longer preparation time, often have their eyes up, looking at the conductor more than instrumentalists, who have less rehearsal time. Singers expect (and need) to have the conductor also inspiringly looking at them and fully communicating the music to be sung. We must also readily admit that, the more the conductor looks at the performers, the more they respond by watching the conductor and the more responsive they are to the demands of the music and the expectations of the conductor. Look at them. Inspire them!

Memorize while learning the music.   If the chorus is to memorize the music, help them during the *learning process* by frequently asking them to sing *a structural phrase or section* from memory. Don't wait until it is completely learned to begin the memorization process. By the time it is completely polished, it can also be completely memorized. If the chorus sings from memory, conduct from memory. Do not, however, take a chance at making mistakes, thereby causing errors in the performance, by conducting from memory. If, however, we have done our score analysis before the first rehearsal, we should be able to memorize it solidly while the chorus learns and memorizes it. (If the chorus uses music, the conductor may use music, but must be looking up 95 percent of the time.)

Employ vocalizing warm-ups and full-body movement.   Begin every rehearsal with effectively planned warming-up vocal exercises. Teach voice! And remember that the entire body is the vocal instrument. The entire body sings. *The more the body is involved, the better the vocal output will be.* Robert Fountain—conductor of the great Oberlin College Choir of the 1950s and 1960s, later at the University of Wisconsin in the 1970s and 1980s—placed great emphasis on movement by the singers while they are learning a choral composition. They would dance, march, swing, sway, skip, and jump. They did whatever seemed and felt appropriate for the music to be fully expressed by the complete body. Then, when it came time to actually perform the composition, the movements would imaginatively take place *within* the body, which continued to bring the music to life. The whole system of Jaques Dalcroze eurhythmics is a wonderful source for the exploration of this area. Singers, by the way, can employ movement even while sitting. Standing gives them more options, but they can also move sideways, front and back, and in and out of phrases while seated. Slight, minimal movement is also appropriate in performance. Singers are people, not mannequins.

Don't conduct the accompanist or soloist.   Qualified accompanists do not need to be conducted during long introductions, interludes, or final keyboard endings. If it is necessary, begin and end the section or phrase with them, but it looks quite silly for a conductor to be conducting one person, and quite frankly, we're just not needed. Accompanists know how it should be played. They've been doing it, over and over, during weeks of rehearsals. Short introductions, interludes, and endings may, of course, be the exception to this. Don't conduct soloists. They don't need it. If they do, they shouldn't be singing a solo. Exceptions would include specific instances in which communication between soloist and conductor would ensure greater success in potentially problematic passages when an orchestral accompaniment is used. These situations would be predetermined.

Be businesslike.   Although the atmosphere of a rehearsal needs to be positive, cheerful, and friendly, it also needs to be dignified and business-like. This is not an informal gathering of music-makers getting together for fun. It is a very serious artistic endeavor, from which great accomplishments are expected. The fun and fulfillment of a rehearsal or concert come through great accomplishments and the realization of the artistic potential of each singer or player. To achieve all this takes a lot of very hard work, concentration, and technical progress. It is a business! Be dignified. Be professional. Be the *conductor!*

Employ special techniques for learning difficult music.   Sit or stand in section circles. It is extremely productive to have each section sit or stand in a well-spaced circle, to reinforce group strength and effort regarding sight-reading, accuracy, tone quality, phrasing and individual assertiveness. That is, a circle of sopranos, a circle of altos, a circle of tenors, and a circle of basses. The room might be set up this way in advance of the rehearsal, or the singers can be asked to "go to circles" (standing) spontaneously at any time during the rehearsal, for five to ten minutes for a difficult section (or for as long as twenty to thirty minutes). If longer than that will be necessary, the chairs should be set in circles before the beginning of the rehearsal for the comfort of the singers.

When singing in circles, the singer's work is reinforced, not only on either side, but also from every direction across from the singer. It's as though everything that happens within the section comes to the center of the circle, then like a fountain, is dispersed out over all the singers, so that each gains from the others' contributions.

In general, it is counterproductive to ask singers to stand throughout an entire rehearsal. In choruses that do, you usually see singers begin to falter physically toward the end of the rehearsal. Their posture and energy begin to fade noticeably. To stand occasionally, however, is very refreshing for the singers.

Sing musically on natural syllables.   Sing on a neutral syllable such as "doo-doo-doo" (with a soft, non-percussive d) or "lah-lah-lah." Relieve the singers' minds from concerns of text, allowing them to focus completely on the fundamental accuracy of the pitches and rhythms and phrasing. *Teach phrasing immediately, right along with pitch and rhythmic accuracy.* To do otherwise will necessitate re-learning mechanical, meaningless notes and rhythms later to transform them into musicality. Do it in this beginning process so we can firmly establish the following concept: We shall never sing consecutive notes, words or syllables in an unmusical, mechanical or meaningless manner. Remember the major concept of rhythmic interest, forward motion, and phrasing: *We shall never sing consecutive notes, words, or syllables with equal emphasis.*

Sing quietly.   Sing no louder than *mp–mf* while learning a new song. Why waste the singer's vocal strength on music that is not yet known? In addition, the softer singing will allow both singers and conductor to hear more effectively the degree of accuracy with which the piece is being sung.

Sing slowly.   Sing slowly enough that the singers (and you) can easily hear that which is being sung, giving them a much better chance of success with difficult passages. Do not be in a hurry to learn the music. Take the time to thoroughly learn it, allowing the process to be as comfortable as possible.

Use "count-singing" to solidify rhythmic togetherness.   Rather than using words, or the neutral syllables (doo and lah) recommended earlier, we can use the numbers indicated in the time signature. That is, if the song is in three, sing "one-and-two-and-three-and," repeatedly throughout a phrase, section, or entire piece. If the song is in four, it would be "one-and-two-and-three-and-four-and."

When a rest appears in the music, there is silence. Do not continue counting through rests. The chorus sings the melody, as written in their part, but they continuously sing the numbers instead of words or other sounds. This process can be very effective in tightening up rhythms and lining up other ensemble problems. It can also become monotonous, and boring if used more frequently than necessary.

Speak or clap difficult rhythms.   Don't proceed into a "train wreck." Stop before it happens. Slowly and calmly clap or speak difficult rhythms until they are secure. Then, slowly and quietly sing them. Then gradually sing them faster. Finally, you will be up to tempo and at the appropriate dynamic level.

Have the entire chorus sing one part.   If one section needs considerable work on its part alone, have all the women, all the men, or the entire chorus sing with them to strengthen the learning process with additional security and confidence. This is especially helpful for small sections. In addition to helping with extra confidence, it keeps the others in the chorus actively involved and gives them an opportunity to work on sight-reading.

Have a higher section demonstrate high parts for a lower section. Use the next section higher to give vocal examples of high passages to those of a lower vocal category. For example, if the altos seem to be struggling to sing a high passage well, have the sopranos demonstrate for them. Then, have all women sing it with similar focus. Finally have the altos sing it alone with the quality they have just "grown into." We can work similarly using altos with tenors, and tenors with basses. (Sopranos will just have to imagine an angel chorus.)

Also feel free to use portions of the next section higher to reinforce the strength of a high passage of a lower section. That is, a number of second sopranos can be assigned to help the alto section when their part calls for a few higher notes, second altos can help the tenors in similar situations, and some tenors (if you have any to spare) can help basses when needed.

Have sections help each other. Make consistent use of sections helping each other to maintain strength throughout a composition. If a composer writes several measures for altos only, use all women. By the same token, if a phrase is written for tenors only, consider using tenors, baritones, and altos, or, if written for basses only, use all men.

Most choruses would sound better by employing this procedure. Put yourself in the place of the audience or congregation, and you'll immediately know that, in most cases, this would more positively affect the listeners than the way it was originally written. Let it be the rule, rather than the exception. I often say, "no one in my chorus does nothing; if there is nothing written for them, they're helping someone else." That, of course, is an overstatement. I, however, do employ the concept very often.

Sitting and Standing Arrangements

Sitting and standing arrangements vary depending on the strengths and weaknesses of the chorus, the style of the music, and the conductor's preferences. Conductors' preferences will vary from one extreme to another, with one giving great attention to many important details, and another allowing the singers to sit anywhere they please. Most conductors find themselves somewhere in between. Use the following considerations when determining the placement of singers within an ensemble.

Arrangement Considerations

Height. The first consideration is the singer's height. Singers cannot function well if they cannot see the conductor or be seen by the conductor. Therefore, it goes without saying that the chorus should be seated with the shortest singers in the front, gradually working toward the back with the taller singers. This is also more pleasing visually for the audience.

One way to arrange them quickly and effectively, if height is the only (or first) criterion by which the formation is to be set, is the following: have each section line up according to height with the shortest person in the front of each line, and the tallest at the back. Then have them fill in the designated area assigned to their section, row by row, beginning with row one. Reverse the procedure if you wish to begin with the taller singers in the back row. If any of your sections are singing in duets (sa, sa, sa, sa or sb, sb, sb, sb etc.), have them enter in pairs, with the same procedure. I have used this method dozens of times for festival and all-state choruses, and even with my own choruses. It's efficient and can be very effective done quickly.

Strengths and weaknesses.   Place opposites next to each other. That is, strong readers next to weaker ones, bigger voices next to smaller ones, experienced singers next to inexperienced ones, wider vibratos next to straighter voices, and so on. These opposites tend to help each other in positive, productive ways. When possible, seat singers with those with whom they will enjoy singing. We cannot always work out all these criteria compatibly but we can try.

Voices that compliment each other.   Weston Noble (Luther College, Decorah, Iowa) has developed a remarkable system for testing or comparing singers within a section. He listens to them sing with other individuals of the section to determine which singers they feel and sound best or most comfortable with. He has them sing with a variety of other singers and has them change from one side to the other (the singer's left and right). He will ask them for their preference regarding this. He then determines which singer sounds best with another and on which side they should be placed. I've seen and heard it. It works. This is just another valid option (though quite complex and time-consuming) for the conductor to consider when making decisions regarding seating the chorus.

Intonation.   Keeping the sopranos and basses near each other, to aid in keeping the melody and harmonic foundation in tune, is a definite advantage to intonation overall. In addition, keeping the inner voices, altos and tenors, together similarly helps intonation (and is an advantage when altos may be helping the tenors with singing *occasional* high passages).

Section strength.   If smaller sections, such as tenors and occasionally basses, need to be blocked together for supportive strength, place them in the center, singing straight out toward the audience.

Spacing.   The smaller the group, the more space is possible between singers. Don't place more than one row of singers on a flat floor-level area. Elevating the back rows greatly enhances both sight and sound.

For example, an ensemble of sixteen, in two rows of eight, will look and sound much better with the back row elevated. It might be even better if they stood in three rows: five, six, and five, with sixteen to twenty-four inches between singers.

An ensemble of twenty-four would do well in three rows of eight, with the same generous spacing.

This all falls under the category of "soloistic ensemble singing." Be confident in your singers; they can do it. They don't need to be placed close together to succeed. Let them perform (collectively) as individual artists.

With larger groups, *use all the risers*, really spreading the singers out as much as possible to make a professional appearance and presentation. Give the singers the challenge, the confidence, and the freedom to *truly perform*. Professional soloists in a Beethoven *Missa Solemnes* quartet do not stand shoulder to shoulder. They have performing space and the freedom to really present themselves and their music. Let's give our choral singers the same consideration and opportunity.

Various Arrangements

As we discuss the various diagrams, remember that we need to let the chorus and the music be determining factors in our choice. Often, it may be appropriate to change standing formations during a concert of general song repertoire.

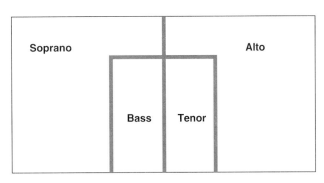

Figure 9.1

More women than men. Figure 9.1 shows a situation in which there are considerably more woman than men. Place the men in front, where they can be heard well by both the audience and the conductor. With young singers, it is especially important to have the boys within close proximity of the conductor/teacher. Keep the basses next to the sopranos, and tenors near the altos. This helps to keep the sopranos melodic intonation in tune with the basses' harmonic foundation. It also helps to unify the inner voices of tenors and altos.

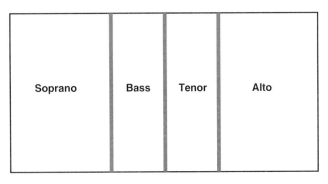

Figure 9.2

Better balance of men and women. The set-up in Figure 9.2 is a progression from that in Figure 9.1, in that there are now more men involved in singing. We will continue to keep them in the middle so they will be more easily heard. In less advanced ensembles, we don't want the men in back, where they are at a disadvantageous distance from the conductor. Columns are often effective because a portion of each section is directly under the watchful and inspiring eye of the conductor and they are singing straight down into the heads (and minds) of their fellow section members.

Large choruses performing with orchestras. The arrangement shown in Figure 9.3, in columns, is ideal for large choruses that perform with orchestras. This places the sopranos in the conductor's eyesight-line with the first violins, the altos with the second violins, tenors with the violas, and the basses with the

| Soprano | Alto | Tenor | Bass |

Figure 9.3

celli and basses. This set-up is also very effective in festival situations with large choruses. Each section is singing straight down the heads of their section-mates, reinforcing each other's efforts, and again, a portion of each section is close to the conductor.

Men behind women. The arrangement in Figure 9.4 is for those conductors who want to have the men behind the women. It is, by far, the most attractive arrangement, because the audience views all the women together (in the front rows) in their concert dresses, and all the men (across the back rows) dressed in their tuxedos. This uniformity has a professional appearance. In addition, the chorus is more effectively able to hear each other in this arrangement than they can in columns. Basses would be behind sopranos, and tenors behind altos, for "listening" reasons previously mentioned.

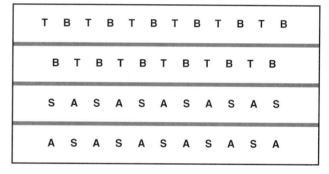

| Bass | Tenor |
| Soprano | Alto |

Figure 9.4

Semi-scrambled formation. Figure 9.5 shows a semi-scrambled arrangement for the conductor who wants a scrambled sound (and wants the chorus to experience the joy of singing independently, which comes with singing in a scrambled formation) without negating the visual beauty of the chorus that I mentioned in Figure 9.4. The men are scrambled, but stay in the same rows, and the women do the same thing.

```
T B T B T B T B T B T B
  B T B T B T B T B T B
S A S A S A S A S A S
  A S A S A S A S A S A
```

Figure 9.5

Fully scrambled formation. Figure 9.6 shows a fully scrambled formation, for advanced ensembles, in which the chorus sings in quartets. Notice, however, that I have placed the quartet members in such a way that sopranos are always standing next to basses, and altos are next to tenors (for reasons mentioned in the discussion of Figure 9.1). This is extremely fulfilling for the singers and builds great individual security within each one. This is not ideal for music written with major section entrances that need to speak out clearly, but when appropriate, the homogeneous sound is absolutely beautiful.

When cueing scrambled arrangements, cue straight ahead, or to the entire chorus; those that need the cue

```
S B A T S B A T S B
  B A T S B A T S B A
  A T S B A T S B A T
  T S B A T S B A T S
```

Figure 9.6

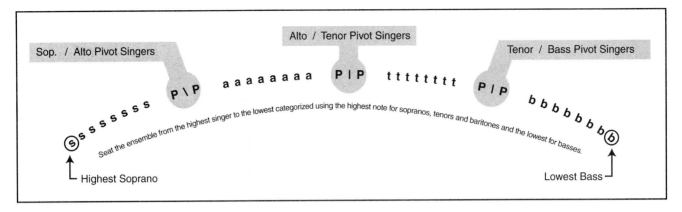

Figure 9.7

will take it without a problem. Some conductors find it effective to continue to cue the area where the sections used to be when in block arrangements, but this could be confusing to singers.

Chamber ensembles. Figure 9.7 shows an arrangement for chamber ensembles of sixteen to thirty-two singers. The highest soprano is on the conductor's extreme left. The lowest bass is on the extreme right. The entire ensemble is seated from the highest singer to the lowest, with each singer categorized by his or her highest (or lowest) note of quality.

This formation is for use while the chorus is learning the mechanics of the songs, rather than for the final refining or performing. The conductor stands directly out in front of the center of the semi-circle, at the most advantageous spot to effectively hear the ensemble. The piano is placed *behind* the conductor, and to his or her left. It is there when needed, but not a distraction to the conductor's focus on listening to the singers. Robert Shaw occasionally used this arrangement during beginning rehearsals of his chorale.

This semi-circle also shows the placement of "pivot singers." Those are singers who often help strengthen another section. That is, the highest baritones will frequently sing tenor when the part descends and needs extra support, tenors do likewise for the higher passages of the bass section, pivot altos help in higher tenor passages, and so on, throughout the chorus. This maintains uniform strength of sound in the melodic line of each part throughout an entire composition. Robert Shaw usually stopped to give the directive; other times, he simply motioned to the singers he wanted to pivot, then later motioned them back to their own parts again, all without stopping the rehearsal. The pivot-concept could be advantageous to any chorus on most compositions. Try it. Assign as many pivots as needed.

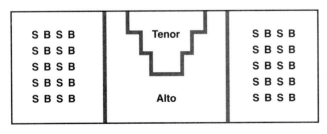

Figure 9.8

More sopranos and basses. The formation shown in Figure 9.8 can be used if there are more sopranos and basses than altos and tenors in the chorus. This formation "diffuses" the soprano and bass sounds, keeps them together for intonation purposes, and projects the altos and tenors. (I used it with the Eastman School of Music Chorale for the recording of Alfred Mann's edition of Handel's *Messiah.*)

More women than men. This (Figure 9.9) is somewhat similar to that shown in Figure 9.8, but in this situation, there are more women than men in the chorus. It is appropriate for choruses that are more advanced than those in Figures 9.1 and 9.2. The sound of the women is diffused, and seating them in duets enhances the soprano tone. The men's sound in strengthened by being centered and seated in a block formation. It works very well.

S A S A			S A S A
S A S A			S A S A
S A S A	Bass	Tenor	S A S A
S A S A			S A S A
S A S A			S A S A

Figure 9.9

Rehearsal Planning

There is an old saying that goes something like, "Any road is sufficient for the person who doesn't know where he's going." This is particularly applicable to conductors when it comes to the *organization* (or lack of it) regarding *rehearsals*. We need two kinds of plans:

- A minute-by-minute plan for each rehearsal and
- A long-range plan that successfully takes us from the first rehearsal to the concert

If I could offer you a system of rehearsal planning that would absolutely guarantee well-prepared concerts, would you want it? Of course you would. That's exactly what we will discuss. Thorough preparation consists of (1) knowing what it will take to sufficiently prepare a concert, and (2) always knowing whether or not we're on our chartered course toward its successful completion.

We will create a hypothetical situation in which we are planning for a high school chorus to rehearse for a seasonal holiday concert. This will help you frame your thinking when the time comes to plan your own series of rehearsals for a concert.

The Facts

1. The concert will feature several ensembles in addition to the chorus, thereby allowing the chorus to present only six songs.

2. The chorus is capable of completely learning approximately one song per week.

3. Based on my knowledge of the chorus's sight-reading ability and vocal proficiency, I will select two *easy* songs, two *medium* songs, and two *difficult* songs.

4. The chorus rehearses 50 minutes daily.

5. Each rehearsal begins with approximately 12 minutes of vocalizing warm-ups and business details, leaving 38 minutes of actual song-rehearsing time available each day.

The Strategy

1. Thirty-eight minutes multiplied by five days per week and six weeks equals a total of 1,140 minutes for the rehearsing of these six songs. That equals 190 minutes per song.

2. Subtract one-fourth of that total *from the easy songs* and add it to the *difficult ones*. This results in the two easy songs getting approximately 142 minutes each, the medium songs will receive the original 190 minutes each, and the two difficult songs now receive approximately 237 minutes each.

3. I will now evaluate each song very carefully to establish firmly that it can be learned in the allotted time. If not, I will simply change the problematic selection(s) or reduce the program by one song, doing five instead of six. I will proceed with the original plan of six only if it seems reasonable to do so. It does.

4. The concert is Saturday, December 18, so we begin the six-week preparation period Wednesday, November 3 (because there will be three days vacation during November 24, 25 and 26). The total number of rehearsal days is 30.

5. Now, I will create a grid outlining a minute-by-minute schedule for the *allotted time of each song* (see Figure 9.10). The songs will be placed in an order based solely on contrasting easy songs with the more difficult. The number of minutes per song, on any given day, will be determined by my expectation of productivity. (In this hypothetical situation, however, pay no attention whatsoever to the actual number of minutes assigned to these imaginary songs. They are meaningless. Only the *principle of the concept* is of any significance here.)

6. It might be productive to duplicate and distribute the schedule to the singers. This will enable them to know in advance what is planned and to know that we do *have a plan*. It will also be a source of information to let them know what they missed should they be absent. In addition, if I need to be absent, my assistant conductor will know exactly what is to be rehearsed in my absence.

Figure 9.10

	W	Th	F	M	T	W	Th	F	M	T	W	Th	F	M	T	M	T	W	Th	F	M	T	W	Th	F	M	T	W	Th	F
	3	4	5	8	9	10	11	12	15	16	17	18	19	22	23	29	30	1	2	3	6	7	8	9	10	13	14	15	16	17
Song "A" Easy	18	18	18		8	8			8	4		3		3	6		6		7	4	7	8		5		5		3	3	
Song "B" Easy							10	20	20	15	10	4	8	8	3		4		6		7	6	7		4		4		3	3
Song "C" Med				15	24	18	18	10	10	10		6		10	8	8			10				10	7	10			12	5	5
Song "D" Med											28	28	15	20	14		15	20	10				10		10		10		5	5
Song "E" Diff	20	20	20	23	6	12	10	8		9			12		10	9	8		8			10		10		10			10	10
Song "F" Diff																15	26	17	14	11	17	15	13	18	22	8	29	16	12	12

Assistant Conductor

Having an assistant conductor is very important. This will make it possible for continuity and progress in the conductor's absence. It will also help make sectional rehearsals possible. In high school when the conductor is absent, a substitute teacher can help with *class order* while the student assistant does the *conducting and teaching*.

We can almost always find a musically gifted and trained student who, with special private tutoring from us, can become a very fine assistant conductor. With our admonition for the chorus to select a fellow singer possessing maturity, musicianship, and leadership qualities, let chorus members *nominate* several potential assistant conductors. Observe each one conducting a song the chorus already knows, and then make your selection from these nominations. This greatly helps the conductor and might start some young student on his or her way to a wonderful life in the field of choral music!

Ongoing Evaluation

Using a chart similar to the one shown in Figure 9.10, I can evaluate my preparation progress, at any time, to see if I am successfully staying on my chartered course. I can review the number of minutes spent on preparation of a given piece, evaluate its progress, and determine whether or not the remaining allotted time is sufficient to complete solid preparation. If the answer is "yes," I continue as planned. If the answer is "no," I must alter the plan by

- Omitting a song that I have not started
- Scheduling some sectional rehearsals to catch up
- Scheduling an extra rehearsal some evening or weekend for the same purpose of getting back on schedule

The last option is inadvisable because of the considerable inconvenience to the singers. The second alternative is good, if there is extra rehearsal space, and a second conductor and accompanist are available. The first choice may be the most practical. The audience doesn't know six songs were planned so the deleted one won't be missed.

In such decisions, be careful not to become emotionally involved with any "favorite songs." Always have an objective frame of mind regarding the deletion of any one of them at any time.

The deletion of a song means that I will select one that *has not been started* and take it off the program. I don't mean to imply that if a song seems to be lagging behind I would automatically delete it. Valuable time has been spent on it. Continue with it. By omitting another one that hasn't been started (preferably one from the "difficult" category), I now have 237 additional minutes with which to work.

In our hypothetical situation, the most important evaluation will be at the end of the rehearsal, Tuesday, November 23, before vacation and the beginning of difficult song "F." If any song needs more time than has been allotted, now is the time to eliminate song "F," releasing slightly over 237 extra minutes (and bringing a lot of peace of mind).

By the same token, if my progress analysis shows that I am actually ahead of schedule (very rare), I can consider adding an extra easy song to the program, which would then total seven.

The point is that I will always know where I am in the preparation process. I will never have to worry or wonder about it. The chorus will be well prepared. That's a guarantee if I stick to the schedule, re-evaluate frequently, and adjust when necessary.

Rehearsals with Orchestra

The same process applies when rehearsing an instrumental ensemble. Divide the songs into easy/short, medium, and difficult/long. Divide the total minutes by three and then take a fourth of the time from the easier solos and add it to the more difficult ones as we did before. We can further adjust the individual time-assignments based on *extremely* easy/short and *extremely* difficult/long, taking from one and adding to the other (see Figure 9.11). In this case (with orchestra), we *must absolutely stay on schedule*, or we will not complete the rehearsal. The orchestra will not stay overtime because of our lack of planning. The same procedures apply for chorus and orchestra, and dress rehearsals. We must become very proficient at rehearsal planning, pacing, awareness, and moment-by-moment evaluation.

Stay on schedule and give the printed schedule to those involved. This rehearsal schedule for orchestra and soloists will ensure you cover all the material to be rehearsed, *as long as you stay on schedule*. If the allotted time is up, and you are not finished with a particular song, stop and go on to the next one (unless you have only a few seconds left to rehearse). In such a case, plan a few extra moments in the next, or final rehearsal, to briefly go over the part not done in the previous one. The main point: rehearse economically and productively, and *don't go over the time allotted for any given number* unless you know you can make it up in the one that follows.

Place a copy of the rehearsal schedule on each music stand in the orchestra. You will start with full orchestra forces first, then size-down the orchestra as you proceed, indicating when they will be excused. They will be extremely appreciative of your organization and consideration of their time.

Also, give a copy to the soloists in advance. They will appreciate knowing when they can expect to rehearse, when they can rest, and when they will be through and can leave. Try to space out the solo numbers so one singer does not rehearse several demanding solos in a row. Sometimes this is difficult to do while gradually reducing the orchestra for their convenience. Both groups must make occasional compromises. This is all determined by a conductor who must be well organized and considerate of the singers and players involved.

Send soloists your tempo markings for the arias, duets, trios, and quartets well in advance. Explain that one of a conductor's main responsibilities is to unify the overall performance. State clearly that you expect them to be prepared at the indicated tempi. If this is impossible or uncomfortable for them, they should contact you immediately to discuss the tempi in question. Remember, although flexible, the conductor is in charge.

Make a similar schedule for rehearsals of *chorus and orchestra,* and make copies available to all concerned. In rehearsal with chorus and orchestra, give the chorus a

Figure 9.11

Rehearsal schedule

Time	No.	Voice	Orchestration	Dismissal
7:00			(Orch. Tune)	
7:03	1*	Orch.	Full	
7:10	2*	B–T	Full	
7:15	3*	Tenor	No Cl., Trp., & Timp	
7:22	5*	Sop.	Full	
7:27	14*	Trio	Full	
7:35	27-B*	Orch.	Full	
7:42	33*	SATB	Full	(+ Alto)
7:49	11*	Orch.	Full	
7:55	13*	Tenor	No Cl. & Tromb.	
8:03	9	Sop.	No Ob., Trp., Tromb., & Timp	
8:12			BREAK – 15 MINUTES	
8:27	23*	Bass	N. Cl. & Tromb.	
8:37	16	Sop.	No Ob., Trp., Tromb., & Timp	
8:46	20*	Trio	No Cl.	
8:51	4	Bass	Strings + W.W. & Timp.	Trp./Tromb. leave
8:58	27-A	Trio	No Trp., Tromb., & Timp.	Timp. leave
9:04	7*	Bass	No Cl., Trp., Tromb., & Timp.	Cl. leave
9:16	28	Tenor	No Cl., Trp., Tromb., & Timp.	(+ Fl. III)
9:24	19	Trio	No Cl., Trp., Tromb., & Timp.	
9:32			BREAK – 15 MINUTES	Hns./Tenor lv.
9:39	29	S–B	Strings + Fl., Ob., & Bsn., **	
9:43	22*	Bass	Strings + Fl. * & Bsns.**	Ob./Fl II leave
9:51	15	Sop.	Strings only	Winds leave
9:55	17	Bass	Va., Vc., & Bass only	Violins leave
10:00			(END)	

* Contra bassoon plays on these nos.

** Trombone or Timpani are minimal, and not needed for this rehearsal.

rest by interspersing any numbers that the orchestra might play on their own, such as the overture or interlude material. In addition, alternate heavy demanding choruses with lighter, shorter ones. (Figure 9.11 is for Haydn's *The Creation*.)

Chorus Auditions

Auditioning is very serious business for two reasons: first, people's lives are very often directly affected by whether or not they are accepted into a chorus, and second, decisions to accept or reject singers will, in large part, determine the quality and success of the ensemble. These two items make auditioning a very important responsibility for the conductor.

Singers cannot audition at their best if the conductor holding the auditions intimidates them. Therefore, we must put people at ease when they enter to audition. Be friendly. Be appreciative that the person desires to audition for and participate in the ensemble. Be helpful and encouraging during the audition. Auditioning is not enjoyable for most singers. For many, it is a dreaded, nervous situation, especially if it involves sight-reading.

Phases of the Audition Process

Auditions usually consist of vocalizing to determine range and quality, sight reading to determine musicianship, and a solo to determine performance ability.

Vocalizing

- When vocalizing, select relatively easy exercises, so the singer can do them as well as possible. 1-3-**5**-3-1, 1-3-5-**8**-5-3-1, and a 5-tone scale passage (1234**5**4321) are all effective for auditions. Hold the highest note an extra beat so you can actually hear the person sing on that note for a moment.

- Begin altos and basses in C major, taking them eventually up a high E♭, E, or F. Begin sopranos and tenors in D or E♭ major, taking them eventually up to high A♭, A or B♭. Use a moderate tempo. (If the ensemble is advanced, and the competition is keen, you might add a nine-tone scale to further check flexibility, especially for sopranos).

- Determine the singers' vocal category by the *highest note they can comfortably sustain* at a *mp* to *mf* dynamic level. SI: high A or B♭; SII: G or A♭; AI: F, F♯, or G; AII: E♭ or E; TI: A or B♭; TII: G or A♭; BI: E, F, or F♯; BII: D, E♭, or E. Finer ensembles of greater maturity would dictate the higher notes. Bass II's are often determined by the quality of their lowest notes, which is not so often true for Alto I and II, who may have a very similar low range.

Sight-reading

- Select sight-reading material that is practical and not overwhelming. Few things are as difficult as sight-reading under pressure. If the singer is too nervous to do his or her best, the conductor has no way of knowing how proficient he or she might be—in which case, the audition process was a failure for everyone concerned. Make it as positive an experience as possible. The purpose is not to intimidate and demoralize singers but, rather, to discover new talent, or potentially reestablish the ability of former singers.

- Compose singable melodies of moderate challenge for the auditioning process. Incorporate a reasonably extended upper range and sensible rhythmic patterns (dotted rhythms, triplets, sixteenth notes, and so forth). There should not be anything impossible for decently trained singers. In addition, as they sing, play the melody, very quietly, without leading the singer. Tell them that you will do that, but also impress on them that they are to do the leading. They will be immediately relieved. It is easy to tell if they are confidently leading, or insecurely following. Frequently ask them to repeat it. Similar mistakes are very revealing. Help them do their very best. If they don't, it is impossible to tell how good they might have been. The more professional the ensemble is, the more difficult the audition will be. It still, however, should be reasonable.

Typical sight-reading melodies

Example 9.1

Example 9.2

Example 9.3

Example 9.4

Solo Performance

Those who want to sing in a community or symphony chorus or gain a paid position in any chorus should sing a solo in audition. We can obviously know the vocal abilities more thoroughly by hearing at least one solo. In university situations, with sometimes as many as 200–500 auditioning, there is no time for solos; most of the non-music majors wouldn't have one prepared anyway, and might be scared-off from even showing up. Much fine talent could be lost. The same consideration applies to volunteer church choirs, and, of course, school choruses. If solos are expected, be sure to have a professional accompanist available. The singers deserve the best!

Conductors should carry out the audition process in the manner most productive for them and their situation. *But, again, it should be done in a manner that is comfortable for the singer.* Be as concerned for their well being as you are for your ensemble. When you must reject a singer, be sure he or she knows that you appreciated the interest and effort extended. We can never take prospective singers for granted, whether we accept them or not. Be prepared to explain the reasons for rejection, should you be asked. They have a right to ask, and a right to know.

Sample Audition Forms

Sample audition forms appear in Figures 9.12 through 9.15. The first page (Figures 9.12 and 9.14) is to be filled in by the singer, the second by the conductor. Two sets shown here, one for a university situation and one for church or community choruses. The information asked for on the first side of the audition form is of great importance, especially previous choral experience, vocal instruction, and instruments studied (which tells much about musicianship). The blank rectangle in the upper-right corner of the first page is for the conductor to place his or her ranking of the applicant immediately after the audition, based on the standards of the past year(s).

On the reverse side of the form (Figures 9.13 and 9.15) are many categories that could be observed about a vocal performance in an audition. It's important to be able to indicate reactions very quickly, so you do not delay the audition process of others. Many of these specifics have been printed out here so they can be simply checked off or circled, leaving less writing to be done. Do, however, take the time to write details that will be valuable later, when you are making final decisions.

A number is assigned to each singer (in the rectangular box in the upper-right corner of the first page), indicating that singer's placement, at that time, compared with the qualities of singers of the previous year. That is, if the singer is just barely good enough to have qualified last year, the singer receives a number 1. Better than that would be 1 +, 1 + +, 1 + + +, and so on. To compare with the *very best* of last year, the singer would receive a 1 + + + +. If the singer is truly phenomenal, that is professional soloistic level, a 1 + + + + +. Singers who are less than acceptable according to last year's standards will be assigned numbers such as 1-, 2, 2-, 3, 3-, 4. The classification of 4 or 5 would be for someone who couldn't read music at all, or was extremely weak vocally, and therefore

Figure 9.12

UCLA CHORAL AUDITION
Donald Neuen, Conductor

PLEASE PRINT CLEARLY

NAME_____ DATE_____

CLASS: Fr.   Soph.   Jr.   Sr.   MA   DMA   PHD   HEIGHT_____   VOICE PART SI, SII, AI, AII
(Please Circle) **TI, TII, BI, BII**

DEGREE PROGRAM AND MAJOR_____   _____

SCHOOL ADDRESS_____   PHONE (   )_____

_____   _____ZIP _____ STUDENT I. D. #_____

TRANSFER AND GRADUATE STUDENTS: SCHOOLS PREVIOUSLY ATTENDED AND DEGREES EARNED

_____

_____

UCLA CHORAL EXPERIENCE   ☐UCLA CHORALE, ☐CHAMBER SINGERS, ☐UNIVERSITY CHORUS

OTHER MAJOR CHORAL EXPERIENCE_____

_____

PRIVATE VOCAL STUDY: (Number of years, and name of <u>present</u> teacher) _____

_____

MAJOR SOLO VOCAL EXPERIENCE_____

_____

DICTION PROFICIENCY (i.e. languages in which you have competent pronunciation):

Latin_____   Italian_____   German_____   French_____

OTHER FOREIGN LANGUAGES_____

INSTRUMENTS YOU HAVE STUDIED: _____ (Studied for _____ years)

_____(Studied for _____years)

OTHER COMMENTS_____

_____

totally unacceptable even in a "second chorus." Place the number assignments immediately upon completion of each individual audition. This is your *spontaneous ranking.*

When it is time to make the decisions, take the best of those who auditioned based on this ranking system together with considerations based on the indications and comments. If for example, competition is much greater for sopranos than tenors (usually the case), we might accept only as low as 1+ + in the soprano section, while taking tenors as low as 1, 1-, or even an occasional 2. It all depends on the chorus, competition, programming, and the personnel needs of any given year.

Figure 9.13

DO NOT WRITE ON THIS PAGE

1.   **BEST VOCAL RANGE:**

2.   **VOCAL QUALITIES OR PROBLEMS**

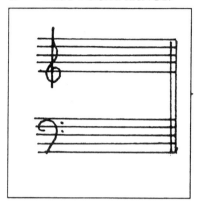

1--Lyrical	1--Average Chorus Voice
2--Pure	2-Vibrato: None, Wobble, Flutter
3--Warm	
4--Natural	3-Chest Voice Break
5--Floating Top	4-Inconsistent Throughout Range
6--Well Focused	
7--Solid Tonal Core	5--Forced/Strained on Top
8--Rich, Full Bodied Tone	6--Lacks Head Tone Dev.
9--Well Developed Head Tone	7--Breathy Tone
10-Pro Solo Type	8--Throaty Tone
11-Brilliant	9--Edgy Throughout
12-Ringing	10--Edgy on Top
	11--Harshness in Tone
	12--Vocally Too Weak

3.   **SIZE OF VOICE:** Very Small - Small - Medium - **Large** - Very Large

4.   **CONTROL/ FLEXIBILITY:**   Top Range
                                                       Throughout:

5.   **PITCH ACCURACY**   ☐ **FINE**   ☐**FLAT**   ☐ **SHARP**

6.   **SIGHT READING AND MUSICIANSHIP:** Perfect - Strong - Average - Weak - None

7.   **PERSONAL COMMUNICATION AND EXPRESSION (1 2 3 4 5 6 7 8 9 10)**
         (Potentially Aggressive Contributor)

8.   **GENERAL COMMENTS:** _____

_____

_____

_____

9.   ☐CHAMBER SINGERS POTENTIAL/DEFINITE

        ☐ CHORALE POTENTIAL/DEFINITE

        ☐ UNIVERSITY CHORUS POTENTIAL/DEFINITE

        ☐ REJECTED

Call-Backs

If the competition is very strong, you might have call-backs of those in the highest rankings from each vocal section (especially sopranos). These singers would sing again, individually, and possibly in groups of 2, 3, or 4, for the purpose of selecting those who seem naturally to sing well together. Do not, however, select one ideal singer and accept only those who match or sing well with him or her. Selections might better be based on a developed vocal *standard*, in the mind of the conductor, not on the ability of one individual singer, which seems terribly unfair and vocally rather manipulative.

Most of the time, a conductor can make accurate selections from the original auditions, and the forms effectively filled out at that time. Call-backs might be needed only rarely.

Figure 9.14

COMMUNITY OR CHURCH CHOIR AUDITION
Donald Neuen, Conductor

PLEASE PRINT CLEARLY

NAME_____ DATE_____

PHONE_____ WK PH _____HEIGHT_____ VOICE PART SI, SII, AI, AII
(Please Circle) TI, TII, BI, BII

ADDRESS_____

_____ _____ZIP _____

COLLIGIATE MUSICAL TRAINING_____

_____

PRIVATE VOCAL STUDY: (Number of years, and name of <u>present</u> teacher) _____

_____

_____

MAJOR SOLO VOCAL EXPERIENCE (If applicable)_____

_____

SIGNIFICANT CHORAL EXPERIENCE (With names of conductors) ☐ THIS CHORUS? YEARS? _____

_____

_____

DICTION PROFICIENCY (i.e. languages in which you have competent pronunciation):

Latin_____   Italian_____   German_____   French_____

OTHER FOREIGN LANGUAGES_____

INSTRUMENTS YOU HAVE STUDIED: _____ (<u>Studied</u> for _____ years)

_____(<u>Studied</u> for _____years)

PRESENT PERFORMANCE ACTIVITIES (church choirs, recitals, instrumental ensembles, opera, etc)_____

_____

ARE YOU OR HAVE YOU BEEN A CHORAL CONDUCTOR? _____ WHERE?_____

OTHER COMMENTS_____

_____

_____

Having Consideration

A conductor can develop knowledge of vocal ability to the extent that he or she can know, after hearing someone audition for only a few seconds, whether or not that person should be considered for membership in an ensemble, and the level of ranking to assign them. That knowledge, in part, can come from focusing on the vocal qualities mentioned in Chapters 2, 3, and 4. If, however, a negative decision to decline is immediately known by the conductor, continue the audition for a few minutes so that you don't appear to insult or demoralize the singer auditioning.

Figure 9.15

DO NOT WRITE ON THIS PAGE

1. BEST VOCAL RANGE:

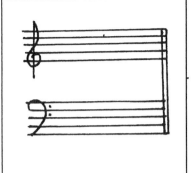

2. VOCAL QUALITIES OR PROBLEMS

1--Lyrical	1--Average Chorus Voice
2--Pure	2-Vibrato: None, Wobble,
3--Warm	Flutter
4--Natural	3-Chest Voice Break
5--Floating Top	4-Inconsistent
6--Well Focused	Throughout Range
7--Solid Tonal Core	5--Forced/Strained on Top
8--Rich, Full Bodied Tone	6--Lacks Head Tone Dev.
9--Well Developed Head Tone	7--Breathy Tone
10-Pro Solo Type	8--Throaty Tone
11-Brilliant	9--Edgy Throughout
12-Ringing	10--Edgy on Top
	11--Harshness in Tone
	12--Vocally Too Weak

3. SIZE OF VOICE: Very Small - Small - Medium - Large - Very Large

4. CONTROL/ FLEXIBILITY: Top Range
Throughout:

5. PITCH ACCURACY ☐ FINE ☐ FLAT ☐ SHARP

6. SIGHT READING AND MUSICIANSHIP: Perfect - Strong - Average - Weak - None

7. PERSONAL COMMUNICATION AND EXPRESSION (1 2 3 4 5 6 7 8 9 10)

8. AGGRESSIVE CONTRIBUTOR (1 2 3 4 5 6 7 8 9 10)

9. GENERAL COMMENTS: _____

_____

_____

_____

10. ☐ **CHORUS POTENTIAL/DEFINITE**

☐ **CHAMBER SINGERS POTENTIAL/DEFINITE**

☐ **PAID PROFESSIONAL POTENTIAL/ DEFINITE**

☐ **REJECTED**

Summary

The conductor needs to give a lot of thought to the rehearsal atmosphere and productivity potential he or she is creating regarding preparation, instructions, positivity, environment, discipline, and energy. Determine effective ways to rehearse that will reap rewards in maximum productivity regarding all aspects of the rehearsal. Plan seating arrangements based on height, the music, and strengths and weaknesses of individual singers. Auditions should be as positive and relaxed as possible, thus enabling the singers to comfortably present their abilities at an optimal level.

Thoughts on Handel's Messiah

Why is there an entire chapter on *Messiah*? In the United States, *Messiah* is performed more often and with greater regularity than any other classical composition. Christian churches and most university, symphony, and community choruses perform it; many do it annually. Because of its familiarity, few conductors feel the need to study the work with a scholar. The consensus? "Everybody knows *Messiah*."

The problem is that, yes, everybody knows *Messiah*—based largely on the conductors they've sung it with over the years. Because few conductors have studied it with a Handel scholar, most learn it ad hoc, rather than building their knowledge on accurate information and analysis. Unfortunately, many conductors simply do not feel the need to know more about this major work.

So, let us now take time to look at *Messiah* from the perspective of Alfred Mann's teaching. Let's learn from the scholar who probably knows more accurate information about George Frideric Handel (and *Messiah*) than anyone of the last century. Mann spent twenty-five years preparing his edition of the conductor's score and orchestra parts—ultimately the finest available. This edition was first published by Rutgers University Press, then Jerona Publishing Company (Hackensack, New Jersey), and the Conductor's score (only) by Dover Scores (available at most music stores). G. Schirmer and most other vocal scores will work well with Mann's score and orchestral parts, although measures need to be numbered in the vocal scores.

Messiah Performance Information

The following thoughts derive from my eighteen years of association, study, and many *Messiah* performances and lecture and demonstration sessions with Alfred Mann. I hope that they help stimulate your own study of this great piece.

❧ A Tribute to Alfred Mann

The thoughts I express in this chapter on Handel's *Messiah* are based on extensive personal study with Alfred Mann, the world's foremost Handel scholar. At this writing he is eighty-two, retired from the Eastman School of Music faculty (a position he held after retiring from Rutgers University in 1980). He is living in this second retirement in Fort Wayne, Indiana, near his son Adrian Mann, principal bassist with the Fort Wayne Philharmonic Orchestra.

Alfred and I were colleagues, dear friends, "brothers," and teacher-student during my twelve-year tenure as Professor of Conducting and Director of Choral Activities for the Eastman School of Music from the fall of 1981 to the spring of 1993. We remain very close friends, and he continues to be my musical advisor on important matters of performance practice and stylistic interpretation from the Renaissance through the Classical stylistic periods.

Alfred generously gave as much time as students needed to learn the knowledge and wisdom he had to offer them. No matter what was asked, he could answer the question and fulfill the need, often without even referring to the score. He knows the scores and he knows the answers.

One of his greatest qualities was indescribable patience. Another was his unending care for the student. In addition, he was always centered, with both feet firmly on the ground, never being swayed to the left or the right by those who would find it immaturely stimulating to go to extremes on historical or stylistic interpretation issues. He was always refreshingly wise in a way that exuded common sense, practicality, reason, and a keen sense of humor. The result? You could trust Alfred Mann—as a musical scholar, musician, and person. How rare, and how wonderful!

While we were colleagues at Eastman, he offered an annual special course for my graduate choral conducting majors (MM and DMA). In fact, he dedicated his recent book, *Bach and Handel: Choral Performance Practice* (Hinshaw Publishing Company), to "Donald Neuen and his students." We all became the grateful "family" of Alfred Mann. Even now, in Fort Wayne, Indiana, he is happy to assist visiting choral conductors in similar matters if they have the initiative to find their way to him. He will gladly teach through his last breath. He is an incredible scholar, phenomenal teacher, and a kind, patient, and loving human being.

Messiah was written for the concert stage, not for a sacred church service. Therefore, it needs to be approached from that point of view. *Messiah* is not an emotional outburst of fundamental religion, and it is not the Christmas story of Jesus' birth. Rather, *Messiah* is an expressive and objective presentation of the life of Christ that progresses from the original prophecy to the summation of Christ's impact on the lives of believers. It portrays the overall *concept* of *Messiah*.

Beauty in Simplicity

A conductor need not superimpose emotional sentimentality on either the textual or musical message. In its beautiful simplicity, it is complete in every way. Honest, appropriate, expression and passion, yes—sentimentality, no.

That simplicity was no accident. Handel intended it to be that way. He did not want soloists to employ ornamentation and embellishment. While in Italy, composing opera, Handel had to put up with aria singers embellishing and ornamenting his melodies. It was the long established custom there, proving one singer superior to another. When he went to England to compose oratorio, he no longer had to suffer the embellishment of his beautiful melodies, and, in fact, did not. In *Messiah,* for example, he very specifically indicated "ad libitum" at measure 8 of the opening tenor solo: "Comfort Ye."

Had he expected embellishment, he certainly would not have had to indicate it. Had he wanted it more frequently (than once) throughout, he would have repeatedly asked for it. He wanted it once: No. 2, measure 8, period. Ornamenting and embellishing are interesting and virtuosic things to do and sometimes, interesting to hear. In this case, however, it is simply inappropriate. Ask your soloists to set their egos aside, and sing the melodies the beautiful way in which they were composed.

> ### ❦ To Ornament or Not to Ornament
>
> An occasional appoggiatura is acceptable. Remember, however, that it weakens the word. For example, to use an appoggiatura on the final word of a phrase such as "saith the Lord," weakens the word "Lord." Even when the final word has two syllables ("spo-ken"), it is weakened by an appoggiatura. So, if the phrase is declamatory, do not use it. If the phrase or thought is of a rather passive nature, and you wish to use the appoggiatura, fine.

Double Dotting

Double-dotting, for the most part, is not appropriate in *Messiah*. To double dot the opening Sinfony would seem to indicate a tempo slower than is appropriate. That was one of the reasons for using the double dot: to bring slow tempi to life. The Sinfony should probably be performed at approximately 54–60 for the quarter note. Also, there were occasions in Handel's writing where he did use the double dot. So, if he had wanted it, he would probably have written it. The exceptions: the opening of chorus No. 24, "Surely," and the final two measures of No. 27, "All they that see him." In both cases, the sixteenth rest should be observed as a dotted sixteenth rest per the notation in measure 6 of No. 24 and beats 3 and 4 of measure 10 of No. 27.

Nine Styles of Choral Composition in *Messiah*

To attempt to understand the performance style of Handel in *Messiah*'s choruses necessitates an awareness of actually *nine* different styles.

Triple meter
No. 4, "And the glory of the Lord"
No. 9, "O Thou that tellest good tidings to zion"

Both choruses need an exhilarating and uplifting triple-meter dance feeling of forward motion. Conduct No. 4 in one (although not *too* fast) and No. 9 in two.

Duet texture

No. 7, "And he shall purify"

No. 12, "For unto us"

No. 21, "His yoke is easy"

No. 26, "All we like sheep"

Handel originally composed the music used in these choruses as secular love duets. Their sound therefore should have a duet/quartet texture, much lighter and more chamberlike than other choruses. Handel added some *new material* to these choruses in sometimes solid block-style homophonic writing at section endings, then returned to the duet texture. In these moments, a somewhat heavier texture is needed; then return to the lighter style when Handel does—as for example, "Wonderful Counselor, the mighty God, the everlasting Father, the Prince of Peace" in No. 12.

Full anthem style

No. 22, "Behold the Lamb of God"

No. 24, "Surely"

No. 26, "All we like sheep"—the ending (added later)

No. 53, "Worthy is the Lamb"—opening portions

These choruses may be sung with a full-bodied tone, at times approaching the fullness of later composers (especially No. 24), totally the antithesis of the duet texture choruses. Never to be overdone, or approaching the physicality of Beethoven, some choruses may certainly approach the sounds of Haydn, Mozart, and even (in No. 24, "Surely") Brahms.

Pure Renaissance style

No. 25, "And with His stripes"

This chorus is written in the linear style of the Renaissance, with each section consistently having its own melodic material, and the accompanying forces duplicating the voice parts. It should probably be taken in a moderate, single beat per whole note and sung with the subtle, serene, linear beauty of most sacred renaissance music.

Turba choruses

No. 28, "He trusted in God"

No. 41, "Let us break their bonds asunder"

A dramatic style in which the singers (chorus) take on the role of crowds of people in action. These may be sung very physically and aggressively dramatic.

Madrigal style

No. 51, "But thanks"

This little thanksgiving chorus follows the lovely duet for alto and tenor, No. 50, "O death, where is thy sting?" It should be sung in a very free flowing, light madrigal style, capitalizing (subtly) on the off-beat emphasis of up-beat eighth notes throughout.

Angel choruses

No. 17, "Glory to God"

No. 33 "Lift up your heads"

Both evoking an image of angels singing, these choruses should reflect that uplifting, buoyant, somewhat lighter style, that flows forward as freely as envisioned angels. The heavenly rejoicing of No. 33, following the resurrection, might allow a bit more fullness of sound than No. 17 (although No. 17 may expand in sound as it progresses to the end).

Baroque rhythmic choruses

No. 35, "Let all the angels"

No. 37, "The Lord gave the word"

No. 39, "Their sound is gone out"

No. 44, "Hallelujah"

No. 46, "Since by man came death"—the allegro portion ("by man came also the resurrection")

No. 53, "Worthy is the Lamb"—the "amen" portion

These choruses subtly possess the vital spirit of rhythmic energy found in fine jazz with its vibrant spirit and element of continuous forward motion.

The only *a cappella* moment in *Messiah*

No. 46, "Since by man came death"—measures 1–6 and 17–22 (*Grave*)

This might be sung effectively with minimal or no vibrato, depicting the sound of "death," then return to a normal full-bodied sound in the allegro portions that follows. It demands an incredible long line of controlled tone, pitch, balance, and blend.

The performing ensemble.   The size of the forces is not nearly as important as the spirit with which the work is performed. A chorus of 24 could be sluggish and lack true baroque energy and vitality. On the other hand, a large chorus of 200 might be trained to sing effectively and appropriately in all nine styles presented above. A small chamber orchestra of period instruments might possibly play without enthusiasm and spark, and a larger ensemble playing on modern instruments could conceivably perform with brilliance, precision, and clarity. Size alone will not determine success. The knowledge, wisdom, and expertise of the conductor, singers, and players will. The size of the forces simply might depend entirely on the size of any given chorus or concert hall—or, on the wishes of the conductor. The *spirit* of Handel (Baroque) is what matters.

I tend to prefer a slightly larger ensemble than some do. I feel that larger groups can be taught to perform with chamber quality subtlety, a vibrant spirit, baroque spirit and precision, and also have the exciting power needed to occasionally really *sing*! I feel the same regarding the orchestra. Strings at 8-8-6-6-2, 4 oboes, 2 bassoons, 2 trumpets, timpani, and harpsichord are ideal for a larger chorus of 80–150. Cut the number of strings in half for the solos (except for "Comfort Ye," "Every valley," "Behold I tell you a mystery," and "The trumpet shall sound," which call for full strings).

I can also appreciate a smaller performing force of 32–64 fine singers, and an orchestra of 6-6-4-4-1, 2 oboes, 1 or 2 bassoons, 2 trumpets, timpani, and harpsichord.

(The harpsichord was generally used in pieces written for the concert hall, and the organ used for those written specifically to be performed in church). I would still recommend reducing the orchestra to 3-3-2-2-1 for solos, unless you're performing in a large concert hall, in which case the smaller orchestral sounds are a bit too thin.

I prefer not to hear or conduct forces smaller than those mentioned in the previous paragraph. I believe that a chorus of 12–24 and strings of 3-3-2-2-1, often fail to make a convincing statement or positively affect the listener.

If budget constraints prohibit a full orchestra, do not hesitate to make do with what you have. For example, in a church situation with extremely limited funds, an ensemble of organ, string quintet, and one trumpet is perfectly acceptable—certainly not ideal, but acceptable. Also workable would be organ, 4 first violins, and 1 trumpet. Do not worry about those who might criticize you! As Alfred Mann says, "If we do our job well, and the singers and audience gain a positive experience of singing and hearing a great work performed *well*, that's what's important." Never give credibility to the negative criticism of purists. Frequently, they lack common sense, practicality, and a spirit of generosity. Although most present-day performances feature a quartet of soloists, and that is just fine, Handel's final preference is shown in Table 10.1. My preferences are shown in Table 10.2.

Table 10.1   Handel's *Messiah* Soloist Preferences

Soprano (No. 1)	Nos. 18, 20, 45, and 52 (prima soprano)
Soprano (No. 2)	Nos. 31, 32, and 38 (lighter more lyrical voice)
Soprano (No.3)	Nos. 14, 14-A, 15, and 16 (lightest voice)
Mezzo-soprano	Nos. 6 and 36
Alto	Nos. 8, 9, 19, 20, 23, 49, and 50
Tenor	Nos. 2, 3, 27, 29, 30, 34, 42, 43, and 50
Baritone	Nos. 47 and 48
Bass	Nos. 5, 10, 11, and 40

Table 10.2   Neuen's Preferences for Soloists

Soprano	All soprano sections shown in Table 10.1 assigned to sopranos, except Nos. 31 and 32, which I believe are more effectively sung by the tenor (in the sequence of 27, 29, 30, 31, and 32).
Alto	Alto sections shown in Table 10.1 assigned to alto (not mezzo-soprano)
Tenor	Tenor sections shown in Table 10.1 assigned to tenor, plus Nos. 31 and 32.
Bass-baritone	Bass and baritone shown in Table 10.1 assigned to both bass and baritone, plus Nos. 6 and 36 (mezzo soprano shown in Table 10.1). The singer definitely needs to be a bass-baritone, not one or the other. (Although a baritone will probably do a better overall job than a bass will.)

Sequence of Scenes

It is important to remember that *Messiah* is a *process* concerning the overall *concept* of Christ. Therefore, when setting up programs and program notes, we should make an effort to help the audience understand the chronology of events as they relate to the biblical passages. All too often cuts may be made in performances of *Messiah* that negate the evolutions of the process and confuse the chain of events that Handel so carefully documented. Table 10.3 will help us understand the story and help us make cuts that keep significant scenes intact. For example, the Hallelujah Chorus responds to neither Christmas nor Easter. It is the celebration of the successful gospel mission portrayed in Nos. 38–43.

Table 10.3   Sequence of Scenes in the *Messiah*

Part 1

1	Orchestra	Sinfony	Introduction

Prophesy

2	Tenor, acc. recitative	Comfort ye	The Old Testament announcement of Messiah
3	Tenor, aria	Every valley	
4	Chorus	And the glory of the Lord shall be revealed	

Concept of Messiah

5	Bass, acc. recitative	Thus saith the Lord	
6	Bass, aria	But who may abide the day of His coming	
7	Chorus	And He shall purify	

Contemplation of what we've been told

8	Alto, recitative	Behold, a virgin shall conceive	The suggestion of the beginning of a story
9	Alto, aria | Chorus	O thou that tellest good tidings to Zion	
10	Bass, acc. recitative	For behold, darkness shall cover the earth	The dramatic contrast of light into darkness
11	Bass, aria	The people that walked in darkness	
12	Chorus	For unto us a Child is born	Revelation of Christ's birth

The Nativity Scene

13	Orchestra	Pifa	Scene change
14	Soprano, recitative	There where shepherds abiding in the field	A reflection or a vision of Christ's birth
15	Soprano, recitative	And the angel said unto them	
16	Soprano, acc. recitative	And suddenly there was an angel	
17	Chorus	Glory to God	Praise from the Angelic host
18	Soprano, aria	Rejoice greatly, O daughter of Zion	Continued vision
19	Alto, recitative	Then shall the eyes of the blind be opened	He came to heal, feed, comfort and bring truth
20	Alto and Soprano, aria	He shall feed His flock like a shepherd	
21	Chorus	His yoke is easy	To live the life of truth, righteousness and love is not difficult. The burden is light.

Continues

Table 10.3 continued

Part 2

Passion of Christ

22 Chorus	Behold the Lamb of God	Depicting Christ at the time of his approaching death
23 Alto, aria	He was despised	
24 Chorus	Surely He hath borne our griefs	Our redemption
25 Chorus	And with His stripes we are healed	Purpose of the crucifixion
26 Chorus	All we like sheep have gone astray	Admission of our guilt and Christ's innocence
27 Tenor, acc. recitative	All they that see Him, laugh him to scorn	Mocking crowds
28 Chorus	He trusted in God that He would deliver Him	
29 Tenor, acc. recitative	Thy rebuke hath broken His heart	Recognizing Christ's sorrow
30 Tenor, arioso	Behold and see if there be any sorrow	

Crucifixion and Resurrection

31 Tenor, acc. recitative	He was cut off out of the land of the living	A brief crucifixion and resurrection moment
32 Tenor, recitative	But Thou didst not leave His soul in hell	

Scene of Heaven

33 Chorus	Lift up your heads, O ye gates	Rejoicing in heaven concerning the resurrection
34 Tenor, recitative	Unto which of the angels said He	
35 Chorus	Let all the angels of God worship Him	
36 Bass or Alto, aria	Thou art gone up on high	The ascension

Gospel Mission

37 Chorus	The Lord gave the word	The spreading of the word—Pentecost
38 Soprano, aria	How beautiful are the feet of them	
39 Chorus	Their sound is gone out into all lands	

Rebellion to the word

40 Bass, aria	Why do the nations so furiously rage	Rebellion and raging against the spreading of the word
41 Chorus	Let us break their bonds asunder	

The Lord and His word shall prevail

42 Tenor, recitative	He that dwelleth in heaven	The gates of hell shall not prevail against the word
43 Tenor, aria	Thou shalt break them	
44 Chorus	Hallelujah	Gospel mission victory

Part 3

Affirmation of faith in the resurrection and life after death

45 Soprano, aria	I know that my Redeemer liveth	Personal testimony
46 Chorus	Since by man came death	Mankind's role in the prophesy, the eventual resurrection, and eternal life

47	Bass, acc. recitative	Behold, I tell you a mystery	
48	Bass, aria	The trumpet shall sound	

Victory over death

49	Alto, recitative	Then shall be brought to pass	Victory over death
50	Alto and Tenor, aria	O death where is thy sting	
51	Chorus	But thanks be to God	Chorus of thanksgiving for eternal life

Final statement of God's power for us and closing anthem

52	Soprano, aria	If God be for us	An expression of confidence in God's care, and final praise to Messiah.
53	Chorus	Worthy is the Lamb—Amen	

Orchestration

It is essential to know the orchestrations of the various movements of *Messiah* as we set up our orchestra rehearsals. Nothing will earn the respect of players more quickly than an obvious effort on our part to respect their time. In Table 10.4, we can see that only the continuo is required for an entire rehearsal, therefore, we plan accordingly.

Table 10.4   **Rehearsal Plan for** *Messiah*

Ensemble	Modification	Messiah *Chorus No.*
Full orchestra	Strings, oboes, bassoons, trumpets, timpani and harpsichord	44 & 53
Full orchestra	Without timpani	No. 17
Full orchestra	Without trumpets or timpani	Nos. 1, 4, 7, 9 (second half), 12, 21, 22, 24, 25, 26, 28, 33, 35, 37, 39, 41, 46, & 51
Full strings and continuo		Nos. 2, 3, 13 (violin I, II, and III), 47, & 48 (with trumpet solo)
Reduced strings and continuo	Use half of the strings	Nos. 5, 6, 9 (first half), 10, 11, 14–16, 20, 23, 27, 29, 30, 31, & 40
Unison violins and continuo	Use either all first violins or half of first and second violins	18 (few I–II divisi portions), 32, 36, 38, 43, 45, & 52
Continuo personnel only	Cello, occasionally bass, and harpsichord only	Only: Nos. 8, 14, 15, 19, 34, 42, 48 (B-section), 49, & 50
Selections without bassoons		Nos. 2, 5, 8, 13, 14–16, 19, 29, 31, 34, 42, 47, 49, & 50

Messiah Tempi

After extensive study with musicologists Alfred Mann and Julius Herford and conductor Robert Shaw, Table 10.5 represents my conclusions regarding tempi throughout *Messiah*.

Table 10.5   Tempi throughout *Messiah* Choruses

Number	Note	Tempo
1	♩	54–60
allegro	𝅗𝅥	84
2	♩	54–60
3	♩	96–104
4	𝅗𝅥.	48–54 (in 1)
5	♩	96
6	♪	96
prestissimo	𝅗𝅥	84–90
7	♩	96–100
8	recitative	
9	♩.	56–60
10	♩	54
11	♩	72
12	♩	96–100
13	♩.	48
14	recitative	
14-A	♩	76
15	recitative	
16	♩	90
17	♩	96–100
18	♩	108
19	recitative	
20	♩.	48
21	♩	96–100
22	♪	86[1]
23	♩	48–54 (definitely in 4)
b section	♩	72–76
24	♪	88–96
25	𝅝	54–60 (in 1)[2]
26	♩	100–104
adagio	♩	60–64
27	♩	66
28	♩	108
29	♩	48–52
30	♪	76
31	♩	90
32	♩	66–70
33	♩	96–100
34	recitative	
35	♩	96–100

Number	Note	Tempo
36	♩	96
37	♩	92–96
38	♩.	48
39	♩	96–102
40	♩	132
41	♩	104–108
42	recitative	
43	♩	104–108
44	♩	120
45	♩	92–96
46	♩	44–48
allegro	♩	108
47	recitative	
48	♩	108–116
49	recitative	
50	♩	84–88
51	♩	94–96
52	♩	104–108
53 largo	♩	60
andande	♪	96–100
larghetto	♩	90–96
allegro moderato	♩	108–114

[1] Nos. 22, 23, 24 might all be considered in 4, with the quarter note being the major pulse of all three (at approximately the same unified tempo of 44–48, as an outgrowth of the half note being considered the major pulse of duple rhythm tempi in the Renaissance period. On some occasions Alfred and I did this when we had a capable ensemble and ample rehearsal time. On other occasions we did Nos. 22 and 24 in eight, as indicated earlier.

[2] No. 25 would be in 2 if in 4/2 time signature, with the whole note getting the beat.

Summary ⌒

Messiah was written for the concert stage, not for the church, therefore sentimentality and exaggerated evangelism are inappropriate in its interpretation.

- Ornamentation and embellishment of solo melodies were not Handel's intention—with only one exception that Handel specifically indicated (*ad libitum*) on No. 2, measure 8, "Comfort ye."
- Double-dotting in the opening Sinfony was probably not Handel's intention.
- Handel uses nine different compositional styles in the choruses:
  1. Triple meter (Nos. 4 and 9)
  2. Duet texture (Nos. 7, 12, 21, and 26)

3. Full anthem (Nos. 22, 24, ending of 26, and 53)

4. Renaissance (No. 25)

5. Turba (Nos. 28 and 41)

6. Madrigal (No. 51)

7. Angel (Nos. 17 and 33)

8. Baroque rhythmic (Nos. 35, 37, 39, 44, allegro of 46, and "Amen" of 53)

9. A cappella (No. 46, grave sections)

- Size of forces may vary. The more important factor is the degree to which they are trained to sing—with a true baroque *spirit*.

- The size of the orchestra may also vary in proportion to the chorus and concert hall. However, it is usually wise to cut the strings by half for solo arias.

- Handel used a variety of solo assignments, therefore we may also. The usual, however, is a quartet of four.

- *Messiah* is written in a very logical sequence of scenes, and when possible, it is good to keep these scenes intact, understanding and conveying their message.

- The original orchestration calls for strings, oboes, bassoons, trumpets, timpani, and harpsichord.

- The author's tempo suggestions are simply a point of departure for the reader. (Few things, if any, are definitive.)

Artistic Musical Conducting

*A*t the outset, let's establish that we are not interested in the age-old misconception of a giant chasm between choral "directing" and instrumental "conducting." The subject is *artistic musical conducting*. A knowledgeable conductor finds few differences between working with vocalists or instrumentalists. We should envision ourselves as *conductors* who conduct *musicians musically*. The style and overall general appearance of who we are and what we do are basically the same whether we are in front of an orchestra, band, or chorus.

Know the techniques of your performing forces.   Although our basic conducting technique remains consistent, the techniques of the musicians we lead will differ. The conductor should have an effective working knowledge of the skills of the ensemble being conducted, be it a clarinetist, violinist, timpanist, trumpeter, or the human voice. So although expressive, passionate, clear, and precise movements are consistently effective with any ensemble, a lack of comprehensive knowledge of either the score or the performing forces will render the most beautiful stick technique useless.

Conduct the music.   A fine instrumental conductor effectively communicates precise beats, expressive melodic lines, driving rhythms, dynamic changes and nuances, significant harmonic moments, and all other attributes of a composition. The choral conductor does exactly the same thing.

In the past, choral conductors often felt they needed to teach and conduct in a rather elementary and dictatorial manner because singers couldn't respond if they didn't. Thus, the practice evolved of physically conducting (dictating) syllables, words, and notes, rather than beat patterns and musical phrasing. We now know differently. Thanks to the professionalism of outstanding contemporary choral conductors, we have come to see that singers will respond to artistic musical conducting if given the opportunity. To spoon-feed the chorus denies the conductor a mature musical expression and the singers a chance to use their intelligence. Instead of lowering conducting standards to match the level of a given ensemble, the conductor must raise the awareness level of the ensemble. If we are to eliminate the "second-class category" of choral conducting and become truly fine conductors, able to stand in front of choral or instrumental forces with ease and confidence, we must establish the following concepts.

Three elements of successful conductors

1. A great mind
2. Passion that comes from the very depths of the soul
3. Effective conducting techniques

Great Conductors

Great conductors have abundant knowledge and deep passion. We can all further develop our minds, which are limitless in their potential for growth and expansion. Those who wish to grow, do so. Those who don't, stagnate. The successful conductor continues to expand his or her mind for as long as life lasts.

Knowledge

Understand the music.   Whether conducting a Broadway tune, folk song, spiritual, motet, or major work for chorus, soloists, and orchestra, the conductor needs to approach the score with deep commitment and integrity. Our goal is to know everything there is to know about the score. We cannot teach that which we do not know. That which is not taught, does not happen! The conductor must be able to teach a piece with a comprehensive understanding of its wholeness. That includes

- Stylistic interpretation
- Structural and harmonic analysis
- Compositional techniques and instructions
- Phrasing analysis, and conducting (editorial) markings
- Performance problems for singers and players
- Technical and dramatic understanding of the text
- Physical coordination problems of the conducting challenges
- Rehearsal planning for potential success

Remember Robert Shaw's answer when he was asked how much time he spent studying scores? "Every waking hour." Great minds are not so much born as they are self-developed. Most conductors are, to varying degrees, involved in things other than music. Each must wrestle with and successfully find the right solution to the problem of sufficient study time. Whatever the situation, it must result in really knowing the music. To be a conductor is to be a leader. To lead is a privilege that brings with it the responsibility of knowing the subject.

Understand the techniques used by the performing forces. If you are conducting singers, you must understand the art of singing. If you are conducting instrumentalists, you must have a working knowledge of the instruments. Strings require a different language (of bowing and articulation) than winds do, women's voices present different challenges and problems than men's do, and young singers must be treated in a very special way. It goes on and on. The main issue is that efficiency of rehearsals and the quality of performances must not be limited by *technical ignorance* of the conductor. We must enable the ensemble to perform better and more effectively because we are there, with the knowledge to help them through solid teaching, whether they are singers or instrumentalists.

Many instrumental conductors fall short when conducting singers. Those who have majored primarily in an instrument and find themselves conducting a chorus in a church, school, or community must accept the responsibility of learning the techniques of fine singing. It is often taken for granted that any trained musician can effectively conduct a chorus. Not so. Only a trained musician, who also *understands great singing and how to teach it,* should be permitted to conduct a chorus.

Choral conductors who want to conduct major combined choral and instrumental works also need to accept the responsibility of learning certain instrumental techniques. In this instance, I would suggest private study, with a string player, on the work to be performed—even on a regular basis until you feel confident with string bowing techniques. If, however, the work is with chorus, brass, and percussion, then study with brass and percussion players. The point is, study with someone! Know what you're doing. You don't need to know how to *play* the many instruments, just how to speak intelligently about the music *they* are playing. Although choral singers often need to be taught how to sing, instrumentalists do *not* need to be taught how to play. They already know that and resent conductors who attempt to teach it. They simply need to know how we want the *music* to be played.

Passion

Many teachers of conducting believe that passion is something that simply cannot be taught—that conductors either have a talent for passion or they don't. I do know that passion is *the* most difficult aspect to teach if it is not a natural part of a conductor's makeup. True passion, and the free expression of it, may need to develop as a person grows from a very young child through the late teens. If parents and teachers have encouraged a child to *feel* and to *express* feelings uninhibitedly, passion is likely to develop.

To realize full passion, we must reach into our souls for the deepest feelings of true substance known to humankind. When this is discovered, so too will be the deepest feelings of *great music.* I can say with certainty that no matter how passionate we think we are, there is always room for greater depth.

A great conductor knows the difference between energy and passion. Be aware that there is a vast difference between energy and passion. Energy is the motivating fuel of life. It is the basic enabling force of all growth and progress. Without energy, there is no life! Energy, therefore, is the very basis of all great singing.

Passion, on the other hand, is deep emotion, a reaching inward for something incredibly special, a powerful impulse for attaining a desired goal. Real passion comes from the deepest core of the human spirit. This quality is most rare among conductors, especially American conductors, who often base most of their emphasis on energy and technique alone, completely unaware of the substantive potential of true passion. American society is preoccupied with speed and action. Americans seldom slow down enough to even think about the possibility of passion, let alone seek and find it deep within themselves.

Stick Technique: Very Important, But a Second Priority

Many highly successful conductors lack what we might call artistic conducting techniques. How, then, did they succeed? Through intelligence, knowledge, and expressiveness. The gestures of some of the world's greatest conductors would never be found in a conducting textbook, yet their *minds* have enabled them to produce incredible results with choruses, orchestras, or bands. They know what they need to know, and they know how to express and teach it. Does this mean that precise, disciplined, and consistent conducting techniques are not important? Absolutely not! It simply means that they are secondary in importance to a fine, well-developed mind.

I will hasten to add that minimal-technique conductors frequently need to *overteach* to compensate for bad conducting techniques. Instrumentalists and singers often have to *overcome poor conducting* to do what has been asked of them.

When a conductor really knows what he or she is doing, regarding every aspect of the music, and has an overwhelming passion for it, there will be greatness. *Intelligence and knowledge must dominate.* These are the very essence of true substance and long-lasting success. It is especially important that choral conductors, who by definition are involved with text and textual feeling, understand that pure emotion, personality, and charisma are not, in themselves, a substitute for intelligence and knowledge.

A True Reflection of the Score

A really successful conductor *becomes the music itself,* a feat that can only be achieved when all aspects of the score are known and understood. Few conductors are able to reach that level—in which they actually *become* a true reflection of the score. It is not easy. Complete knowledge of the score and a total reflection of it are the two main factors that separate great conductors from all others. To reflect the score means several things.

All movements should be appropriate and meaningful without affectation. No gesture should be unnecessary, unmusical, undefined, or unnatural. None should be obtrusive, distracting, or simply for show. There should be no meaningless, idiosyncratic, or habitual movements or gestures. Specific musical thoughts or ideas in the score should dictate every movement or gesture.

Conducting is a predetermined, highly developed artistic skill, and its specific characteristics emerge anew with each new score.

Musical phrases constantly change—so should our conducting. If a composition has substantial quality, its musical lines are in a process of continual change. There will seldom be one full measure, let alone a phrase, in which there is not a new musical thought or nuance to express—a change or contrast in dynamics, rhythm, melodic direction, harmony, instrumentation, voicing, or textual expression. Something of musical or textual interest is constantly happening or changing in great music. The feeling and expression of the conductor must follow these musical ideas. To look the same for several consecutive measures or phrases is simply not musical conducting. This would fall into the category of mechanical time-beating. *Time-beating is the antithesis of musical expression!*

> ## ℰ *What Orchestral Players Say*
>
> In recent interviews, I talked with the principal players in several major symphony orchestras. They quickly acknowledged that they would always prefer a more precise, skilled, artistic style of conducting, but that they seldom get it. As a result, the players acknowledged that they don't watch the conductor except when absolutely necessary. They say it would be confusing (isn't that unfortunate?). They must settle for their first priority only: that the conductor knows what he or she wants, knows how to get it from the players, and does so convincingly.

The conductor must be comfortable expressing feelings. The conductor must not only be comfortable showing the full spectrum of feelings, but actually enjoy and receive fulfillment through it. This expression is very similar to the great actors' visible, dramatic display of inner emotions. You can actually see in their physical expressions those feelings that they are experiencing deep within their minds, hearts, and souls. We must hasten to say that this does not suggest that the conductor should *exaggerate* the honest expression of the music to the extent of sentimentality or superficial theatrics. It means that whether the music is *piano/dolce*, or *forte/marcato*, the conductor needs to be able to reflect the music and text accurately, effectively, and consistently, whether they express simple beauty or heavy dramatic impact.

The conductor must be able to focus intensely. A conductor must develop focus that enables him or her to *become* the music. One must be so completely engrossed in the music that nothing else exists at that moment, so centered in the music that to disturb this focus, to be called away from this *musical existence*, would almost cause a state of disorientation. Developing this degree of focus takes great effort and practice for most conductors. It is one thing for a great *actor* to bring himself into this state as he executes his role. It is quite another challenge for a conductor to do it, while consciously retaining a *spontaneous teaching awareness.* The conductor must possess this teaching awareness so he or she can

- Hear and analyze what the musicians are *actually producing*

- Connect this actual production with his or her conceptual vision of what the music *should be*

- Transform the rehearsal into a performance of the conceptual vision through effective teaching

The Physical Gestures of Conducting

The actual conducting movements should be as learned and consistent as the technical executions of a pianist, violinist, or singer. These people do not spontaneously improvise a skill. Conductors should not either. A technique is a learned proficiency that, when successfully and consistently employed, results in the perfection of a desired performance—whether in athletics, the arts, or any other physical activity.

The mastery of any language will produce a greater potential for the successful expression of one's thoughts and feelings. So, too, with the conductor's language that *visually* expresses musical ideas. And, as with speaking, the level of the conductor's language proficiency will either enhance or hinder this musical communication. If we are to refine the technical aspects of our conducting language, what, then, are the most important concepts for which we will strive? In the following discussion, I present those concepts for your consideration. Some of them might seem elementary, but take nothing for granted. Videotape your rehearsals and concerts. Be your own best critic. See and know yourself as a conductor.

It is very important to the success of our expressive potential that the left hand doesn't only mirror the right hand. Each hand has its own responsibilities and its own "language."

The Right Hand

The primary function of the right hand is to present a consistent beat pattern while maintaining full expression and allowing the occasional cue within the context of clear, concise beating. (That is, any given beat can potentially be a cue, if directed toward specific singers or players.) The right hand can, for the most part, be as expressive within a beat pattern as out of it. Beat patterns do not have to be limiting, mechanical, awkward, or pedantic. It just takes practice to incorporate expressive beauty, or exciting energy, within consistent patterns. All the passion, expressiveness, energy, and power needed could, if necessary, be done with the right hand alone. Often, as in the conducting of an aria accompaniment, the right hand may be sufficient by itself. Try it.

The Left Hand

For the most part, the left hand should not duplicate the movements of the right hand. As a concertmaster of a major symphony orchestra told me, "When both hands do the same thing, it becomes more confusing; we [the players] have to look at two things instead of one." When parallel or mirror gestures are eliminated, the left hand is free to be instructive and expressive on its own, to present *additional communication* rather than redundantly mimic the right hand.

The left hand is one of the conductor's most powerful tools. Unfortunately, the left hand is often relegated to simply mirroring the right hand. Gestures such as cues, accents, sforzandi, stresses, rhythmic pulses, dynamic changes, and so on, along with—occasionally—nothing at all, form an entire language of the left hand, totally *independent* of the right hand.

The left hand should move independently from the beat pattern consistently given by the right hand. The two hands should, for the most part, avoid identical, parallel, or mirror movements. The basic function of the right hand is consistently to display the beat pattern to the members of the ensemble. *Essentially, the left hand assists with other musical responsibilities.*

Left-hand communication may include

- Cueing.

- Dynamic changes and contrasts. This is a major responsibility of the left hand.

- Sforzandi, stresses, accents, and other rhythmic pulses.

- Releases. The left hand should do the releases, rather than the right hand or both hands doing releases. Any movement of the right hand should be for making music, not stopping it. (Instrumentalists are conditioned to play the next passage if they see right-hand movement.)

- Long phrases. For lengthy, flowing phrase indications, the left hand can begin at the right shoulder, then, very gradually move to the left, leading with the back of the hand over several notes or measures.

- Nothing at all. The left hand does not have to be employed at all times. It is very refreshing and clear to view a conductor who, for the moment, is conducting only with the right hand. Some passages simply don't need both hands. This is especially true of many moments in solo accompaniments and absolutely true of recitatives. It is also often true for the *beginning* of a song. One clearly communicative hand is frequently much better than two.

Figure 11.1a

When you are not using your left hand, keep it at your side—not hanging straight down, but with a slight angle to the elbow as though there were a snap on your wrist connected to your waist. Let this be the home-base position for the left hand when you're not using it. The more you insist on using your left hand *independently of your right hand*, the more the left will find to do naturally and effectively.

Intensity. Lower your left hand to the waist for either the beginning of a crescendo indication (see Figure 11.1a) or to call for greater depth and substance of sound (see Figure 11.1b). It is important that the extending of the left hand to ask for a crescendo is done with intensity toward the ensemble. Do not move out too far or too quickly. *Distance and speed dissipate intensity and effectiveness.*

It is extremely important that the left hand indicate *every crescendo and diminuendo—every one*! In Figure 11.2a, the left hand is asking for a diminuendo. It is turned over, and moving back toward the body. Figure 11.2b indicates the beginning of telescoping the gesture up toward the face so the performers can see the *facial expression* at the same time as they see the conducting gesture and pattern.

Figure 11.1b

Figure 11.2a

Figure 11.2b

Figure 11.3a

Figure 11.3b

In Figure 11.3a and b, the left hand is moving toward the left, with the back of the hand leading, to express a long-line melodic phrase. This can be slowly, gradually, and gracefully extended over three or four notes, or up to two to three measures, then re-started. It is a very effective use of the left hand, and seems to actually draw out the phrase from the ensemble.

The Baton

When using a baton, the position of the arm, hand, fingers, and baton should be as natural, relaxed, and free as possible. Allow the baton to become a true *extension of the arm,* not an unnatural, obtrusive, obstacle-like *addition to it.*

When should you use a baton? Anytime it might effectively enhance the communication of the conductor with the performers, for example, in

- Large ensembles for the simple reason of visual clarity
- Intricate or complex rhythmic music in which clarity is paramount
- Contemporary music in which mixed meters prevail and necessitate greater clarity
- Instrumental ensembles that are accustomed to the precision of a baton

Although this list consistently mentions clarity and precision, a baton can also be perfectly effective for the person who simply prefers to use one, and is completely comfortable with one—even in situations in which the baton might not be necessary. Baton use is often a matter of personal preference. Robert Shaw, for example, used a baton all the time, even with a small ensemble singing a folk song or Christmas carol.

The decision *not* to use a baton should be based solely on musical, logistical, and situational reasons, rather than on one's inability to use a baton effectively. If we take the time and expend the effort to become proficient and comfortable with the use of the baton, then we can base the decision on wisdom and intelligence, rather than on fear and insecurity. All it takes is practice.

The main reason for using a baton is the need for more precision and accuracy than hands and fingers alone can provide. It is a more precise object than the hand. When precision is needed, use a baton. When it is not, do as you prefer.

Baton Size

The distance from your shoulder to your elbow, and from your elbow to your hand, is approximately 12 to 14 inches. If the baton is to be a natural extension of your arm, it should not exceed 14 inches and it should also have a *small, tapered handle.* The nicely tapered handle helps it to feel natural, as if nothing were in your hand. We should not feel as though we are *holding onto* something or *gripping* something foreign.

Ideally, the baton should evoke the feeling of a feather. If the weight of the handle is equal to that of the shaft, the baton will balance perfectly at the point where the handle meets the shaft—further establishing the baton's weightlessness in the hand. Anything larger is usually unnecessary, clumsy, and obtrusive (except on the football field, when a marching band conductor might be attempting to keep nearly 300 marchers and players together). A slightly longer baton might also be desirable when you are conducting a full symphony orchestra and a large chorus.

Proper Baton Positioning in the Hand

Give great thought and consideration to the best way to hold a baton. Give it the same importance that a violinist gives to the technique of bowing. Use these steps to get yourself into the ideal position to hold and use your baton. Before we begin, be aware of two important precepts:

1. First, everything we do must be *natural*.
2. Second, it may take practice and time to get used to the technique so that it will *feel* natural.

If you are a beginner you will have an easier time because you have not formed any idiosyncratic habits. If you are an experienced conductor, however, you might need to *retrain* your body to do these movements well and comfortably. Be patient and diligent and you will succeed. New physical techniques in anything (golf, tennis, or conducting) may take a while to feel comfortable.

Figure 11.4

Identify your natural, relaxed hand position. Hang your right arm down at your side in a totally relaxed position (see Figure 11.4). The hand will be naturally rounded (rather than the fingers hanging straight down). The hand will be at a slight angle, with the thumb pointing slightly toward the left, just barely touching your leg. This is a natural position for the hand. The thumb aiming straight out (forward) is *unnatural.* If you were to relax and hang both arms down to your sides, they would both be this way. If you were to swing them naturally front and back, they would swing slightly toward the center in front, and slightly out from the sides when going back.

As your hand hangs, relaxed, at your side, gently touch the pads of the thumb and first finger. This is exactly where you will eventually grip the baton, at the point at which the two pads gently touch. Notice that the other three fingers remain relaxed, curved, and with a slight *breathing* space between each one. This is a very important aspect of what we are about to do. Embed this position—relaxed, curved, with breathing space—solidly in your mind. Picture it.

Grip the baton. Bring your hand up, keeping the fingers in exactly the same relaxed, curved, breathing position as they were when at your side. *Make no changes whatsoever.*

Figure 11.5

Place the baton in it, gently gripping the baton with the pads of the thumb and first finger at the point where the shaft meets the handle. Drop your hand to your side again. Consciously make sure it is in exactly the same *relaxed* position as it was without the baton. The baton should be pointing slightly toward the left, aiming out in front of your left foot, not because you make it do so, but because it will do so naturally (see Figure 11.5).

If your hand and baton were to aim straight forward, your wrist would have to twist in an unnatural, slightly forced position. Check your fingers for natural curve and spacing. The breathing space should be only wide enough to comfortably slip a piece of paper between the fingers. Do not spread your fingers. Remember: The baton and arm must be as natural a collaboration as possible. *The physical act of conducting must be natural.*

Maintain this relaxed position with your arm raised. Raise and lower your arm several times, maintaining the same relaxed hand position and angle from the hand to the wrist. When you raise your arm think of *leading with your elbow* (not with the baton or your hand). Your hand and the baton will follow and rest in position (see Figure 11.6).

Figure 11.6

Follow these steps when raising your hand, arm, and baton into position to begin conducting: (1) Inhale as you bring your arm and the baton up, so you have a feeling of *rising* with the arm (elbow) and baton. *You are becoming one with the baton.* (2) Lead with your elbow, then wrist, then the hand and baton, somewhat like a swimmer lifting the back of his or her arm out of the water, elbow first, in the motion to take another stroke.

The last movement is the tip of the baton coming to rest at a very slight angle upward, maybe only one or two inches higher than the handle held in your hand. If the baton points downward, it looks somewhat negative; if it is perfectly perpendicular with the floor, it appears passive; if it is slightly raised, it positively indicates that something is about to happen.

If you bring the arm and hand up in a natural manner, the baton will be pointing toward the second violin section (or the stage-right side of the chorus) at a 45° angle in your hand. Avoid allowing the baton to point either straight ahead or toward the first violin section (90 degrees). Remember to raise the tip of the baton slightly.

Find the 4 o'clock position.   The *4 o'clock* position refers to the position of the right elbow in relation to the upper body. When we look at the figure from behind (Figure 11.7), we can clearly see that the elbow is at approximately the same angle as a clock hand pointing to 4 o'clock. If the elbow is up at three o'clock, the angle is too high. The beats, therefore, are also too high. If the elbow is too low, at five or six o'clock, the conductor looks weighted down and constricted and is expressively very limited. The performing ensembles, reflecting their conductor, will feel the same way. Basically, four o'clock is just right. It represents freedom, relaxation, and *buoyancy.* The arm is "living" and encourages freedom in breathing (singers and winds) and bowing (strings).

In Figure 11.8, we can see the 4 o'clock position from the front. When positioned this way the baton is pointing slightly to the conductor's left (into the violin II section), and the middle of

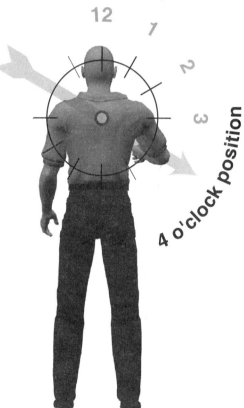

Figure 11.7

Figure 11.8a (near right) and 11.8b (far right)

the baton shaft is in line with the buttons of the shirt, centered, not off to either the left or right.

As in other photos, notice the curved, relaxed, natural position of the fingers, and the consistent relationship between the hand, wrist, and forearm. The arm is free, *as though floating in a swimming pool* with the water at nearly chest high level. The freedom of potential movement is at every joint of the fingers, wrist, elbow, and shoulder. The entire arm floats. The elbow is out from the side at a four o'clock position. The conductor has freedom of movement and the singers and players see a visual image of potential breathing expansion, great posture, and an exhilarating feeling that the body is about to do something special.

Figure 11.9a demonstrates the same positioning we've been discussing, but viewed with the hand inverted, exposing the palm and baton handle. Notice that the end of the handle, although aiming toward the palm, *does not touch it* (the handle is probably too long if it touches the palm). This enables the baton to float in the hand and helps maintain a naturally buoyant connection between the baton and arm. In Figure 11.9b, we see where the baton handle would touch the palm if it were pushed to do so. The baton should not be able to be pushed out the right side of the hand. (If it is, that would happen because the baton points toward first violins at a 90° angle.)

Maintain a level wrist.   Remember to keep the wrist level in the home base position. In fact, you will notice a coin placed on the level wrist in Figure 11.10—this demonstrates that, in a completely relaxed, home base position, the conductor can beat through the pattern without the coin falling off.

Within the full range of conducting gestures, the wrist and palm will eventually move and turn in a *wide variety of motions.* That is as it should be. Now however, we have established a *home-base position* (see Figure 11.6 on page 211), from which we

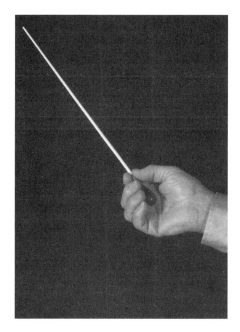

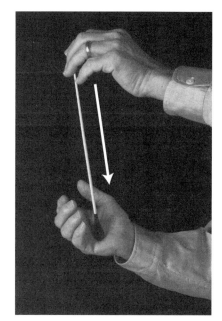

Figure 11.9a (far left)
and 11.9b (near left)

Figure 11.10

will eventually depart for musically expressive reasons and then return. If we do not have a practical home base position, our opportunity to ask for something new or different (which should speak out clearly) is limited.

Remember that the position of the hand, wrist, and fingers remains the same when resting at the side and when raised (Figure 11.11). Notice the baton shaft is centered with the tie.

Once we have established a comfortable baton grip, we need to develop our *home-base conducting position*. This is the position from which we will often depart and to which we will *always* return. We are establishing a manner of conducting in which there are no idiosyncrasies or habits of any kind, a manner that indicates only relaxation and freedom to our singers and players. This manner allows the music to dictate completely all movements that appropriately vary from this and then return.

If we attempt to bring out something special when our conducting gestures are already filled with unusual movements and idiosyncrasies, the result will be futile. To employ a special gesture from a natural, home-base position is as though

Figure 11.11

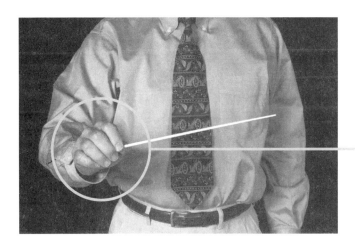
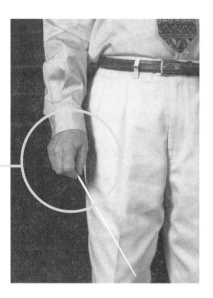

someone were speaking calmly and then suddenly makes a dramatic statement. It commands the attention of your ensemble.

Feel the natural flow of the home-base position.   With a level wrist, and the stick pointing at a 45° angle to the left, you have a natural, uninterrupted flow from the right shoulder all the way out to the tip of the baton. Notice in Figure 11.12 that each of the three angles (at the shoulder, elbow, and wrist) are similar. To aim the baton straight forward would unnaturally interrupt this flow. The tip of the baton is slightly raised to alert the ensemble subliminally that something is about to happen.

Retain this natural home-base position as you conduct through various beat patterns. That is, in 4/4, do not close up your arm for beat 2, then open it wide to the right for beat 3. Without being rigid, stay in the same basic relaxed position throughout, letting your body move *ever so slightly* to the left for beat 2, and to the right for beat 3. When going to beat 3, lead with your elbow, bringing the baton along last (retaining the original curved position of similar angles)—rather than

Figure 11.12

opening up the arm, leading with the baton, and pointing it to the right. Let your *body* become *slightly involved* in the motion of the beat patterns. Your arm and baton alone do not do the conducting; rather, you and your whole body conduct. This, by the way, is a very important concept. Musicians do not follow only the baton or hand—they see and react to the *entire physical being* of the conductor, from the waist up. They also react to the *facial expression* and specific *manner* of the conductor.

In addition, to avoid problems, be aware of any idiosyncrasies or repetitive movements that might distract the performer from your primary, natural, relaxed clarity developed for the home-base position of the baton and arm. All sorts of variations will *appropriately* follow once this is securely established.

Review checklist for baton-hand-arm positioning

1. Hang your right arm down at your side in a totally relaxed position. The hand will be naturally *rounded* (as opposed to the fingers hanging straight down) (see Figure 11.4 on page 210).

2. The hand will be at a slight angle, with the thumb aiming slightly toward the left, just barely touching your leg. This is a natural position for the hand. The thumb aiming straight out (forward) is unnatural. If you were to hang both arms relaxingly down to your sides, they would *both* be this way. If you were to swing them naturally front and back, they would swing slightly toward the center in front and slightly out from the sides when going back.

3. As the hand hangs down, relaxed, at your side, gently touch the pads of the thumb and first finger. This is exactly where you will eventually grip the baton—at the point at which the two pads gently touch. *Notice that the other three fingers remain relaxed, curved, and with a slight "breathing" space between each one.* This is a very important aspect of what we are about to do. Let this relaxed, curved, with "breathing" space positioning be solidly entrenched in your minds. Picture it.

4. Bring your hand up, keep the fingers in *exactly the same* relaxed, curved, "breathing position as they were when at your side. *Make no changes whatsoever.* Now place the baton in it, gently gripping it at the point at which the shaft meets the handle, with the previously mentioned *pads* of the thumb and first finger.

5. Drop your hand to your side again. Consciously make sure it is in exactly the same relaxed position that it was without the baton. *The baton should be slightly pointing toward the left, aiming out it front of your left foot*—not because you *make* it do so, but as with the thumb earlier, it will do it naturally. Check the fingers for the natural curve and spacing. This "breathing" space is only enough to comfortably slip a piece of paper between the fingers—we are not *spreading* the fingers at all (see Figure 11.5 on page 210).

6. Bring the baton up with the following thoughts:

    a. Inhale as you bring the baton up, so *you* have a feeling of rising *with* the arm and baton—you are becoming *one* with the baton.

    b. Lead with your elbow, then wrist, then the hand and baton—somewhat like a swimmer lifting the back arm out of the water, elbow first, in its motion forward to take another stroke.

c. The last movement is the tip of the baton coming "to rest" at a very slight angle *upward*—maybe only one or two inches higher than the handle held in your hand. If the baton points downward it looks somewhat negative, if it is perfectly perpendicular with the floor it is passive, if it is slightly raised, it positively "says" that something is about to happen!

7. If you bring the arm and hand up in a natural manner, the baton will be pointing toward the second violin section, that is, a 45-degree angle in your hand. Avoid allowing the baton to point straight-ahead (180 degrees), or toward the first violin section (90 degrees). Remember that the tip of the baton is *slightly* raised (see Figure 11.6 on page 211).

8. The middle of the shaft of the baton should be lined up with the buttons of your shirt. Avoid having the baton (hand) too far to the right, as is often the case with choral conductors—too far to the right, and consistently too high, up near the right shoulder.

9. The wrist should be level with the floor, not turned with the palm facing either the body or away from the body. The entire forearm, in this home-base positions, is parallel to the floor. In fact, place a coin (quarter) on your wrist; it should be able to *stay there* as you slowly conduct through a beat pattern. See the coin and level wrist in Figure 11.10 (see page 213).

10. Your hand should be *rounded,* following your level forearm, just as it was somewhat *rounded* while hanging down at your side in the original position of Figure 11.4 (see page 210).

11. Your arm is free, as though floating in a swimming pool with the water at chest high level. There is the freedom of potential movement at every joint: fingers, wrist, elbow, and shoulder. *The entire arm "floats."* The elbow should be out from the side at what might be described as *four o-clock position.* This gives the conductor freedom for movement, and a visual image to the singers/players of potential breathing expansion, great posture, and an exhilarating feeling that the body is about to do something special.

    If the arm is up at a three o'clock angle, it is simply too high, the beats, therefore, are also too high, and it just looks like a bird flapping its wings. If the arm is too low, at five or six o'clock angles, the conductor looks weighted-down, constricted, and is expressively very limited. The performing forces will feel the same way. Basically, *four o'clock* is just right. It represents freedom, relaxation, and buoyancy. The arm is "living" (see Figures 11.7, 11.8, pages 211, 212).

12. Be sure your fingers and thumb remain curved, relaxed and "breathing" (see Figure 11.10 on page 213).

13. Check approximately equal angles (not exactly, but similar) at the shoulder, elbow, and wrist, with a *natural flow* from the *shoulder to the point of the baton* (Figure 11.12).

14. Retain this natural "home base" position as you conduct through various beat patterns. That is, in 4/4, do not close-up your arm for beat two, then open it wide to the right for beat three. *Without being rigid,* basically stay in the same relaxed position throughout—letting the body move *ever so slightly* to the left for beat two, and to the right for beat three. When going to beat three, lead

with the elbow, bring the baton along *last* (retaining the original curved position of similar angles), rather than opening up the arm, leading with the baton, pointing it to the right. Let the body become slightly involved in the motion of the beat patterns. It is not just the arm and baton that does the conducting, it is YOU the BODY, the PERSON.

Checklist for what can go wrong

1. When your arm is hanging down to the side, your thumb might be aiming straight forward, or your fingers might be pointing straight down or tensely pressed together.

2. When holding the baton, your first finger might be touching the pad of your thumb at its *first joint* rather than at its *pad.* This extended finger looks unrelaxed and somewhat tense.

3. Your fingers are tightly clenched as a fist, not relaxed and "breathing" (Figure 11.13).

4. Your thumb or first finger joints pressed *inward* rather than curved and relaxed.

5. The baton aims 90 degrees to the left, with *fingertips* on top of the baton handle (Figure 11.14), which allows the baton to be pushed out the back of the hand, instead of the manner shown in Figures 11.8a and 11.10.

Figure 11.13

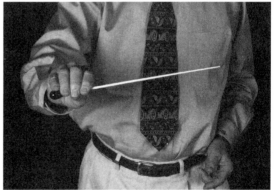

Figure 11.14

6. Baton aiming 180 degrees forward, with the wrist *bent* enabling it to do so (Figure 11.15).

7. The middle of the baton off to the right, rather than lined up with the buttons of your shirt (as in Figure 11.11).

8. Your wrist turned over—thumb up, palm to the right (see Figure 11.15).

9. Your elbow hangs down at five or six o'clock or is held too high at three o'clock (rather than effectively "floating" at four o'clock).

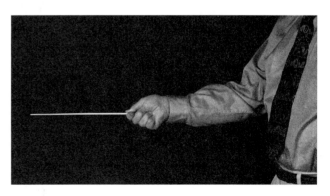

Figure 11.15

10. Your wrist is frozen—remember that there needs to be relaxation, freedom, and *potential movement* at each joint: fingers, *wrist,* elbow, and shoulder.

11. Your hand, arm, and baton positions change from their original relaxed manner as you move through beat patterns. (Remember, though, that this is the *basic position,* from which you may *often vary* to do anything you wish (for musical reasons), then return.

Be aware of any idiosyncrasies, formation, or movement that might distract from our *primary* natural, relaxed clarity developed for the basic home-base approach to the baton and arm position. *All sorts of variations will appropriately follow once this is securely established.*

Beat Patterns

Design your beat patterns with an eye to clarity and overall effectiveness. Get rid of any involuntary idiosyncrasies or habits such as accents, bounces, rebounds, syncopated up-beat motions on each beat, curlycued up-beats, and so on. All these movements communicate musical (or nonmusical) ideas that might not be indicated in the score. If you use these motions through force of habit, then you will have nothing *new* to offer when the music calls for something *special.*

If you use a home-base manner of conducting (that indicates nothing except freedom, naturalness, and clarity), then you can consciously and *additionally* indicate every special musical moment called for in the score. After such a special musical moment, return to the home-base manner again. Thus, every musical gesture you make will speak clearly to the performers and call for a response from them. We should confirm that there will often be numerous *consecutive* special musical moments. In such instances, you might only be able to return to our home-base manner of conducting infrequently.

The physical movements in conducting should truly reflect the score and indicate only what is there. The singers and players perform only what is in the score; they don't carelessly improvise. The conductor, too, must read the score and physically react accordingly, expressing only what is there. To do less is inadequate; to do more indicates ignorance or borders on an ego-centered podium drama that is distracting to both musicians and audience.

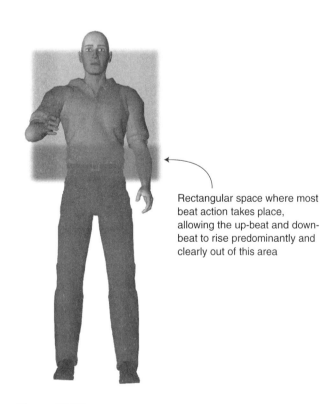

Rectangular space where most beat action takes place, allowing the up-beat and down-beat to rise predominantly and clearly out of this area

Figure 11.16

The Conducting Zone

Our standard conducting zone is from the eyes to the belt and slightly wider than the shoulders (see Figure 11.8b on page 212). This is the area in which most of our beat patterns will take place. It will logically expand when dynamics increase to forte and fortissimo and decrease for softer dynamics.

We should keep most of the conducting *action* lower in the conducting zone (see Figure 11.16), thereby allowing the crucial upbeats and downbeats to stand out clearly.

The Standard Beat Patterns

Over the years, conductors and teachers of conducting have come up with many different beat patterns. However, some patterns have proven to be consistently effective and legible to singers and players alike (see Figure 11.17). Stick with these standard patterns most of the time, and every ensemble will be able to clearly understand your conducting gestures at the *first rehearsal*.

Figure 11.17

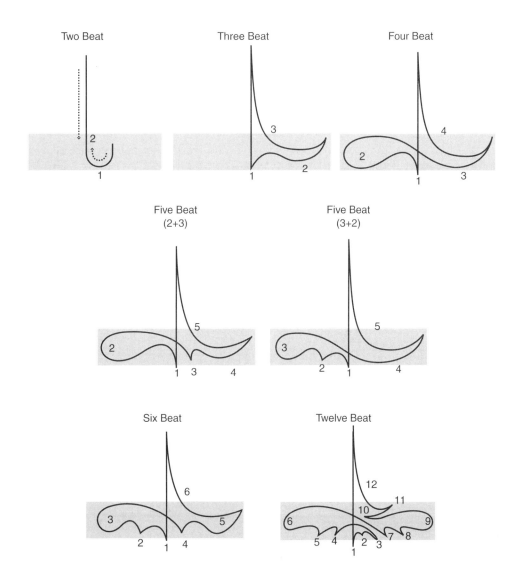

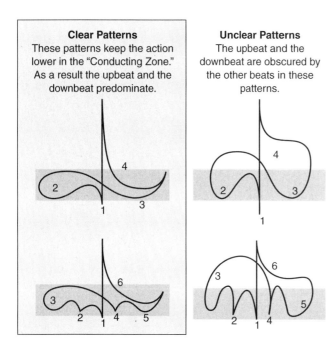

Figure 11.18

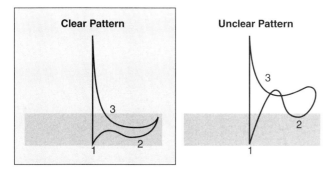

Figure 11.19

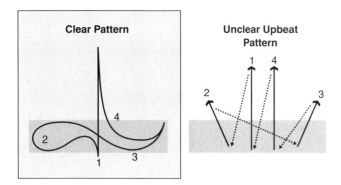

Figure 11.20

Beat patterns should be absolutely clear and discernible by quick, flash-like glances from musicians who might have to keep their eyes on the music, especially in orchestras playing with limited rehearsal time. The upbeat and the downbeat are the most crucial and should dominate. We must clearly identify a conducting zone and keep the *horizontal* beats *lower* in the zone so that the up-beat and down beat have greater visual clarity. See Figures 11.18 and 11.19.

Avoid idiosyncrasies. Give the beats clearly without extraneous curling or movements of any kind. As with all rules, we may occasionally stray and then return, but our basic conducting manner should consistently offer the ensemble *clarity* with *expression*. One goal does not exclude the other. We might, at times, go more in one direction than in another, but seldom to the exclusion of either.

Avoid *up-beat* conducting. In this manner of conducting, all beats seem to go up. The gesture approaches the point of the beat (ictus) by getting there early, using an ahead-of-time, syncopated manner, then rebounding upwards for each beat (see Figure 11.20). (Occasionally, this upbeat-style of conducting may be very effective in some slow tempi, but its effectiveness is very limited.)

Up-beat conducting began in Europe and is still very prevalent among European conductors, others who have been trained there, and those who have emulated them. I believe this is the result of young conductors subconsciously going to the beat ahead of time in an insecure effort to get the performing forces to follow them.

In the conductor's mind is the pleading call, "Come on, play!" or "Come on, sing!" The conductor gets to the lower, proper point of the beat ahead of time, a syncopated half-beat early (the gesture of "pleading"), and then proceeds upward for the actual moment of the beat or pulse, in the hope that all will arrive there together. It works. But it is unnecessary, and eventually causes musicians to stop watching the conductor. Musicians learn that it is safer to *feel* the actual point of the beat (ictus) as a performing ensemble, rather than being confused by watching the conductor.

It takes greater confidence and control to place the beats accurately at their proper points, and be secure that the performers will follow. I have never seen a text advocating up-beat conducting with diagrams to

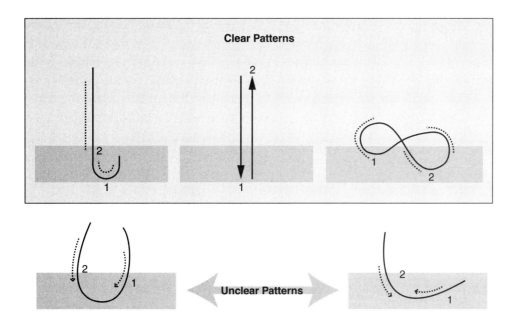

Figure 11.21

match. Insecure conductors just do it. Use it rarely, in appropriate slower tempi, but otherwise *avoid it.*

Distinguish two-beat patterns. Be careful that beats 1 and 2 of the two-beat pattern are clearly discernible. The "U" formation on the left in the unclear pattern (Figure 11.21) makes it impossible to tell the difference between the downbeat and the upbeat. The extended version on the right is also unclear.

The two-beat pattern is often very effective if it resembles a candy cane, or umbrella handle (with a small curved lower area). Another very clear and precise motion is the straight down and up motion, with a slight stop at both the bottom and top. (If clarity is *not critical,* and a rolling musical line is important, a figure-8 pattern might be useful.)

Subdivide for clarity, not confusion. We often employ subdivision (4/4 in 8, 3/4 in 6, 2/4 in 4, and so on) when the tempo is slower than 48 and the conductor's gestures become so slow that they are of no value to the ensemble. The music in this case is frequently tranquil or serene, and therefore, is most effective if done in a subtle way (unless a *forte or marcato* style is indicated). See Figure 11.22.

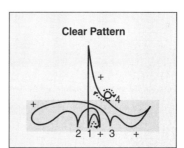

Figure 11.22

- Keep the action low.
- Think legato and linear; avoid large and unclear beats.
- The circular fourth beat motion is for a legato flowing motion.

By the same token, reduced beating (4/4 in 2, 3/4 in 1, 6/8 in 2, and so on) might be considered when the tempo is faster than 144–156. Although faster beating can sometimes be effective, at faster speeds the movement of the hand or baton can become so fast that it is of little or no value to those watching it.

We could say much more about beat patterns, especially subdivision, but remember that the intent of this segment is merely to establish significant *concepts* from which you can develop a multitude of techniques. Each of us must spend a great deal of time and effort seeking and determining what is practical, economical, clear and concise and, at the same time, musically expressive. From the musicians' point of view, it is well worth every minute we spend. We can be our own best teachers.

Dynamics

Dynamics Determine the Beat Size in the Pattern

Although fast-tempo conducting cannot be large (you will look as though you're beating yourself into a heart attack) the dynamics generally dictate the size of the beat. That is, loud = large, and soft = small. The obvious wrong example would be the large-beat, flailing conductor asking for pianissimo. There are six dynamic levels, ranging from *pp* to *ff,* so there should be six corresponding beat sizes. Consider, for practical purposes, the suggestions shown in Figure 11.23 for the area of the beat zone.

Practice various exercises in 4/4; do four measures in each of the six dynamic levels. Then practice a crescendo-diminuendo exercise over two 4/4 measures. Be

pp — within the size-span of a softball; with only finger and minimal wrist movement

You should notice that the center of the pattern is quite high. This way the eyes of your ensemble members will be drawn to your eyes.

p — within the size-span of a volleyball or soccer ball; now using some lower arm movement

mp — within the size of a basketball (or slightly larger), using full lower arm and elbow movement, and some (but not much) upper arm movement

mf — the size-span now expands in **gre**ater proportion, to **an** area from shoulder **to** shoulder, and from the eyes down to the waist, using the full arm and shoulder movement

f — expanding outward from the shoulders, and upward from the eyes; continue using the full area of arm and shoulders, plus natural upper body movement

ff — using the full upper body, from the waist upwards, everything that feels comfortable and seems sensible. Be "as big as the music."

Figure 11.23

sure that the size of your beat reflects the indicated dynamic level. When reducing the size of your beat for softer dynamic levels, raise it up toward your chin for clearer visibility. The ensemble can then see both your *beat* and your *face* at the same time. *This is very important* because musicians will always *subconsciously* look at a conductor's face. They are looking at the *person,* not at a hand or baton. The *person* is primary; the baton or hand is secondary.

Do not compromise this concept because of the size (large) or proficiency level (low) of an ensemble. Rather, raise the ensemble to your standards. Five hundred singers can see a *pp* beat if they really look for it. And you can quickly train inexperienced singers to watch and respond to artistic conducting; simply insist that the ensemble rise to your standards of artistic conducting.

Preparatory Beats

Effective preparatory beats require thought and focus. The conductor should neither neglect them nor take them for granted. Each new work demands special attention to (and practice of) the preparatory beats. Each preparatory gesture contains the visual indications for the

- Exact tempo
- Dynamic level
- Appropriate style

Do not take the need for absolute accuracy in all three categories lightly. Many conductors unintentionally give a slightly faster upbeat than the actual tempo of the following beats, or they give a larger preparatory beat than soft dynamics might indicate (especially if it is *ppp, pp, p* or *mp*). The preparatory beat should genuinely indicate the style: *legato, staccato, marcato, sostenuto,* and so on.

Give the preparatory beat time, thought, and practice. On a difficult beginning, it might be helpful to think the preparatory beat before giving it. If there is time, such as at the beginning of a piece, think a few beats (in tempo) before starting, and then join your thought process uninterruptedly with your conducting gesture. If the tempo is quite slow, it might help to think sixteenths or eighths, even if the music calls for notes of longer duration.

Given the proper preparatory beat at the beginning of a piece, movement, or new tempo indication, musicians will seldom need a verbal explanation of the three points listed. If they are well trained, they will be accustomed to following exactly what they see. If they have to ask, or need an explanation, we have not done our job well.

Beat Styles

Establish *beat styles* that correspond directly to musical ideas. Musical ideas continually change in compositions, *sometimes within a single measure*, and conducting gestures need to change with them. We will discuss five important beat styles

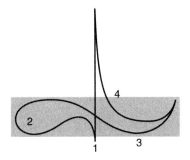

Figure 11.24

representing five very common styles of musical expression: *expressive legato* (the normal or regular beat style), *light staccato, full staccato, marcato,* and *nonexpressive* (in which the conductor indicates no expression—nothing other than where the beats are).

Expressive-legato. The expressive-legato beat shown in Figure 11.24 seems to predominate far past its useful boundaries, often reaching, incorrectly, into such other styles as *staccato* and *marcato.* This style is used much too frequently.

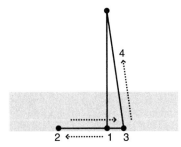

Figure 11.25

Light *staccato.* Either an absolute stop-beat or slight click-beat is appropriate for staccato, staccato-like, rhythmically complex, or syncopated music in the dynamic range of *pp, p,* or *mp* (Figure 11.25). For both the stop and click beats, use only the hand and wrist for *pp,* slight forearm movement for *p,* and full forearm and elbow for *mp.*

There is no bounce or rebound at all in the *stop-beat.* It is one of the most effective beat styles in all conducting, but, unfortunately, the least used.

The light staccato click-beat has a *very slight* "click," or bounce, at the point of each beat (see Figure 11.26).

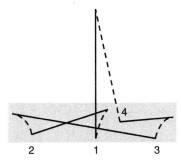

Figure 11.26

The full *staccato* or full bounce beat. This looks exactly like the light staccato click beat, but with a larger, full arm, full bounce motion to each beat (Figure 11.27). The extent of motion, of course, depends on whether the dynamic is *mf, f,* or *ff.* The louder the music, the more arm and, eventually, shoulder are used. This beat style is for music that is really "alive" with bouncing, buoyant rhythms or pulses in the louder dynamic levels.

The *marcato* beat. We will also use a stop-beat for marcato passages (Figure 11.28). This looks exactly like the light staccato stop-beat, but is much larger. It is for *mf, f,* and *ff* dynamic ranges. The marcato beat comes to an *absolute stop* on each beat and is for solidly *marcato* music. The conductor's hand and arm are very intense, almost rigid, showing definite strength and power on each beat—no bounce or recoiling.

Thus, there are two kinds of *stop-beats,* the light staccato and the marcato. They are extremely valuable, incredibly clear and precise, and all too seldom used.

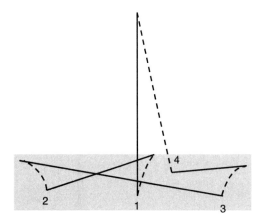

Figure 11.27

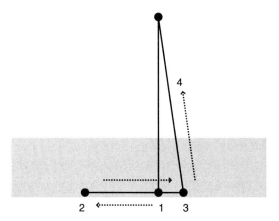

Figure 11.28

Employ the hand, wrist, and (for *mp*) forearm for the light staccato, and the full arm for *marcato*. Use them as often as the music calls for them—your musicians will be grateful. Employ a stop-beat pattern anytime that absolute clarity is crucial.

The nonexpressive beat.   As shown in Figure 11.29, this beat resembles the light staccato and marcato stop-beat, but the nonexpressive beat has no expression whatsoever. It is so seldom used that I almost hesitate to mention it, but it can be valuable when, for example, the choir or orchestra is performing whole notes tied to whole notes (or continuous tremelo), underlying a solo voice or instrument, and there is no accent or pulsation desired from measure to measure, beat to beat or note to note. The only purpose of this beat is to keep the entire ensemble together and subtly aware of the beat. The same function is served when conducting expressionless passages in recitative continuo.

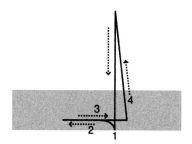

Figure 11.29

Beats 2 and 3 must move more slowly than do 4 and 1 to be properly paced. We must not arrive at the point of the beat ahead of time, which would necessitate a momentary stop or rebound. The pattern should be perfectly even and flowing throughout all beats without interruptions that might cause accented responses from the ensemble. Notice that the downbeat is the only beat that has real definition to the point of the pulse (ictus). All other beats are in a constant flowing motion.

Use the beat-style exercise shown in Example 11.1 to practice your beat styles. Practice it slowly and carefully. Sing it (on la-la) until you can sing it *very* expressively—thoroughly learning it in 4-measure phrases. Once you can sing it well, begin expressively conducting *as you sing*. Work on only four measures at a time, until you can do it all with *exaggerated expressions* and clarity. You will notice that most style changes occur for the conductor one beat or part of a beat *before* they do for the singer. That is because the conductor must give the singer (or player) preparation *in advance*.

Fermatas

Conducting fermatas can be problematic if the conductor does not abide by the following rule: *The stick (right hand) comes to an absolute stop on the beat on which the fermata is placed.* The stick stays there, absolutely motionless, until it is time to go on. The conductor's *left hand* takes responsibility for crescendi or diminuendi during the fermata and for the release at its end.

When it is time to proceed, the right hand simply gives the preparation beat and we proceed. This technique enables the conductor to be in complete control of the duration and intensity of the fermata. The right hand is perfectly still. The left hand is making any interpretative gestures that the conductor wants to communicate during the fermata.

With the right hand still, rather than moving outward to indicate more intensity or a slight crescendo, time is on the side of the conductor's interpretive instincts, not on how far out the right hand might be already extended, or how awkward it might look or feel. A still right hand also prevents a musician from

Example 11.1

accidentally going on too soon because the conductor's right hand moved—something to which orchestra players are trained to react impulsively. The right hand may give the preparatory beat to proceed, either at the same time that the left hand is giving the release, or after it, as the music calls for.

This method totally eliminates the need to explain to the ensemble what is about to take place with an upcoming fermata. If your right hand freezes and doesn't move until you give a preparatory beat to go on, the ensemble will follow very well, and there will be nothing to explain. Again, between the freeze and the preparation to go on, you can do as much or as little as you wish with your *left hand*. Everything the conductor does should be obvious, needing no explanation. That may sound ideal, but it is our job to indicate our intentions in a manner that is clearly understood. This is called *mastering our language*.

Compound versus Simple Meter

The terms compound meter and simple meter refer to the way the beat is divided within a given time signature.

Simple Meter

Simple refers to meters that divide each beat into groups of two; 2/4 (simple duple), 3/4 (simple triple), and 4/4 (simple quadruple) are all examples of simple meter (see Example 11.2). The beat doesn't need to be a quarter note. Time signatures like 4/16, 4/8 and 2/2 also represent simple meters.

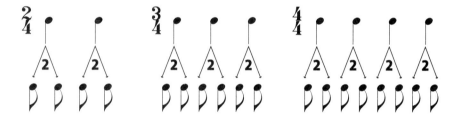

Example 11.2

Compound Meter

Compound describes meters that divide the beat into groups of three: 6/8 (compound duple), 9/8 (compound triple), 12/8 (compound quadruple). (See Example 11.3.) As with simple meter, many other time signatures classify as compound.

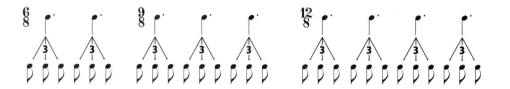

Example 11.3

What's the beat? The term *beat* can be a little confusing when we discuss these concepts. In our examples of simple meter we call the ♩ note the beat. This is obviously correct because it is indicated by the time signatures. On the other hand, in our compound examples, we often consider the ♩. note the beat, grouping the three ♪ notes together. You would usually conduct the compound meters above as: 6/8 in two, 9/8 in three, and 12/8 in four. If, however, 6/8 were conducted in 6, then it would be simple sextuple (six ♪ notes divided into two ♬ each).

Conducting Compound Meters

Although the patterns for 6/8 in two, 9/8 in three, and 12/8 in four look the same as their simple meter counterparts on paper, there is a difference in their look and feel when you are conducting. The beats (each containing three ♪ notes) in compound meter should have an *upward* lift. Do not think *down*. Everything lifts, as though you were touching an iron to determine if it is hot—or the way a percussionist lifts the stick to play out of the drumhead to allow it to fully vibrate for better tone. It is important, however, that this lift does not slowly transform your pattern into totally "upbeat conducting." The beats are not larger, and they do not have a larger rebound; they simply have a different *feeling* and a different physical (lifting) character that will be obvious to the players or singers.

Complex Meters

In both simple and compound meter, the beats can be divided by the common denominator two or three. This is not possible in such meters as 7/8 or 5/8 (see Example 11.4). Therefore we must analyze the music and divide the beats into a *combination* of twos and threes. Using 5/8, for example, we could conduct 2 beats, one based on a quarter value (1-2) and one based on a dotted-quarter (1-2-3). The conductor should practice with a metronome set on the tempo of the ♪, and keep it constant. Within a measure, the groups of two and three can occur in any order.

Composers often make meters complex by changing the divisions of the beat for musical reasons. This is common in pieces that are already using other complex meters. Often the meter will change every bar, and this creates a challenge for the conductor. In this 9/8 example we see that the measure is divided ♩ + ♩. + ♩ + ♩ or 2 + 3 + 2 + 2. Again, simply keep the ♪ constant.

Example 11.4

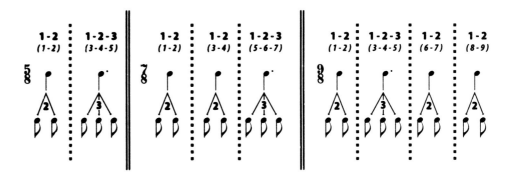

Conducting Complex Meter

This is not as difficult as one might think. The key is to understand the rhythm and/or melody first, and practice conducting second. There are three steps in determining how to conduct this type of music.

1. Identify the number of beats in a measure. Look at the measure shown in Example 11.5 and determine how many beats it has. 7/8 will have three, 5/8 will

Example 11.5

have two, 11/8 will have five, and other meters can have a variety of possibilities. Fortunately, most modern editions contain all the information we need to decipher the rhythmic and metrical intent of the composer. However, sometimes we will be on our own. Then we must analyze the material carefully.

2. Identify the divisions of the beats. To a large degree this is already done, so now, count the measure out loud (see Example 11.6).

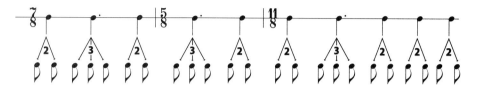

Example 11.6

3. Assign the appropriate pattern. If our measure has three beats, we will use a three-pattern (see Figure 11.30). We will need to assign the appropriate strokes of the beat to a combination of simple and compound meters. Remember that the strokes with a compound assignment need to *float* more than do those with a simple assignment. This is the only way the ensemble will be able to understand what we are telling them.

Although it is important to feel a floating sensation in any compound-meter conducting, it is *critical* in complex meters. Ensembles tend to rush the compound beats and land early on the following beats. If our conducting demonstrates a clear float, and we insist that they *feel* that float as they rehearse and perform, we can eliminate this problem.

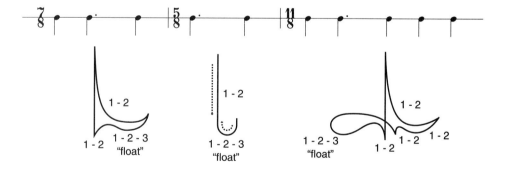

Figure 11.30

Mixed Meter

When a piece contains a variety of meters it is said to have mixed meter. This can be as simple as going from 3/4 to 4/4 and back, or it can become extremely complicated. When the meters become complicated, composers must give additional information to assist us in reading their intent. They do this in the form of simple equations above the barline separating measures of two differing meters. Refer to the notation shown in Example 11.7 and the respective descriptions of the examples.

Example 11.7

In Example 11.7a, the 𝅗𝅥 note = the 𝅘𝅥 note. As a result the two measures will sound identical. If the equation were (𝅗𝅥 = 𝅘𝅥) then the 3/4 measure would be twice as fast as the 3/2 bar.

In Example 11.7b, the 𝅘𝅥𝅮 note = the 𝅘𝅥𝅮 note. Therefore, as in the complex meter discussed earlier, the downbeat of the 5/8 bar needs to have the floating feeling because it is a longer beat than both the previous and the subsequent beats.

We will treat the 3/8 bar in Example 11.7c the same way we would treat a single compound beat in a measure of 5/8 or 7/8. Once again the 𝅘𝅥𝅮 note is constant.

In Example 11.7d, the 𝅘𝅥. note = the 𝅘𝅥 note. Therefore, the notes will become slower because there is one less note (2 instead of 3) per beat. The metric relationship is like triplets in simple time (3 versus 2) or duplets in compound time (2 versus 3). As you can see in in Example 11.8a, the 𝅘𝅥. = the 𝅘𝅥; therefore the two bars on the left will sound identical to the two on the right. Example 11.8b illustrates the same concept using triplets instead of duplets.

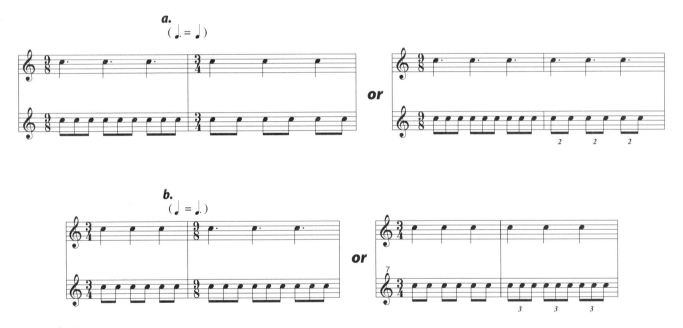

Example 11.8

We can use this information to determine how our conducting will clarify the transitions from meter to meter. We must understand it completely before our first rehearsal, then explain it clearly so that a change in the beat or a change in the divisions of the beat does not confuse the performers.

A Balance between Listening and Conducting

During early rehearsals, the conductor needs to refer to the score frequently to check mechanical accuracy. Therefore, we will place more emphasis on listening than on physical conducting (Figure 11.31). The more physically active a conductor becomes, the less he or she is able to hear discernibly. Try doing active calisthenics exercises while listening to music and observe how much less discerning your hearing is. Energetic conducting is very similar. The more movement, the less we hear. By the same token, when an ensemble is learning new music, singers need to spend more time reading the music, so they are less able to watch us. Save the more passionate conducting for later when the ensemble knows the music well. The first priority is to become a great listener and teacher. I do not mean to imply that the conductor does not communicate and inspire with great motivation and energy from the very first rehearsal. Of course we do! I mean that the ultimate passion must wait a bit, so that we can, in fact, hear everything we need to hear while teaching the fundamentals of the piece. But nothing negates our primary job of *inspiration.*

As the rehearsal process continues, we can pay more attention to conducting, communication, and expression (passion), which will rest on the foundation of accurate mechanics built in previous rehearsals. Once it is safe to begin emotional communication at full pace, it is time to increase the eye-to-eye intense focus with a nonstop effort.

Being an effective communicator does not mean that the conductor must memorize the entire score and look up 100 percent of the time. But he or she must know the score well enough that, with the aid of occasional quick glances at structural points of reference, the conductor can employ eye contact 90 to 95 percent of the time. A conductor should never follow the score note-by-note or measure-by-measure. If we have done our homework—structural analysis, worksheet, and memorization of key passages—and if our scores are clearly marked, reference glances should suffice. Proper preparation enables the conductor to focus on the music and the musicians.

Direct, intense, continual communication might be thought of as a "yellow-highlighted" focus—as though the conductor had gone through the entire score and

Figure 11.31

mentally highlighted, without interruption, the primary and secondary themes, cues, and other ideas that need attention. The result? Give a cue and *stay with that person or section until you are needed elsewhere*, then cue someone else and *stay there until needed elsewhere*, and so on.

Cues and Eye Contact

Intense focus and nonstop communication, eyeball to eyeball, from the conductor to the musicians, is the essence of effective leadership and inspiration. People tend to respond in like manner. If the conductor doesn't consistently look into the eyes of the ensemble, they, in turn, will not look back. There is no greater inspiration than that of your leader looking you straight in the eye, with great positive intensity, asking you to give all you have to give. *If there is one guaranteed success factor in choral conducting, it is consistent eye-to-eye inspirational communication.*

The "Cue and Stay" Strategy

The concept: *cue and stay, cue and stay, cue and stay—briefly glance down at the score—cue and stay, cue and stay, cue and stay—briefly glance down at the score—cue and stay, cue and stay, cue and stay.* While staying, intensely motivate the person or people you are conducting. The effect should be absolutely riveting! The attention given to the singers should bring them to the point of contributing 100 percent on every note, word, and syllable. When you stay with a section or members of the ensemble for a period of time they realize that they are accountable. A glazed stare through the entire chorus will engage them little more than if you were looking down at the score. You must look into the eyes of singers (and players) and motivate them directly.

Figure 11.32 illustrates a phrase of the structural analysis of "Awake the Harp." Highlighting indicates the measures where you should *stay.* In these portions, the conductor will cue and stay until the next cue arrives. (The importance of the structural analysis becomes clear: A diligent analysis of the score itself determines the attention of our conducting.)

The goal is to stay with a voice or section until you are needed elsewhere. Occasionally, but very rarely, the conductor will conduct everyone, the entire ensemble. My rule is this: *Most of the time, conduct someone (or section) in particular; occasionally conduct the entire ensemble; but NEVER conduct no one.* This last point means that we should not conduct the music as if no one were there, as if we were conducting a recording. *Always communicate directly with someone!*

In the heart, mind, and soul, the conductor should always have something of inspirational value that needs to be communicated actively to the musicians, encouraging a similar response from them. Along with teaching fundamental accuracy and expressive interpretation, the conductor exists to inspire and enable the singers and players to perform at higher levels than previously existed because the conductor is there to stimulate them. Know the music and how to teach it. Then truly conduct!

Figure 11.32

Summary

To conduct is an intellectual, emotional, and physical *art*. We must not take any aspect of it for granted. We need to dig in and search in great depth for every detail that needs to be known, developed, and successfully communicated.

Our overriding goal is to conduct in a manner that is both consistently clear and precise—and filled with honest appropriate passion and inspiration. We must come to know and be secure with everything in the score and the essential techniques of the performing forces.

Once again, we must *know* what to teach, *how* to teach it, and how to *inspire* the musicians to want to do what we teach.

The Role of the Conductor

*W*ho are we? What function do we serve? What is our real purpose? What is our job? Without defining this in a very analytical manner, we may be on the wrong course without even knowing it. Let's try to gain a thorough understanding of ourselves and our mission. After all, ours is not a career; it is a mission—a mission to serve and preserve the arts, a mission to enhance life with the beauty of great music, certainly one of the noblest missions.

First, we will discuss some of the conductor's various roles. Then we'll discuss how to be an artistic choral conductor and how to evaluate oneself as a conductor. We'll end this chapter with some thoughts on a career in music.

Servant

- Serve the composer and the score through integrity, dedication, knowledge and thorough preparation.
- Serve the choral art through a relentless effort toward quality and excellence in all things.
- Serve the singers and players through technical and musical knowledge, the ability to teach and inspire, artistic musical conducting, and thorough preparation.
- Serve the audience through appropriate, interesting, stimulating, and varied programming.

Teacher

- Teach with ever-increasing effectiveness, the right pitch at the right time, in the right manner and style.
- Teach vocal technique as a vital part of every rehearsal.

- Teach comprehensive musicality in a consistent manner—especially the area of phrasing, based on the principle that no two consecutive notes, words, or syllables should receive equal emphasis.
- Base rehearsing on
  - Solid preparation
  - Intense listening
  - Quick recognition and analysis of problems
  - Fast, effective solutions and corrections
  - Moving on!
  - Motivation, inspiration, challenge and accomplishment

Motivator

- Motivate singers and players to want to strive for everything that is presented, especially quality and excellence in *all* things. They should do it because they are motivated by the conductor—because they *want* to—not because it has been dictatorially legislated.
- Motivate singers to perform—not simply sing, but to really *perform*, with their entire beings involved in the production presentation, projection and communication. There is a monumental difference between accurate singing and *performing*. Know the difference, teach it, and motivate it.
- Motivate increased interest (recruitment) of new singers and solid community support of the total program and concerts. The buck stops with us; either we produce or we don't. No one else will do it for us. It's our job and our responsibility.

Leader

- Lead with the realization that the conductor must accept full responsibility for the success of the ensemble and the total choral program.
- Lead the entire situation! This is no place for democracy. The conductor is the one trained, knowledgeable, and qualified to make significant musical, vocal, and organizational decisions. Accept this responsibility while being sensitive to the feelings and well-being of the ensemble members.

Student

- Study endlessly—throughout life—with musicologists and composers to gain greater knowledge regarding appropriate interpretation, performance practice, and stylistic interpretation.
- Study videotapes of one's own conducting and teaching—as well as the conducting of other professionals—for continuous *growth* in the areas of teaching and artistic musical conducting.

An Artistic Choral Conductor

At the beginning of this book we discussed that we can become, with hard work and dedication, artistic choral conductors. By now, it should be quite clear that we have taken on a huge task. We should hasten to concede that there is far more to great conducting than we have ever imagined, certainly more than can be expressed in a single chapter or book.

As we work our way through this world of choral music, remember that, from time to time, we will face frustration. When those times come, re-read these concepts and remind yourself that we have the solutions within reach—it is only a matter of going after them.

Most choruses have the potential for greatness. Most can become a truly fine chorus if the conductor is capable of leading them to their potential. The "buck" stops at the podium. The only limitation of a chorus is its conductor. The conductor's only limitations are those we place on ourselves.

Instill Energy

Energy is paramount! Positive energy and an alive spirit are the foundation of every aspect of great singing. We either have it or we don't—there is no middle ground. The conductor has to be the source and example of this energy and must never accept less from the chorus.

Teach Singing

Singularly, the most important thing we teach is *singing—great singing.* We must teach singing sounds that are vibrant and filled with true substance—sounds that will make a positive and thrilling impact on the listener and be fulfilling for the singer. The obvious foundation here (after energy) is to properly *open the mouth* and *sing!* Produce real tone, place it in the head, and uniformly shape individual vowels. Sing!

Insist That Your Choruses *Think*

After energy and great singing, the most important thing we must accomplish with our choruses is to get them to *think!* All artists have to think. Singers, however, more than any others, seem to "get by" without thinking (or with minimal thinking). The reasons: (1) they've not been consistently required to think, and (2) usually ten to forty or more singers surround them singing the same part. If they don't think, they'll get by fairly well anyway.

Once I tried to convince a group of elementary and junior high school vocal teachers to set up a graded system to determine what each singer should know at any given grade level. The response? "That's for the high school teachers to do, we're just supposed to teach them to enjoy music." And, with that, they refused. I hasten to say that there are also many terrific elementary and middle/junior high school teachers in the field who are doing a solid job of comprehensive teaching, and doing it well! But, I must also mention that, as a university choral conductor since 1963, in almost every round of fall choral auditions, some singers who possessed fine vocal talent embarrassingly stated that they had never been taught to read music—although they had participated in chorus all through their pre-collegiate schooling—some as featured soloists.

Instrumentalists have to think or they will play the wrong notes. Singers must be taught that singing well is the only acceptable way to sing—and to sing well, one must intensely and consistently *think*. Singers must understand, retain, and *do* what they've been taught! Admonish the singer to "think until your brain perspires! Don't do anything well *accidentally*—do it well because you think and do, think and do, think and do."

Teach Musicianship

Solid musicianship is a must. The conductor must teach it (unless, in very advanced ensembles, it is already established). All interpretative efforts must be placed on a foundation of 100 percent accuracy of pitches and rhythms—each singer, each song. If our singers (or some of our singers) aren't able to read music, we must teach them to read.

Self-Evaluation

If we have an awareness of the *potential progress* that can be made within the art of conducting and teaching, we can often be our *own best teachers.*

We must remember to have audiotapes and videotapes made of us and our ensemble(s) during rehearsals and concerts. Study the tapes intensively. If we have solidly established the significant choral concepts in this book, we are then armed with the ability to evaluate these tapes and correct ourselves and the ensemble in most areas. We might often feel too busy to do this, but be assured, that we will gain immeasurably from the practice. We seldom know for sure what our ensemble sounds like, nor what we look like. Tapes don't lie. They will present us with the opportunity to hear and see reality.

I often tell a chorus that singers are seldom aware of the lack of quality they might be producing. They simply *sing*. "What comes out is what we get." They seldom *think* before making sounds, and they often don't know they're supposed to do so. Refer often to the value of singers really listening to themselves and being consciously aware of producing the ideal tone you have taught them.

The same applies to those of us who conduct. Are we, as conductors and teachers, really consciously aware of what we are doing? We certainly cannot rely on the compliments or criticisms of others. We must know for ourselves. We need to live up to *our own* standards, not someone else's.

Compliments usually come from those who enjoy what we're doing, but who often know far less than we do about it. Thus, their standards might not be high enough for us to use as a basis for our progress or accomplishments. On a scale of one to ten, a compliment from someone who has only the musical knowledge at the

Choral-Evaluation Form

I. ***Tone quality (energy, beauty, and placement/resonance)***

    A. Entire chorus in general

    B. Sopranos

    C. Alto

    D. Tenors

    E. Basses

II. ***Pitch accuracy and intonation***

    A. General accuracy of written pitches

    B. Specific intonation:

        1. Entire chorus

        2. Sopranos

        3. Altos

        4. Tenors

        5. Basses

III. ***Rhythmic precision***

Rhythmic interest and forward motion

IV. ***Diction***

    A. Understandability

    B. Clarity of consonants

    C. Unified vowel formation

    D. Syllable and word inflection

    E. Word meaning emphasis

V. ***Ensemble balance and blend***

    A. Section-to-Section

    B. Within a given section

VI. ***Interpretation***

    A. Tempi

    B. Style

    C. Phrasing (note groupings, crescendo-stress-diminuendo emphasis)

    D. Dynamics

    E. Musical expression

VII. ***Other factors***

    A. Personal communication of singers

    B. Choice of music

    C. Stage presence

    D. Appearance

Figure 12.1

✒ Videotape Rehearsals and Concerts

Our singers have little if any idea what they look like when they sing. They also do not know the full extent of how they sound. Make videotapes of both rehearsals and concerts and play them for the singers. One picture is worth a thousand words. Also make a videotape with the video solely on you during an entire rehearsal or concert. Study it, and become your own best teacher. You'll be amazed at what you see, and what you can teach yourself.

level of five would think that a chorus at the level of five and one at the level of ten are both equally proficient. (There are also singers in our ensemble who lack sufficient knowledge to appreciate fully how fine or weak the group really is.)

Sometimes I have received a standing ovation for a concert I presented, yet I was disappointed in aspects of both the performance and my own conducting. On the other hand, sometimes the performance might have been truly splendid, but the response was less than enthusiastic. *We* need to be the standard bearers, the benchmark, regarding our own excellence. We must *know enough* to do this, then *do it*—via videotape.

Some years ago, I devised a workable adjudication form especially designed for choral purposes (see Figure 12.1). We can use this form to evaluate our own rehearsals and concerts. Duplicate it. Use it. "Adjudicate" yourself. This form contains most of the important concepts of this book. Be objective, analytical, and realistic. Grow!

A Career in Music Is a Privilege

To spend one's life in the field of music is a rare and special privilege. To get up every morning and know that "today I am going to make great music with enthusiastic musicians" is an indescribable joy! The medical field prolongs and saves lives. We musicians, if we do our job properly, help people *enjoy their lives*. Our music can stimulate their minds and souls like nothing else. Ours is one of the most fulfilling lives-to-live on Earth. Make the most of it. Accept the responsibility of excellence that comes with the privilege of happiness. Give your singers the opportunity to be really special—really great!